ECUMENICS:

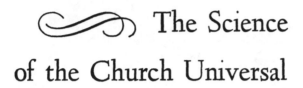 The Science
of the Church Universal

John A. Mackay

Prentice-Hall, Inc., Englewood Cliffs, N. J.

Dedicated to
my fellow members of the Theological Education Fund Committee
and to all in every land and clime
who seek through the Gospel
the establishment of the one Church
in obedience to the one Lord

ISBN 978-1-4391-9402-7

Library of Congress Catalog Card Number 64–22800   T 23538

Prentice-Hall International, Inc., *London*
Prentice-Hall of Australia, Pty., *Sydney*
Prentice-Hall of Canada, Ltd., *Toronto*
Prentice-Hall of India (Private) Ltd., *New Delhi*
Prentice-Hall of Japan, Inc., *Tokyo*

Contents

PART IV   THE CHURCH AND THE WORLD

Call for a New Science

prologue

Among the epoch-making events, some calamitous, some creative, that have marked the course of history in the past half-century, there is one which is more outstandingly significant than all the rest. It may be described thus.

A new reality has come to birth. For the first time in the life of mankind the Community of Christ, the Christian Church, can be found, albeit in nuclear form, in the remotest frontiers of human habitation. This Community has thereby become "ecumenical" in the primitive, geographical meaning of that term. History is thus confronted with a new fact.

The Church's advent on the bounds of the *"oikoumenē,"* "the inhabited earth," the restoration to currency in contemporary speech of the word "ecumenical," together with increasing concern about the so-called "Ecumenical Movement," have made both possible and imperative the creation of a new science. The time has clearly come to move beyond the "Science of Missions," which stirred Christian thought in the first decades of the present century, and beyond the "Theology of Mission," which has begun to stir it today. The moment has arrived when the worldwide Christian Community must be studied in its essential character as a missionary reality, together with all that is involved when this ecumenical society is true to its nature and fulfills its destiny. This is the task of the Science of Ecumenics.

The field of discourse of the Science of Ecumenics embraces everything that concerns the nature, functions, relations, and strategy of the Church Universal, when the latter is conceived as a world missionary community. Questions pertaining to the Church's essence, its mission, its unity, and its relations in the world, which have hitherto been dealt with separately, and have been discussed under diverse designations, will be treated together as constitutive phases of a single discipline.

The suggestion that this book should be written was made to the writer at a meeting held on the outskirts of Paris during the summer of 1959. The occasion was the annual gathering of the Theological Education Fund Committee. This committee had been created by the International Missionary Council a short time before, as a result of the vision and concern of a distinguished churchman, Charles W. Ranson. Its operation was made possible through the financial co-operation of a leading American foundation and of a large number of Churches. The design of the committee was to use the funds placed at its disposal to promote the cause of theological education in the lands of the "younger" Churches.

As the suggestion referred to came from men and women who were in basic agreement with the ideas which a fellow committee member had happened quite casually to share with them, I desire, in gratitude for the inspiration they gave me, to dedicate to them, singly and together, this volume on the Science of the Church Universal. My gratitude is due in a special manner to Dr. Marcus Ward and to Canon Max A. C. Warren for most helpful observations regarding the original manuscript.

The pages that follow will combine elements of the subjective and the objective. They will voice echoes of the author's struggle over four decades to grapple with the ecumenical concept and its significance. They will crystallize the fruits of his thinking as the incumbent of a Chair of Ecumenics, the first of its kind,[1] which was created in May 1937 by the governing board of a theological institution [2] because of the sympathy of its members for his con-

[1] O. G. Myklebust, The Study of Missions in Theological Education (Oslo: Egede Instituttet, Forlaget Land Og Kirke, 1957), II, 64–65, 91.
[2] Princeton Theological Seminary.

cern. These pages will also provide a construct of the writer's thought to the present time, as he has continued to wrestle, in the light of the Eternal and confronting the temporal, with the role of the Church in God's design and man's predicament.

JOHN A. MACKAY

Chevy Chase, Maryland
February, 1964

The Science
of Ecumenics

PART I

Historical Perspectives

chapter 1

THE REDISCOVERY OF THE CHURCH

A crucial event in the contemporary history of Christianity was the Conference on Church Community and State, which met in Oxford, England during the summer of 1937. This assembly, convened at a time when the clouds of World War II were gathering, proved to be historic in more ways than one. Under the leadership of that prophetic figure, J. H. Oldham, the new significance of the Church in Christian thought and the Church's central role in history were set in bold relief.

Several things had happened. In the late Twenties, Christian thinkers moved beyond the general consideration of Christianity and of Christian ideas and began to focus attention upon the Church, which had become an almost forgotten theme. There were several reasons for the reborn interest in the Church which marked that period.

In the first place, a concern for Biblical theology had been developing. Scholars had begun to explore the theological significance of the Biblical concepts of the "Covenant," the "Covenant People," the "People of God," the "Body of Christ," the "Fellowship of the Spirit." In the second place, there was a growing awareness that the Church had become a worldwide reality. As a result of the Missionary Movement of the past century and a half, the Gospel had been carried to all nations. As the fruit of missionary effort, a large number of new Churches had come to birth. Many of these Churches were already autonomous, and the problem of their relationship to the mother Churches was becoming increasingly real. In the third place, the Christian Church in Nazi Germany had become the center of violent controversy and persecution. The German universities had already succumbed, but the Confessing Church stood fast. At Barmen in 1934 it issued an historic declaration. The Church defied the Fuehrer. It proclaimed the sovereign Lordship of Jesus Christ and the spiritual rights of the Community of Christ, whatever might be the secular government under which Christians lived. The fact that the German Fuehrer had refused to allow representatives of the Lutheran Church in Germany to attend the Oxford Conference gave fresh meaning to the reality of the Church. It confronted the conference with the problem of the Church's witness in a state hostile to its claims. For these reasons a new Church-consciousness was born, which inspired the organizers of the Oxford Conference.

What could be more natural, therefore, than the centrality given to the "Church" in the official title of the conference of 1937? It was the first time in modern history that a gathering of Christians from many lands had undertaken to consider the "Church" and its relationship to the secular order. The fifth of the five sections into which the conference was divided had, moreover, as its theme, "The Universal Church and the World of Nations." The sombre conviction that the nations of the world were heading for conflict led this section to deal with the subject of war. It desired to set forth the Church's attitude on what appeared to be imminent.

Not only, however, did the Oxford Conference give new status to the Church as a spiritual reality and pose it as an important theme for discussion, the confernce gave birth also to a watchword, which was soon to be re-echoed around the world, and with which Oxford, 1937 will always be associated: "Let the Church be the Church." These words, which appeared originally in a paper prepared for the conference by the chairman of the section on "The Universal Church and the World of Nations," were picked up and blazoned forth by Archbishop William Temple, who prepared the Conference Message. The Archbishop had been an active member of Section Five.

In the document, "A Message from the Oxford Conference to the Christian Churches,"[1] the watchword is echoed twice. "The first duty of the Church," the message reads, "and its greatest service to the world, is *that it be in very deed the Church*—confessing the true faith, committed to the fulfillment of the will of Christ, its only Lord, and united in Him in a fellowship of love and service."[2] The words sound again in a passage which deals with the threat of war. The passage in question runs thus: "If war breaks out, then pre-eminently *the Church must manifestly be the Church*, still united as the one body of Christ, though the nations wherein it is planted fight one another, consciously offering the same prayers that God's name may be hallowed, His Kingdom come, and His will be done in both, or all, the warring nations."[3]

It happened, in the Providence of God, that the writer of these lines was the person, who by an inspiration of the Spirit and in an agony of concern, had originally penned the words, "Let the Church be the Church."[4] In the pre-conference document which he had drafted for the members of Section Five we find this passage, "*Let the Church be the Church.* Let the Church *know herself*, whose she is and what she is. Discerning clearly her own status as the Community of Grace, the organ of God's redemptive purpose for mankind, she must by a process of merciless self-scrutiny become what God intended her to be. Nothing less than that, nor yet anything more than that. . . . It must be her ceaseless concern to rid herself from all subjugation to a prevailing culture, an economic system, a social type, or a political order. Let the Church live; over against all these, let the Church stand."

This yearning that the Church should become in its historical existence the dynamic instrument of God's will, which it actually

[1] J. H. Oldham, *The Oxford Conference—Official Report* (Chicago: Willett, Clark & Company, 1937), pp. 45–52.
[2] *Ibid.*, p. 45.
[3] *Ibid.*, p. 47.
[4] See report of the General Secretary of the World Council of Churches, W. A. Visser 't Hooft, to the Central Committee of the W.C.C. at its meeting in New Haven, Connecticut, July 30–August 7, 1957, *Minutes and Reports,* p. 81.

was in its eternal essence, had become with me in those years a veritable passion. The mood followed a period in which I had come to despair of the Church. During the period in question I came to feel that the answer to the New Testament ideas of a true Community and of a crusading fellowship, was a no-Church Movement such as we find today in Japan. But in the early Thirties a new sense of the Church as a dynamic missionary Community was born within the soul of the writer.

As I recently pondered once again upon the Oxford watchword, in view of the invitation that had come to me to write this book, I discovered words I had penned in 1934, three years before Oxford. In the Mission Study volume for that year, the same yearning is described. "The supreme need is that the Christian Church be a fellowship. Let the Church be the Church, let it be true to its inmost self, that is, to the reality of fellowship. The early Christian Community was a *koinonia*, a fellowship, before it was an ecclesia, or assembly. . . . Let the idea of fellowship be worked out to the fullest degree in the Christian community, locally, nationally, and internationally." [5]

THE REBIRTH OF THE ECUMENICAL IDEA

Equally important is the fact that it *was the Oxford Conference of 1937 that restored to currency the term "ecumenical."* The word had been resuscitated in Protestant circles in 1900. The great missionary conference which convened in New York City in 1900 bore the title, "The Ecumenical Missionary Conference." "Ecumenical" was interpreted by the leaders of the New York Conference as involving a dynamic missionary confrontation of the *"oikoumenē,"* "the inhabited earth." Said one of its sponsors: "This conference is called 'ecumenical,' not because all portions of the Christian Church are represented in it by delegates, but because the plan of the campaign which it proposes covers the whole area of the inhabited globe." [6] The Honorable Seth Low in opening the first public session of the conference put it thus: "This conference is ecumenical because it is concerned with the

[5] *That Other America* (New York: Friendship Press, 1934), pp. 195–96.
[6] *Ecumenical Missionary Conference* (New York, 1900), I, 10.

whole world. So far as Protestantism is concerned, it is ecumenical because all Protestant Christendom is to take part in it." [7]

But the term ran into trouble and fell again into disuse. The proposal that the famous Edinburgh Conference of 1910, the historic successor of the New York gathering, should also be designated "ecumenical" was rejected by High Church members of the organizing committee.[8] These brethren were insensitive to a basic historical fact. That fact we will seek to substantiate in the course of this volume, namely that the pristine significance of "ecumenical" is dynamic and missionary in character, a united Christian movement into the *oikoumenē*.

In the "Preface to the American Edition" of the *Official Report of the Oxford Conference* there is a passage which emphasizes the restoration to meaningful, contemporary usage of the word "ecumenical." This preface was written by Henry Smith Leiper, an ecumenical pioneer who later became an associate general secretary of the World Council of Churches. His words are as follows:

> In the generic sense Oxford was Catholic, meaning of course, universal, all-inclusive, interracial, supranational. A better word, less subject perhaps to misunderstanding, is the one so frequently applied: Oxford was *ecumenical*. That old word from the Greek was reborn and brought back into circulation, along with the fundamental idea for which it stood in the early Christian centuries . . . the idea of the whole household of faith.[9]

The "Message from the Oxford Conference to the Christian Churches," which, as has been stated, was written by Archbishop Temple, does not, it is true, contain the term "ecumenical." It was not many weeks after Oxford, however, that the Archbishop gave utterance to the famous saying which is associated with his name: "The Ecumenical Movement," said he, "is the great new fact of our time." It is significant, moreover, that the "Report of the

---

[7] *Ibid.*, p. 15.
[8] William Richey Hogg, *Ecumenical Foundations* (New York: Harper & Row, Publishers, 1951), p. 109.
[9] *The Oxford Conference (Official Report)*, Preface to the American Edition, VII.

Section on the Universal Church and the World of Nations" (of which section William Temple was a leading member) contains several references to "ecumenical" and to things "ecumenical" in the context of "movement." The subsection of the report, entitled "The Ecumenical Church," begins thus: "A special ground of faith and courage amid the perplexities of our age is that the Christian Church is becoming truly ecumenical. The Missionary Movement of the past century carried forward the sense of world mission inherent in the Biblical records, making the bounds of the Christian Community co-extensive with the inhabited globe. This movement has been the principal sign that the Church was alive to the God-given vision of the Church Universal. Moreover, the Churches are realizing anew that the Church is one."

Later in the report "ecumenical" is distinguished from "international." "The term 'international,'" we read, "necessarily accepts the division of mankind into separate nations as a natural, if not a final, state of affairs. The term 'ecumenical' refers to the expression within history of the given unity of the Church. The one starts from the fact of division and the other from the fact of unity in Christ." Then come these significant words: "This fact of the ecumenical character of the Church carries with it the important consequence that the Church brings to the task of achieving a better international order, an insight which is not derived from ordinary political sources. To those who are struggling to realize human brotherhood in a world where disruptive nationalism and oppressive imperialism make such brotherhood seem unreal, the Church offers not an ideal, but a fact, man united not by his aspiration but by the love of God. True ecumenicity, therefore, must be the goal of all our efforts." [10]

In the final section of the report, which bears the subtitle, "The Church's Witness," a strong plea is made for "ecumenical education." The gauntlet is thrown down to theological faculties and seminaries. Here are the words of the challenge: "The Church is by nature ecumenical, but few of its members have as yet come to realize the full implication of this fact. In order to give content to this Christian affirmation, we must attempt to educate Church members in the understanding of the actual witness, life, and

[10] *The Oxford Conference (Official Report)*, pp. 152–53.

problems of other churches than their own. Theological faculties and seminaries have a particularly important task in this connection. They should introduce into their program the study of the contemporary theology—dogmatic as well as practical—of all branches of the Christian Church, and enable their students to enter into personal contact with the Church life of other confessions and in other countries. The future of the Ecumenical Movement depends largely on whether a generation of Christians can be formed, who, while rooted in their own traditions, are willing by much patience, scrupulous fairness, and also by critical insight and complete frankness, to labor for a deeper understanding between the Churches." [11]

But if this desirable goal was to be reached, some form of "ecumenical organization" should be envisaged. In support of this objective, the report concludes thus: "We commend with thankfulness the efforts of these movements which are working for the cause of international understanding through the Churches. We rejoice in the decision taken by the conference to recommend the creation of a World Council of Churches and we urge that the study of the problems dealt with in this report be included in its aim." [12] Eleven years later, following the close of World War II, which Oxford had presaged with dread, there was born in the city of Amsterdam what is now universally known as the World Council of Churches—destined to become the chief symbol and organ of the Ecumenical Movement.

The Oxford Conference of 1937 thus inspired a fourfold development in contemporary Christianity. First, it gave new significance and relevancy to the reality of the Church in its dynamic and worldwide aspect, initiating the watchword, "Let the Church be the Church." Second, it restored to currency the term "ecumenical," which it enriched with a new connotation that embraced the mission of the Church and the unity of the Church as integral facets of the "Ecumenical Movement." Third, it called upon those responsible for theological education to make provision for a study of the Church in its diverse traditions and denominations throughout the world, and to set in high relief the Church's responsibility

[11] *The Oxford Conference (Official Report),* p. 170.
[12] *The Oxford Conference (Official Report),* p. 171.

and role in the world of today. Fourth, it recommended the formation of a World Council of Churches.

LANDMARKS ON THE ECUMENICAL ROAD

It was not long before the new vision of the Church Universal,
which marked the Oxford Conference, began to influence Protestant Christianity. In December, 1938 a significant gathering
took place in Madras, India under the auspices of the International Missionary Council, which had itself come into being in
1921. The historic Jerusalem Conference, which met under the
same auspices in April, 1928, had dealt in a most basic way with
the centrality of Christ in the Christian religion, with the approach of Christianity and Christian missions to the non-Christian
religions, with Christian co-operation, and with the emergent
phenomenon of secularism as a new religion. But comparatively
little was said at Jerusalem about the Church, or about the
Churches and their mission. The time was not yet. The sense of
the Church had not been reborn, and the younger churches were
not yet a significant force.

THE CHURCH'S MISSION TO THE WORLD

But in the wake of Oxford and its emphasis upon the Church,
the growing importance of the new churches in Asia, Africa, and
Latin America, together with the increasing threat of a disrupted
world, led to the selection of "The World Mission of the Church"
as the central theme of the Madras Conference. A large and unprecedented proportion of the nearly five hundred delegates present at Madras were from the "younger" Churches. A sense of the
reality of the Christian Church as a world community had been
created. Memorable discussions took place, and creative decisions
were made regarding the Church's world mission. Less than eight
months after the conference adjourned, World War II was un-
leashed. It was destined to thunder on for six years. Following the
close of the war, a broken humanity became more tragically rifted
than at any time in history. Symbols of the rift are the continuing
breach between East and West, the dismal dividedness of Germany, Palestine, China, Korea, Viet Nam, and now the ominous

developing rift in the Western Hemisphere, with Cuba as an outpost of the Communist world.

Happily, however, the members of Christ's Church Universal continued to remain united in spirit during the war years, and at its close they were more eager than ever to give concrete communal expression to their growing sense of oneness. It is most significant that the first conference of a worldwide character to be held under any sponsorship after the actual fighting came to an end in 1945 was convened in Whitby, Canada by the International Missionary Council. Madras 1938 was followed by Whitby 1947. The observation is in order that it was much easier to get Christians of the warring nations to meet and confer with one another at the close of World War II than it had been at the close of World War I. Why should this be? The reason is plain. The sense of the Church that was reborn at Oxford and the concrete experience of belonging to the world Community of Christ, which was engendered at Madras, had their effect. It was thus easier for British and German Christians on the one hand, and for American and Japanese Christians on the other, to re-establish bonds of friendship when the guns had ceased to roar and the bombs to fall in the summer of 1945.

When missionary-spirited and Church-minded Christians assembled in 1947 in the small Canadian town of Whitby, not knowing what the future had in store or what plans should be made, they concentrated upon a series of questions that brought together the Eternal and Temporal. They were challenged to consider the "Unity of Mankind" in a divided world. They were confronted with a "World in Ferment." They were invited to consider the "Church in Its World Setting," and the meanings and implications of a "Revolutionary Church." They were charged to meditate upon the "Word of Redemption"; upon the "Given Word," which is the message of the unvarying Gospel; upon the "Articulate Word," which involves the "Problem of Communication"; upon the "Dynamic Word," the reality of the Holy Spirit, who makes Himself manifest in "Proclamation" and in "Fellowship." Discussion followed presentation. Towards the end of the two-week meeting, the members of the conference were grasped by a phrase that was destined to become a dynamic watchword and betokened the beginning of a new era. The new watchword was "Partners in Obedience." Christ's followers throughout the globe, members of the "older" and the "younger" Churches were to go forward "with Christ to the Frontier." And this they were to do because of the "greatness and universality of the missionary obligation."

The closing days of the Whitby Conference were marked by the birth of a new sense of the Church's "frontier," which was proclaimed as being something much more than a geographical boundary. Those present were determined to go forward together in holy partnership, in obedience to Christ's mandate, and as members of a world Community of faith. The conference came to an end with the approval of two significant statements. One was entitled "Christian Witness in a Revolutionary World"; the other, "The Supranationality of Missions."

The affirmation that the Christian Church is true to its nature only when it accepts its missionary obligation continued to be made by the International Missionary Council at two subsequent conferences convened under its auspices. The first of these met in Willingen, Germany in 1952; the second in Accra, Ghana in 1957. Through these conferences a potent impetus was given to study the theological basis of the Church's Mission.

In the meantime, the new status of the "younger" Churches as members of the Church Universal and as responsible participants in missionary partnership became evident in three significant regional gatherings. These were the Conference of Latin American Churches, which met in Buenos Aires, Argentina in 1949; the East Asian Conference, at Bangkok, Thailand in 1950; and the All-African Church Conference, at Ibadan, Nigeria in 1958. All three conferences were convened and controlled by members of the Churches located in the regions indicated. In each of these gatherings a small group of men and women representing the "older" Churches were present as special guests and consultants. But all who attended worked together as members of one holy fellowship.

THE CHURCH'S UNITY IN THE WORLD

The emphasis upon the Church's essential unity as distinguished from its common missionary obligation was given organizational expression by the founding in 1948, in Amsterdam, Holland, of a

World Council of Churches. From the time of its creation, the new council became the symbol of the "ecumenical" insofar as the term involved fraternal relations between the Churches with all the implications of true fraternity. The reborn sense of the Church that had become a reality at Oxford had created for the Churches a new issue, the issue of a united front. Significant in this connection are the words of the man who became the General Secretary and principal architect of the World Council of Churches, Dr. W. A. Visser 't Hooft. In an address, "Our Ecumenical Task in the Light of History," delivered in 1955 by this distinguished ecumenical figure we read, "It is not for nothing that the World Council plan was elaborated in the year in which the Oxford Conference of 1937 used as its unofficial slogan, "Let the Church be the Church."

The council stimulated the confrontation of the Churches by questions relating to theological ideas and Church structure. It facilitated also a common approach to social and international issues. The movement formerly known as "Faith and Order," which represented theological concern among the Churches, and "Life and Work," which represented the Church's social concern, became merged at Amsterdam to form the World Council. There was created, in addition, the Church's Commission on International Affairs. The new council and the International Missionary Council (the latter having been constituted in 1921 as a council of missionary councils and not of ecclesiastical denominations) entered into "association." At the same time, a committee was appointed and given a significant name, "The Joint Committee of the International Missionary Council and of the World Council of Churches." It became the task of this committee to deal with relations between the two world bodies, to deepen their sense of comradeship, to stimulate co-operative effort, and to relieve tensions between them. At a meeting in Königstein, Germany in 1954, this committee was reorganized. With the tacit approval of both parent bodies, it undertook the task of exploring the questions of their eventual integration. The vision was born that the body which had been created thirty years before to promote the world *mission* of the Church should become one with the body which existed to promote the Church's *Unity*.

In the meantime the Central Committee of the World Council

of Churches, at a meeting in Rolle, Switzerland in 1951, had given authoritative sanction to that interpretation of "ecumenical" which regards it as a term equally expressive of "mission" and "unity." Following the writer's challenge of the propriety of speaking of the "Missionary Movement" *and* the "Ecumenical Movement," as was done in a paper presented at one of the sessions of the committee, a specially appointed subcommittee, presided over by Bishop Lesslie Newbigin, brought in a statement entitled "The Calling of the Church to Mission and to Unity." That statement, which was duly approved by the Central Committee as a whole, contains this incisive and historic affirmation:

"We would especially draw attention to the recent confusion in the use of the word 'ecumenical.' It is important to insist that this word, which comes from the Greek word for 'the whole inhabited earth,' is properly used to describe everything that relates to the whole task of the whole Church to bring the Gospel to the whole world. It therefore covers equally the Missionary Movement and the movement towards unity and must not be used to describe the latter in contradistinction to the former. We believe that a real service will be rendered to true thinking on these subjects in the churches if we so use this word that covers both 'unity' and 'mission' in the context of the whole world. Both the I. M. C. and the W. C. C. are thus properly described as organs of the Ecumenical Movement."

The movement towards giving a single institutional expression to the two councils gained momentum. In the years immediately following the Königstein meeting, events of great "ecumenical" significance took place. An historic action was taken at the International Missionary Council Assembly in Accra (the capital city of the newly formed Republic of Ghana) during December, 1957. It was agreed by a large majority of the delegates present to recommend to the thirty-five constituent councils of the International Missionary Council that the council should merge with the World Council of Churches. It is but fair to say that some members of the Ghana Assembly expressed very deep concern regarding the wisdom of the proposed merger. They felt that to relate the missionary movement directly to the Churches and to make mission policy subject in any way to ecclesiastical decision would imperil the freedom and vitality of Christian missions throughout the world.

Some of those who expressed this apprehension at Ghana continue to be committed to this idea. It is their conviction that the world mission of the Church should not be controlled by the Churches, but rather by dedicated Christian men and women who are loyal members of their Churches, who are not sectarian in spirit or attitude, but who form missionary societies to carry forward Christ's commission to "disciple all nations." The concern of those men and women has been inspired by one of the sobering facts of Church history. It is tragically true that ecclesiastics and hierarchs in all Churches—Roman Catholic, Eastern Orthodox and Protestant—have not generally been noted for missionary zeal in terms of the true apostolic tradition. It is a lamentable fact that the Church, through putting self-interest above the interests of Christ and His Kingdom, has often failed "to be in very deed the Church." We have cause, therefore, to be grateful to all who share this concern, and give utterance to it, even while we may be unable to accept the policy to which their viewpoint gives rise.

The Ghana decision, which was subsequently endorsed by an overwhelming majority of the national councils, led finally to the union of the International Missionary Council and the World Council of Churches. This event took place in November, 1961 at the Third Assembly of the World Council in New Delhi, India. Not far distant was the city of Lucknow, where in 1953 Asian Christians who attended a meeting of the World Council made it emphatically plain that they wanted to belong only to one world body, not to two. "Association" was thus transformed into "integration," and the International Missionary Council became the "Division of World Mission and Evangelism of the World Council of Churches," convening for the first time in Mexico City during December, 1963.

As regards the World Council itself, it became, at the New Delhi Assembly, more classically Christian and more contemporaneously "ecumenical" in another respect. Pressure from several sources had advocated that the basis for membership in the council should be more fully expressive of the historic Christian faith. The original basis, which had been approved at Amsterdam, was in these terms:

"The World Council of Churches is a fellowship of Churches which accept our Lord Jesus Christ as God and Saviour." The new basis, as adopted at New Delhi, reads as follows: "The World Council of Churches is a fellowship of Churches which confess the Lord Jesus Christ as God and Saviour according to the Scriptures and therefore seek to fulfill together their common calling to the glory of the one God, Father, Son, and Holy Spirit."

In this greatly enriched basis, Jesus Christ as God and Saviour continues to be central. But the attitude towards Christ passes beyond "acceptance" to "confession." Emphasis is laid, moreover, upon the Scriptures as the source of the Church's knowledge of Christ. Churches knit together in "fellowship" are now pledged to be an active fellowship, which might be described as a "Fellowship of the Road." They are committed to take their "common calling" seriously, in order that, through holy togetherness, they may be in "very deed the Church." This they will do "to the glory of the one God, Father, Son, and Holy Spirit." That is to say, they will live to God's "glory," unveiling the splendor of His character, fitting into His eternal "design," and reproducing in their Church life the dynamic, missionary, Pentecostal reality that underlies and is expressed by the Christian doctrine of the Holy Trinity. In this way, coincidentally with institutional development, whereby "mission" and "unity" were "integrated," the council, by adopting the new basis, took on a missionary dimension.

It also took on a new ecclesiastical dimension. How moving and symbolic it was that at the same epoch-making assembly, the delegates from the Churches which, ecclesiastically speaking, have represented the polar extremes in the Church Universal, should enter into fellowship. At New Delhi, the Russian Orthodox Church and two Chilean Pentecostal Churches were received into full membership in the World Council. At the same time, there were present at the council sessions as "observers," and with the full sanction of the Vatican, distinguished clergymen of the Roman Catholic Communion.

The presence of those Roman Churchmen at the New Delhi Assembly gave still greater "ecumenical" significance to the gathering. It also served to raise some very basic questions. Only thirteen years before, his Holiness, Pope Pius XII, had refused, in the most absolute way, to permit any Roman Catholic to attend, in any capacity whatever, the sessions of the Amsterdam Assembly. I vividly recall an incident that occurred at a meeting of the Faith and Order Committee at Oxford a year later. At one of its sessions, the committee was eager to obtain an authoritative Roman Catholic viewpoint on a certain issue. An eminent Catholic theologian was invited to attend and to make his Church's position clear. He consented and came, but on one condition. He could be there only anonymously, and no publicity should be given to the fact of his presence! No less significant was the fact that in a handbook on the Church, published about that time, the chapter on the Roman Catholic Church had to be written by a Protestant, Dr. Newton Flew.

But, as the years passed (and even before the election of Pope John XXIII) Roman Catholic guests began to appear at gatherings convened under the auspices of the World Council, or of some national council related to it. They felt perfectly free to take part in the discussions. It was not long before "dialogue" between Roman Catholics and Protestants became the order of the day, not only in Europe, where it had been common for many years, but also in the Western Hemisphere, North and South, as well as in Asia and Africa.

The culminating phase of this new "ecumenical" phenomenon took place when Pope John XXIII invited Churches of the Protestant and Orthodox traditions to send observers to the Second Vatican Council, which convened in Rome in October, 1962. The atmosphere created by New Delhi and Rome opens up new vistas. It also creates some very basic problems for the future of Christianity and the Church Universal. While crucial issues confront the historical Churches in the Protestant tradition, signs of unrest and of spiritual rebirth begin to multiply in Roman Catholicism. Throughout the Roman World, including Latin America, an entirely new approach is being made to the human situation and to the spiritual problem of man. The old Clericalism, which existed to control life, is being replaced by a new Incarnationalism, which seeks to transform life. The institutional is slowly giving way to the personal, and the formal to the mystical. The laity are being given a more responsible role in the life of the Church. The Bible is being translated and widely disseminated.

Jesus Christ is being rediscovered as a living contemporary reality, quite apart from His presence in the Eucharist. The Church begins to move from the role of being Christ's patron to that of being His servant. Concern is being expressed by some eminent Roman Catholic theologians, such as Dr. Hans Küng, regarding the degree to which the Marian Cult has detracted from the status and obscured the redemptive function that belongs to Christ alone.

Side by side with these signs of rebirth in the ancient Church, we are confronted with the growth, dynamism, new ecumenical spirit, and increasing influence of the Pentecostal Churches. These Churches are growing more rapidly in certain parts of the world than are the Churches of historical Protestantism. They are proving themselves, moreover, to be more realistic than the "older" Churches, and more relevant to the revolutionary conditions that exist in many lands. The Pentecostal emphasis upon the Holy Spirit begins to grip an increasing number of ministers and university students belonging to the historical Churches.

THEOLOGICAL EDUCATION
IN THE ECUMENICAL ERA

In view of all this the time has clearly come for a more basic and comprehensive study of Churchly reality, and of the Church's role in the world, than has been undertaken in the past. It is the thesis of this book that the situation calls for the development of a new field of study. This new field, which is here called the Science of Ecumenics, was introduced into theological education in 1937 at Princeton Theological Seminary. The new Chair of Ecumenics, whose establishment (as indicated in the Prologue) was approved by the governing body of the institution referred to in the spring of that year, was designed to deal with the "Church Universal conceived as a world missionary Community, its nature, functions, relations, and strategy." Included within the general field of Ecumenics were the traditional courses on the "History of Christian Missions," and "Comparative Religion." Later were added such courses as "Comparative Christianity: A Comparative Study of the Christian Traditions," "The Problems of Church and State," "Religions of East Asia," "Christianity and the Hispanic World," "Christianity and the Moslem World," "Christianity and the Peoples of Africa," "The Protestant Churches of Asia," "The New Missionary in Ecumenical Mission."

Certain conditions must be fulfilled, however, if the study of Ecumenics is to achieve its objective of elucidating the Church's mission and promoting the Church's unity. It is imperative that centers of theological education around the world have a clear conception of their mission in an ecumenical era. Theological colleges and seminaries exist to prepare men and women who shall have a luminous understanding of Christian truth and its relevancy to the basic problems of society and culture, and who, in a spirit of total commitment to Jesus Christ, shall be equipped to serve Christ and the Church, wherever their lot may be cast. Theological sophistication without spiritual commitment ends in pompous sterility.

No theological seminary can fulfill its ecumenical role if it is simply an institution for the presentation and discussion of religious ideas and problems. If it were only that, a seminary would be the mere counterpart of educational institutions that are dedicated exclusively to train the intellect of students and to confront them with a vast panorama of knowledge. These institutions interpret the scholar as one who, in intellectual honesty, makes solemn pledge to the Cult of the Uncommitted. He must be open to all truth, but must commit himself to no truth save the truth of open-mindedness.

President A. Lawrence Lowell of Harvard once defined a university as "a society or guild of scholars, associated together for preserving, imparting, increasing, and enjoying knowledge." Abraham Flexner, the founder of the now famous Institute for Advanced Study, in Princeton, where Albert Einstein was a teacher, formulated in these terms his ideal for the institution he dreamed to create. "It should be a haven where scholars and scientists may regard the world and its phenomena as their laboratory, without being carried off in the maelstrom of the immediate."

Let us thank God for such academic centers and for others like them. They have their role. They cannot, however, be an adequate prototype for institutions of theological learning that take seriously the Christian faith.

A theological seminary can be true to its nature and fulfill its destiny only when teachers and students together dedicate themselves and their scholarship not merely to make a *case* for truth, but to serve the *cause* of the One who is Himself the Truth. They will regard the world not only as an object of dispassionate study, but as an arena where they must engage in crusading action. In this most revolutionary hour in world history, when the structure of society is changing, when militant forces of the Right and the Left strive for the mastery, institutions dedicated to the interpretation of the Christian religion and to the preparation of ministers for the Christian Churches are called to be missionary in spirit. That is to say, the atmosphere, the courses, the activities, and the outlook of a theological seminary should have, in the deepest sense, a *missionary* dimension. For if the Church without a missionary dimension cannot "be in very deed the Church," a theological seminary that lacks such a dimension cannot be an effective servant of the Church and the Church's Lord.

A seminary should have also a *communal* dimension if it is to serve the Community of Faith. It dare not be a mere institution: it must be a *fellowship*, a microcosm of the Church Universal. If a theological seminary is to fulfill its "ecumenical" mission, being equally concerned about the Church's *unity* and the Church's *mission*, all who belong to it must themselves constitute a true community. They must move beyond the conception of "star-friendship" that reproduces the motion of planets that go orbiting around the Sun with but a deferential nod to one another as they pass in the cold stellar spaces. This is the protocol pattern of friendship that Friedrich Nietzsche conceived as ideal for super-man.

Equally to be transcended, however, in a theological seminary community is what has been traditionally known in the Hispanic world as "tavern friendship."[13] This is the form of relationship which marks the hilarious encounter of mere social "buddies." They have a good time together, but they never come to know one another deeply, or become relevant to one another's needs. The reality of the Church as the Community of Christ should have its

---

[13] *la amistad tabernaria.*

most vital and dynamic expression among those who belong to a
seminary family. For, if community is not real among the Church's
present and future leaders, how can it ever be real among the
Christian rank and file?

It was the aspiration to constitute a Community of Christ that
led members of the faculty and student body of a historic and
beloved theological institution in a small New Jersey town called
Princeton, to adopt in 1953 a statement concerning Christian
Community. In the belief that this statement may be of interest
to seminaries, Churchmen, and persons in general who are concerned about Christian Community in the ecumenical era, I
venture to transcribe its preamble. It runs as follows:

> Princeton Theological Seminary is more than a school for the
> preparation of pastors and teachers of the Christian Church.
> It is a Community which undertakes to order its common life
> in accordance with the obedience of faith in Jesus Christ Our
> Lord. Insofar as Jesus Christ is the norm and the guide of all
> that happens in the life of the Community, it is possible to
> speak of Princeton Seminary as a Christian Community, and to
> commend the privileges and responsibilities of membership
> to successive generations of faculty, students and staff. Where
> Jesus Christ is the Lord of life, and is at work among those who
> live together in His service, the common life of all becomes
> the concern of each member of the Community; and what hap-
> pens to each member of the Community belongs to the com-
> mon life and the well-being of all.[14]

Engraven on a plaque in the vestibule of the seminary building
known as the Campus Center, are words which seek to interpret
the meaning of "Community" in its institutional and ecumenical
dimension. The words in question are these:

> This building, erected by the sacrificial gifts of alumni and
> friends of Princeton Theological Seminary, is dedicated to the
> creation on this campus of a Christian Community, whose
> members, drawn from many lands and Churches, shall serve
> in all the world the one Church which is Christ's Body.

[14] *Princeton Theological Seminary Handbook,* 1962–63, p. 146.

This book will seek to structure the approach to ecumenical reality which inspired the author's discussion of Ecumenics in a theological seminary classroom. It will also seek to breathe the ecumenical spirit which inspired community relations on that seminary campus.

We are now ready for a basic and objective study of the Science of Ecumenics.

Ecumenics
and Kindred Sciences

chapter 2

When, in the course of history, a new reality comes to birth or an already existent reality is clearly discerned for the first time, the need arises to coin an appropriate name for what has emerged. When it became apparent, for example, in the mid-Nineteenth Century, that human society could not be adequately studied as a mere branch of Philosophy, Augustus Comte created a new science to which he gave the name "Sociology." Both the science and the name had a long, hard struggle before they won academic recognition by the learned; but they ultimately prevailed. Later, as interest in the human mind and its problems increased, the sciences designated Psychology and Psychiatry evolved. Early in the present century, when Geography began to be studied from the viewpoint of the earth's resources, and the peoples of the world from the viewpoint of their characteristics, and both in the interests of military strategy, the Science of Geopolitics was born. When a political theory that gave the State the right to control society and all its institutions received concrete expression, the term "totalitarianism" was minted.

The multiplicity of new terms, especially in the realm of science and technology, has now become so great that scientists admit they no longer understand one another's language. They begin to pass their days in different scientific realms, and have come to the point, as one of them has put it, of "knowing more and more of less and less."

In the sphere of the Church's growth, and because of the emergence for the first time in history of a World Christian Community, we are confronted with a new reality. This new reality involves a new concept, which, in turn, necessitates an appropriate designation. To all that has to do with the Christian Church as a World Missionary Community, together with the responsibilities that belong to it, and the situations that challenge it, we give the name *"Ecumenics."*

The question immediately arises, why this particular term? Admitting the conceptual necessity for some term to designate the science that must deal with the new reality just described, wherein lies the linguistic legitimacy of the particular term suggested and of the significance which it is proposed to attach to it?

THE SECULAR GENESIS OF THE ECUMENICAL CONCEPT

The word "ecumenics" is derived from the Greek word *"oikos,"* which means a set of rooms, and so, a *house* or dwelling. It may mean also a *household* or *family*, that is, the people who live in the house. The verb *"oikeo,"* means *I dwell* or *I inhabit*. From the present participle passive of this verb, and with the term *"ge,"* earth, being understood, comes the word *"oikoumenē," which* signifies *the land that is being inhabited, the inhabited earth.* *"Oikoumenikos,"* from which comes the term *ecumenical,* signifies *that which is related to, or is co-extensive with, the inhabited earth.*

Most fascinating and suggestive is the history of this word *"oikoumenē."* In the speeches of the great Greek orator Demosthenes, the *oikoumenē* signified the Greek world, that is to say, the territory conquered by the armies of Alexander and brought under the influence of Hellenic culture. Beyond the Greek domains lived the Barbarians, who could not be regarded as being truly "ecumenical," or in the best sense "human," inasmuch as they lived outside the real *oikoumenē!*

The Romans, with equal modesty, equated the *oikoumenē* with the Roman Empire. It was the world conquered by the imperial legions of Rome and subsequently brought under the sway of

Roman law. Thus, when Luke, describing the setting of Christ's birth says, "In those days, a decree went out from Caesar Augustus that *all the world should be enrolled*," the Greek word he uses is "*oikoumenē*" (Luke 2:1)ᵢ For the Roman Emperor was the "*Kurios tes Oikoumenēs*," the "Lord of the inhabited earth." The people who lived outside the world of the Caesars, the ancestors of Indians and Chinese, Russians, Scandinavians, and the Celts from Northern Scotland, did not belong to the "inhabited earth," the real world as the Romans understood "*oikoumenē*." And yet, ironically, it was "unecumenical" Scottish Highlanders—kilted, barbarian clansmen—who, according to the historian Tacitus, defeated the Roman army at the Battle of Mons Graupius, in the region known in Scottish geography as the Grampian Mountains.

When the Emperor Constantine made Christianity the official religion of the Roman Empire and the Christian Church became the state Church, the term "ecumenical" became related to the ecclesiastical establishment. The seven great Church assemblies that met at intervals between 325 A.D. and 787 A.D. are known in history as the *Ecumenical Councils*. Following a theological controversy that rent the Seventh Ecumenical Council at Nicea, the unity of Christendom was broken. The Eastern Orthodox Church, with its seat in Constantinople, was constituted as the rival of the Church of Rome for the hegemony of the Christian religion. The Patriarch of Constantinople assumed the title of "*Ho oikoumenikos*," "The Ecumenical One." His successor today is known as "The Ecumenical Patriarch." In Roman Catholic circles, the Pope, too, has been spoken of as the "Ecumenical One." The Roman Pontiff, Pope John XXIII, revived and gave new meaning to the term "ecumenical" in the Roman Catholic Church.

The Second Vatican Council, which convened in 1962 and again in 1963, has been popularly called an "Ecumenical Council," because representatives of Churches other than the Church of Rome were invited to be present as observers. It was thereby recognized that no one Church, whatever its theological pretension or its geographical extension, could claim the exclusive right to the title of "ecumenical." Ecumenical reality was, therefore, not something that you start from, as it was in the Greek and Roman world, but something that you move toward.

This new attitude on the part of the Roman Communion, and

the mood that underlies it, reflect the influence of what has been taking place in the world in general with respect to the significance of "ecumenical." With this we resume consideration of the development of this term.

It is important to realize that, following the increasing disruption of the Christian Church, the term "ecumenical" returned once again to the purely secular connotation which was attached to it in Greek and Roman culture. It appears that the word was first used in England in a secular sense in 1607, to signify *general* or *worldwide*. But the term was little used in current speech in this sense or in any other sense. Early in the Twentieth Century, however, as a result of the breathtaking advances of modern technology, the inhabited earth began to become unified in a quite unprecedented fashion. As the decades progressed and technological inventions increased, men everywhere found themselves to be neighbors and contemporaries for the first time in history. With the advent of the airplane, groups of people who had lived in regions hitherto virtually inaccessible became part of the human family. All physical boundaries could now be traversed, for the world had become a neighborhood. With the coming of radio, the denizens of the remotest parts of the globe, whether lettered or unlettered, became, through the possession of simple technological devices, the contemporaries of all the inhabitants of the earth. The world neighborhood was also a world auditorium. It was this new fact of the world's technological unification that led that brilliant but erratic philosopher, Count Hermann Keyserling, to say that all men were now living in an "ecumenical era," and that the earth had become an "ecumenical organism." Speak a vital word, and it is heard by everyone; touch a vital spot and it is felt everywhere.

In the mid-Twenties, one of Keyserling's books, *The World That Is Being Born* (*El Mundo que Nace*), in a Spanish translation first introduced the writer of these lines to the word "ecumenical" in a context that gave it contemporary relevancy. The *ecumenical* concept became from that hour a luminous and dynamic category in his thinking. In the course of the decade before the Oxford Conference of 1937 he occasionally used the term, with a meaning it is true, he would not give to it today. Loss of faith in the Church during those years led him, for example, to describe as an "Ecumenical Christian" a devoted follower of Christ who belonged to no Church in particular, a Christian who transcended all the Churches as they then existed. But when the Church became a new reality in the author's life, and the nature and role of the Church of Christ took on a new dimension in his thinking, he found in the word "ecumenical" the inspiration for the new concept towards which he was feeling his way.

The crystallization came in the spring of 1937 on the eve of the Oxford Conference and in preparation for it. A Chair of Ecumenics was established, of which he became the incumbent. It was clear that beyond the ecumenical reality created by Greek culture and Roman law and modern technology there had come into being a new global reality which was the creation of the Christian Gospel. That reality was the Church Universal. The time had come when this reality, both as it was and as it ought to be, when true to its nature, should become the subject of special study. The name "Ecumenics" was adopted as the most natural and appropriate to designate a science which was rendered necessary by the Church's arrival at the frontiers of the *oikoumenē*, by fresh concern on the part of the Churches regarding the dynamic, missionary role of the Church, and by increased yearning within the hearts of Christians to achieve spiritual oneness for the sake of Christ's mission in the world. Ecumenics was, therefore, defined as *the Science of the Church Universal, conceived as a World Missionary Community: Its nature, its functions, its relations and its strategy.*

ECUMENICS AND COGNATE STUDIES

The precise significance of Ecumenics and the scope of the study, as here conceived, will become clear if we distinguish the Science of the Church Universal from sciences with which it has something in common but from which it also differs in very basic respects. We begin with Sociology.

SOCIOLOGY

Sociology may be defined as the *science of human society, its origin, history, and constitution.* It embraces in its range everything that has to do with society and its development, including the forms, institutions, and functions of human groups. Sociology can legitimately include within its range all matters relating to culture, social institutions, collective behavior, and social interaction.

The Frenchman Comte minted the term *"Sociologie"* in 1838, and, amid much controversy, succeeded in launching the new science as the "comprehensive, objective study of the associate life of man," making it the summit and crown of all the sciences. Since that time, Sociology has made extraordinary strides. This is especially true in the United States, where this science has tended to become a veritable Divinity. Before the shrine of this Divinity must bow every judgment that is formulated upon the collective life of man. As these lines are being written, sociologists in both North America and Latin America are subjecting the Christian Church and its institutions to a penetrating and legitimate scrutiny within the context of collective life in this changing revolutionary time.

In contradistinction to Sociology, Ecumenics studies the *Divine Society, the Christian Church Universal, its nature, its functions, its relations, and its strategy.* It starts unashamedly from a premise. That premise is a truth which is accepted as axiomatic by every Christian. It may be formulated thus. In human society as a collective entity, there is a Community of men and women, worldwide in its dimension, which the Creator of all things brought into being in a special manner, to which He is related in a unique way, and which He has designed to use, and actually does use, for the spiritual good of mankind.

Starting from this assumption, and being careful to make clear the grounds upon which it founds its belief in the unique character of the Church and the Church's mission within the general sphere of human society (which is the field of the sociologist), Ecumenics subjects the Church as it exists in the world to the most rigorous scrutiny. It seeks to inspire in the Church the practice of self-examination. It looks at the empirical Church as it looks at the contemporary world, in the light of God and His purpose in Jesus Christ, and not in the light of any particular sociological theory of human society. At the same time, Ecumenics avails itself of all the insights, and takes seriously all the concerns, criteria, and criticism that an enlightened sociology can supply, in order that it may be able to provide a luminous and dynamic pattern for what the

Christian Church should be and do in the society of which it is a part.

ECCLESIOLOGY

Ecclesiology is a *theology of the Church.* It is a study of the Church in the light of God and His purpose. A Christian affirmation, and a premise of classical Christianity, is that God Almighty has unveiled His being and purpose for mankind in Jesus Christ. It is affirmed also that the Church is the first fruit of the redemptive achievement of Christ, and that it has been constituted by God as the organ within history whereby the knowledge of God and His will for the world shall be made known to all men everywhere.

We have witnessed in recent decades a veritable renaissance of theological interest and concern. From being a mere appendage to philosophy or a subsidiary of sociology, theology has regained a status in its own right. During the same period, and as part of the same renaissance, the Church, which had largely ceased to be a vital theme in Christian thought, regained its place in Christian concern. It has even become central in theological discussion. As a matter of fact, in this "ecumenical era" no subject so absorbs Christian theology, whether in Protestantism, Roman Catholicism, or Eastern Orthodoxy, as a theology of the Church. That this should be so is an inspiring fact. For one of theology's greatest needs, amid the prevailing confusion in both the Church and the world, is an adequate study of the Church. Such a study would involve everything pertaining to the Church's nature and mission. When the subject of study concerns the *structure* of the Church, or the claim to special status which may be made by a given Church, or the problems of relations between the several Churches, the term *ecclesiology* is commonly used to designate this particular branch of theology.

In what respect must Ecumenics be distinguished from Ecclesiology? *Whereas a theology of the Church in all its phases is supremely concerned with understanding the Church, Ecumenics is concerned with applying the light and inspiration derived from such understanding to the formulation of a strategy for the Church's confrontation with the world.* The everlasting nature of the Church, the claims made by Churches, and the relations of

Churches with one another, in the unity of the one faith, are studied by Ecumenics with a view to developing a plan of action whereby the Church may be "in very deed the Church." *Action and strategy are thus inherent in the conception of Ecumenics.*

CHURCH HISTORY

It is a significant fact that the modern or linear conception of history is a child of the Christian religion. The apprehension of Jesus Christ as the center of history, as He who came in the *kairos,* the supreme moment in the succession of the ages, fulfilling what had gone before and determining what should be hereafter, broke the cyclic view of history which had dominated thought in ancient times. For if history has had a center, and consequently a before and an after, a beginning and an end, it should be imaged not as a circle, but as a straight line. The Church, centered in Christ, created by the Holy Spirit as the successor of the ancient People of God, and appointed to be the mother of the New Humanity that was to come, has become the Community of destiny, God's instrument for the shaping of history.

The Science of Church History, as it has been classically and appropriately conceived, is designed to study the movement of the Church through the ages to the present time. Its approach is thus essentially retrospective. Everything relating to the Church—its activities, its structures, its worship, its personalities, its relations, its ideas, its influence upon culture and society, its successes and failures—are all studied in the perspective of the past.

The Science of Ecumenics, on the other hand, has a *prospective* gaze. It is interested, of course, in all the facts that history can provide regarding the life, thought, problems, and activities of the Church through the centuries. But it is primarily interested in these as a background for intelligent, creative, and even militant action in the living present, with a view to shaping the future. Ecumenics is concerned not merely with what has been, but with what should be. It surveys the past in order that, through listening to the voice of God in His providence, through becoming aware of the permanent forces that operate in history, through being inspired by the Church's achievements and sobered by its errors, it may help the Church today to understand itself and to fulfill its mission as it confronts tomorrow.

As regards Ecumenics and Contemporary Church History, the

distinction between these two academic disciplines is this. *Whereas in a survey of the Church as it is today, the Church is studied as an object of investigation, Ecumenics studies the contemporary Church as the subject of militant, missionary effort in the life and thought of today.* In Ecumenics, teacher and students, as persons who belong to the Church and have a responsibility for the Church, are concerned supremely with the Church as a maker of history. Their primary interest is not mere historical research into ecclesiastical happenings, whether in the present or the past. In this regard, Ecumenics represents (if we may use the term) a decidedly existential, as distinguished from a purely investigative, approach to the history of the Church.

This, however, should be added. When the Ecumenical Movement became "the great new fact of our time," it was interpreted in many Church circles as being primarily, if not exclusively, the quest for Christian unity. A difficulty thus arose with regard to Ecumenics. The term "Ecumenics," which had been minted before the "great new fact" was proclaimed, became adopted in some academic centers. It was used, however, to signify everything relating to "ecumenical," that is, inter-Church relations around the world. As thus conceived, Ecumenics has included all matters connected with the *unity* of the Church, but nothing that has to do with the Church's *mission.* For the reasons already indicated, while the Science of Ecumenics, as dealt with in this book, embraces all questions that concern the unity of the Church, it maintains that the Church's achievement of unity is for the fulfillment of its mission.

HISTORY OF MISSIONS

The Missionary Movement, which, until quite recently, was officially known in Christian circles as the Foreign Missions Movement, is rightly regarded as the greatest and most significant spiritual movement in the history of Christianity. It can be matched only by the movement in the First Century, which carried the Gospel to the bounds of the Roman *oikoumenē* and beyond. It was the Missionary Movement, across the past century and a half, that made the Christian Church *ecumenical* in a geographical sense. It inspired the "ecumenical movement" and made possible a Science of Ecumenics.

This movement began with the founding of missionary societies that functioned independently of the Churches to which the missionaries belonged. In the course of time, however, many of those societies, though by no means all of them, became related to particular Churches which now gave their official sponsorship and support to "Foreign Missions." Following a spiritual awakening, the Churches developed a missionary sense in their members. University campuses were stirred by youthful crusaders, members of the newly formed "Student Volunteer Missionary Movement," whose slogan was, "The Evangelization of the World in this Generation." The newborn missionary sense came to its heyday in the last two decades of the Nineteenth Century and the first of the Twentieth, just before the outbreak of World War I.

In the course of the last half-century, many things have happened in the field of Foreign Missions. As a result of missionary influence, new Churches have been established throughout the globe. Many of these "younger" Churches are autonomous and are members of the World Council of Churches. The new sense of oneness that has been created in the Christian Community scattered through many lands has made the word "foreign" unpopular in Church circles. That fact, together with the expansion of the "Church" and the development of the Churches, has had far-reaching consequences. Missionary societies have taken on new names. "Boards of World Mission" begin to substitute for "Boards of Foreign Missions." The word "board" begins to sound hard and harsh, bureaucratic and imperious; "commission" has been substituted in some instances. In the case of a leading missionary organization in the United States, the historical title "Board of Foreign Missions" is now "The Commission on Ecumenical Mission and Relations." This designation, together with the accompanying watchword of the commission, "Into all the world together," enshrines the thought that the unity of the Church is for the world mission of the Church. It proclaims that the same body that is concerned with dynamic missionary action must be concerned about the relations between all the entities that are pledged to "togetherness."

Consequent upon these developments a whole series of new issues has emerged. These relate to the status and role, and also to the designation, of the "missionary" from another Church and land. They concern the relations between the "mission" and the national

Church, the missionary responsibility of the "daughter" Church and its relations with the "mother" Church, and also the question of priorities that should be given preference in the Church's fulfillment of its mission. Coincidentally with these developments there has appeared a wealth of new literature. Such questions are discussed as the conditions that determine the growth and development of new Churches, the role of the laity, the training of the ministry, and the relationship of Christianity to culture, the Churches, and rapid social change.

All such questions and concerns form an integral part of Ecumenics, as we have defined it. For the Christian Missionary Movement, with its fruits and its problems, should not, and cannot, be treated any longer in isolation from the role of the Church as a world missionary Community. "Missions" must cease to be an activity of some Churches; and "mission" must be recognized as a function of the whole Church. The historical Missionary Movement must thus be set in the perspective of the Church as a whole and of the contemporary world situation. It must continue to be an inspiring force in the thought of the Church, and an abiding pattern in the life of the Church. It must inspire the Church Universal to become what God intended it to be, and what a true Science of Ecumenics should, through the Holy Spirit, help it to become. The inescapable perspective that the Missionary Movement created is: *the mission of the whole Church in the total world situation.*

COMPARATIVE RELIGION

Essential also to Ecumenics is the study of the non-Christian religions. There was a time, some decades past, when it was seriously thought that the great ethnic faiths were reaching the point of becoming effete, or at least of ceasing to be dynamic spiritual forces. The opinion was widely held in academic circles that the influence of western civilization would inevitably spell their doom. There were instances in which chairs of Comparative Religion were abandoned or downgraded. We have witnessed, however, in recent years, a marked resurgence of vitality among the ancient religions of Asia. This is true of Islam, Hinduism, Buddhism, and even Shintoism. Islam and Buddhism have developed new missionary energy, and Hinduism, in some reform movements, begins to become missionary for the first time in its history.

In some instances, the rebirth of religions long regarded as decadent and as having no future has been due to a rising spirit of nationalism in the lands where they have functioned. Old religions are sponsored by new governments in the interests of national policies. In other instances, the resurgence of traditional faiths betokens spiritual hunger and a quest on the part of the people for light, peace, and soul nourishment amid the confusion and uncertainty of the times. We have cause to rejoice that at present there are institutes in Asia supported by the Church where Christian scholars dedicate themselves to a thorough study of the non-Christian religions.

But whatever the reason for this phenomenon, let us ask what is the appropriate relationship between Comparative Religion and Ecumenics?

As an intellectual discipline, Comparative Religion studies the several religions of the world in order to understand and compare their origin, history, characteristics, and ideas. Some Christian academicians hold the view that, when the study of the great religions is undertaken within the precincts of a university, the teacher, whatever be his personal religious belief, should not introduce into his presentation any premise, criterion, or value judgment in terms of which religion or particular religions should be judged.

But whatever view be held as to the particular approach to religion which is deemed consonant with the objectivity, dispassionate analysis, and loyalty to the cult of the uncommitted that mark the contemporary academic atmosphere, this must be said. The approach of Ecumenics to the study of Comparative Religion cannot be that of religious neutrality or of intellectual uncommittedness. It starts calmly, unashamedly, and with intellectual conviction from the premise which is affirmed in Holy Scripture, that the Author and Ruler of the Universe made Himself known historically in Jesus Christ, the God-man and the Saviour of mankind. Ecumenics is keenly interested, however, in discerning in the non-Christian faiths such gleams of insight into Himself, man, and the world as God may have been pleased to enshrine in their history, practices, and ideas. At the same time, while aiming at a scholarly, objective understanding and appreciation of the non-Christian religions, Ecumenics studies these religions specifically as *objects of missionary concern*. For that reason, it devotes thought to the discovery and formulation of an enlightened Christian approach to the other religions. Central in this approach must ever be the manifestation of that wisdom and love in the representatives of Christianity without which the devotees of other religions will never be attracted to the faith of Christ.

GEOPOLITICS

In this survey of studies which we have designated "cognate," because they are related to, or must be taken into account by, Ecumenics, we come finally to Geopolitics. This brings us to the question of strategy, which is as vital in the spiritual realm as it is in the secular. When the problem arises as to what the Christian Church should *do*, as distinguished from what it should *think* and what it should *be*, Christians have much to learn, and also to unlearn, by studying the principles of strategy which secular governments adopt to secure their objectives.

"Geopolitics" is another illustration of a word that was minted to designate a new reality that having been discerned had to be taken seriously.

Webster's Second New International Dictionary [1] thus defines the term: "Geopolitics (or *geopolitik*) is a science concerned with the dependence of the domestic or foreign politics of a people upon the physical environment." This definition, however, in view of happenings during World War II, and of factors that have determined and continue to determine international relations since that war came to a close, fails to be adequate. Following a study of some outstanding works on this subject, and in the perspective of current events, I venture to define this new science as follows: *Geopolitics studies the regions of the earth and their resources, the peoples of the world and their characteristics, with a view to obtaining such information regarding nature and man as will facilitate the conquest and control of both, in accordance with a plan of imperialistic domination.*

[1] Webster's Second New International Dictionary, unabridged (Springfield, Mass.: G. & C. Merriam Company, Publishers, 1947).

The originator of the geopolitical idea was the famous British geographer and one-time Director of the London School of Economics and Political Science, Sir Halford J. Mackinder. In 1904, at a meeting of the Royal Geographical Society, Mackinder read a paper on "The Geographical Pivot of History." That pivot he described as the "Heartland": the vast region bounded on the east by the Ural Mountains and on the west by the Yangtze River; on the north by the Arctic Ocean and on the south by the Himalayan Range. In 1919, on the eve of the Versailles meeting that brought World War I to a close, the British geographer wrote a book entitled, *Democratic Ideals and Reality.* In the course of that volume, he used words which went unheeded by the victors, but which were destined to be picked up in the following decade by military strategists in defeated Germany. Mackinder's famous words were as follows: "When our statesmen are in conversation with the defeated enemy, some airy cherub should whisper to them from time to time this saying,

> Who rules East Europe commands the Heartland:
> Who rules the Heartland commands the World-Island:
> Who rules the World-Island commands the World.[2]

By "East Europe" Mackinder meant the region between the Oder River and the Volga. This area is at present controlled by Russia, whose power extends actually beyond the Oder to the Elbe. The control of the "Heartland" is divided between Russia and China, the latter having recently achieved domination over the whole expanse of the Himalayas. Asia, Africa, and Europe together make up the "World Island." Over against this World Island stands another great island, the Western Hemisphere.

Democratic Ideals and Reality was given no attention by the countries that were victorious in World War I. Not until 1942, when World War II was at its height, did Mackinder begin to be taken seriously by the western Allies. After the lapse of twenty-three years, new editions of his epoch-making book began to appear. But in the interval, his ideas had been picked up in Germany and in Japan. Under the leadership of a military strategist, Gen-

[2] Sir Halford J. Mackinder, *Democratic Ideals and Reality* (New York: Holt, Rinehart & Winston, Inc., 1942), p. 150.

eral Karl Haushofer, an Institute of Geopolitics was established in the University of Munich. Study was devoted to the diverse factors—military, political, economic, and psychological—that should enter the world strategy. Events began to happen in Hitler's Germany. The pages of *Mein Kampf* and the famous *Putsch* of 1933, reflected some of the new ideas. With the passage of time, the new strategy led to attacks on East Europe. Poland fell. Russia was considerably overrun. But the Russians stood fast at Stalingrad, on the banks of the Volga, and defeated the aspirant to World Empire on his way to the "Heartland." Hitler's empire in Europe and North Africa fell. In the meantime, the Japanese, whose military leaders had been profoundly influenced by geopolitical ideas, overran, but later lost, sectors of the Heartland and of the World-Island.

In the period following the close of World War II, mankind has witnessed developments of transcendent importance in the terrain of geopolitical theory and practice. Even while the word "geopolitics" tends to be little used because of its association with German and Japanese imperialists, this science continues to be cultivated sedulously in a greatly developed form. A new world strategy has been born. In both the East and the West a new Imperialism (whatever be the euphemism used to describe it) has also come to the birth. In the struggle commonly known as the "Cold War," every resource—military, political, economic, atomic, psychological, ideological, informational, and even religious—is being used by each of the rival forces that seek to dominate the "World-Island" and the "Other Island," in order to imprint its image upon them.

The time has clearly arrived when the Christian forces of the world should unite in developing a common Christian strategy. Such a strategy would give expression to the insights, objectives and dynamics of the Christian faith. It would summon Christians and the Christian Churches to take their calling seriously, with all realism and dedication, in a world torn by rival forces that struggle on the very brink of doom. In this era when the *oikoumenē*, the whole inhabited earth, is the scene of so much misery and foreboding, the time has come to re-echo and fulfill the word of the great Prophet of the Exile, "Arise, shine; for your light has come, and the glory of the Lord has risen upon you" (Isaiah 60:1).[3]

It is the function of Ecumenics to work toward the development of a Christian strategy for the Church in our time that shall be the spiritual equivalent of *Geopolitics*. Having in mind the description already given of the origin, nature, resources and objectives of this new secular science, let me venture to describe its Christian counterpart: *Ecumenics studies the Christian Churches within the context of God's purpose declared in Holy Scripture, and the human situation as it is today, with a view to the development of a Christian strategy worthy of the mandate of Jesus Christ to bring all nations to His allegiance, and receptive to the infinite resources made available by God to Christ's followers through the Holy Spirit.*

What is said from this point onward will be an exposition of the concept of Ecumenics as embodied in the above description.

[3] Scriptural references not otherwise indicated are from the Revised Standard Version, © 1946, 1952, by Division of Christian Education of the National Council of Churches of Christ in the United States of America.

The Subject Matter
of Ecumenics:
The Church Universal

chapter 3

The way is now clear to address ourselves to the subject matter of Ecumenics. Ecumenics deals, as has been already stated, with *the Church Universal conceived as a world missionary community.* Let us proceed to explicate this concept.

First, what is the Church? The Church is two things. It is an *empirical fact.* It is, also, a *spiritual reality.*

THE CHURCH AS AN EMPIRICAL FACT

A PHYSICAL STRUCTURE

In contemporary society, "Church" means a variety of things. A common meaning is the *building* where Christian worship takes place. The Church as a physical structure is found today throughout the globe in the greatest variety of forms. Its architecture will reflect the religious and cultural background, as well as the social status of those who assemble within it, or of those who erected the edifice. Church buildings run the gamut of design from Gothic and Byzantine Cathedrals to mud or bamboo shacks, from a white colonial shrine to a "little brown church in the vale," or a quiet, simple, meeting house. Churches as structure may change in status. Some which were once centers of living devotion are today museums of religious relics, monuments no longer to the glory of God, but only to His memory. But, happily, the quality and design of a place of worship are not of the essence of the Church.

A LOCAL CONGREGATION

Church is also used to designate a *congregation of Christians accustomed to assemble for worship in a given place.* The local congregation, whether in Philippi or Rome, in countryside or urban center, in inner city or suburban area, is the ultimate empirical unit of the Christian Church. It is a microcosm of the Church as a whole. It forms the cell of the Church Universal.

Great diversity marks the form of organization and the type of worship that obtain in Christian congregations. Some congregations are directed by pastors, priests, or bishops; others recognize no professional ministry. The worship service in one congregation may be highly liturgical, in another it is marked by simplicity and even austerity, with a ban upon prescribed prayers or the sound of instrumental music. In most Christian congregations, it is customary for the Word to be preached and the Sacraments to be administered.

In the United States of America, and in the mission fields of the world where Christianity has become established in the last hundred and fifty years, local congregations have had, and continue to have, a more important status and authority than has been true of similar congregations in the European Protestant tradition. The reason for this difference is that in Europe, following the Reformation, Churchly reality among Protestants began as a movement in the upper sphere of ecclesiastical authority, whereas in Asia, Africa, and the Americas, it began at the grass roots among the people. While a very large number of local congregations are centers of spiritual vitality, this sobering sociological fact is true regarding many others. They are simply religious clubs, each being, as was once remarked by a cynical member of the British Parliament, "a voluntary association for providing services on Sundays for that sector of the community which cares to take advantage of them." In the membership of a congregation are found, in very varying proportions, members who are deeply dedicated to what their Church stands for, members who are mere attendants at Church services, and others who are not really Church members but Church *alumni*. The latter appear in Church only on the great occasions.

A Religious Tradition

Church can also mean a *Christian tradition*. We speak of the Roman Catholic Church, the Eastern Orthodox Church, the Protestant Church. The several hundred denominations of Protestantism are also designated Churches, although some of these prefer to speak of themselves as "assemblies," "conventions," "brotherhoods," or "associations."

It is quite erroneous to think of the number and variety of Protestant Churches as being simply the result of schism. Schisms of course there have been in Christian history, ever since the unhappy break that divided the early Christian Church into two, one with its center in Rome, the other with its center in Constantinople. There are Churches, however, especially in the United States, which owe their character to the racial background of emigrants who set up in their adopted country independent Christian Churches of the particular type to which they were related in the land of their birth. Some Protestant denominations are characterized by loyalty to a particular system of doctrine, others by their adoption of a specific form of Church government, others by the conditions prescribed for Church membership, others by the form of service prescribed for public worship, still others by the attitude which their members are required to adopt in relation to the secular order. There are instances, also, in which an historic event, for example, the American Civil War, was responsible for dividing existing Churches and creating independent Churches within the same ecclesiastical tradition. And, alas, in the Protestant world there are some Churches whose members are limited to people of one race, and from which members of any other race are excluded.

It can be stated as a sociological fact that, so far as theological or ecclesiastical (as distinguished from cultural) considerations at the local level are concerned, the trend in Protestantism today is centripetal in character. The centrifugal movement, which continued for several hundred years following the Reformation of the Sixteenth Century, has given place to a movement towards unity and centrality. This is true locally, nationally, and internationally.

As regards the Roman and Orthodox traditions, certain facts are now apparent to the most casual observer of human affairs. The Roman Catholic Church is no longer so monolithic as it has been traditionally. Diverse trends have become apparent. Clergy and laity become influenced by the spirit of the nation where they live and work, by fresh emphases in culture, doctrine, and human relationship. Roman Catholics in North America, France, and Germany are today deeply concerned about Roman Catholicism as it has developed in Spain, Portugal, and Latin America. They are humiliated by the fact that, due to the doctrine of *Hispanidad,* which equates religion and nationality, Protestant Christians in Spain are regarded as third-rate citizens and have less freedom and status than Protestants enjoy in any other part of the world, including the Communist world.

It should be remarked that the Roman Catholic Church in Spain represents an extreme case of "folk" religion, such as is also found in Latin American countries and in some Protestant lands in Europe. The same phenomenon appears also in countries where Eastern Orthodoxy has been traditionally the dominant faith. "Folk" religion has begun to manifest itself in sectors of the United States. In such cases, the Church comes to be regarded as an influential and venerable social institution whose support is sought by many groups in society, and to which loyalty is given oftentimes for purely sentimental or prudential reasons.

In the world of Eastern Orthodoxy, a new spirit begins to become manifest in the several Patriarchates that control the Russian and Greek Churches, as well as among the Churches traditionally allied with these. Such Churches are the Coptic Church of Egypt and Ethiopia, and the old Jacobite Church of India. A process of self-scrutiny is under way among these Churches. They have become aware that a Church must become dynamically relevant to problems in the secular order, particularly in its own environment, and also that it must break down its traditional isolation and become related to other Churches.

An Ecclesiastical Hierarchy

Still another way of employing the word "Church" represents an important empirical emphasis without involving any specifically Christian viewpoint or doctrine. It is not uncommon for the Church to be equated with, or at least to be an occasional synonym for, Church leaders. The classical, though extreme instance of this usage, is the status of a papal encyclical. When the Pope makes a pronouncement, he speaks constitutionally for the Church of which he is the institutional head. Through him, the Church speaks. In the realm of Protestantism, when messages are addressed to a nation, or to society in general, by a gathering of Church leaders, their voices become, in varying degrees, the voice of the Church. What was said in prophetic proclamation, or agreed upon by a conference or assembly as an appropriate course of action, may not be accepted by the Churches. But the impression becomes pervasive in the popular mind, "The Church has spoken."

It is an undoubted fact that the contemporary trend towards Church unity and relations more truly Christian among the Churches, has created a new phenomenon. It is the phenomenon of a professional, conference-going class. The members of this class play an increasingly important role in the determination of Church policy, denominationally, nationally, and ecumenically. On the other hand, they stand in peril of becoming detached from, and insensitive to, the feelings and ideas of common folk. In this respect, Church leaders, who are in general admirable and dedicated men and women, represent a perilous trend in the Church life of today—the trend, namely, to set the institutional above the spiritual. One of the symptoms of this trend, which begins to provide abundant material for the sociologist and which awakens deep concern among thoughtful Christians, is the current tendency to speak of "Church vocations." Does this represent a movement towards the opposite extreme of the situation that obtained when the reality and significance of the Church were forgotten? Might the Church become Christ's patron? Might Churchianity take the place of Christianity? Might Church vocation become a substitute for Christian vocation? Might the call of the Church take the place of the call of Christ?

With this, we take farewell of the purely empirical and socio-logical. From now onward, we will concentrate our attention upon the Christian Church as a spiritual reality, and consider it in the light of God and His purpose. We shall at the same time aspire after complete realism in confronting the empirical Church with its status and mission in the world.

THE CHURCH AS A SPIRITUAL REALITY

Beyond and beneath everything that is associated with the name "Church," whether it be a physical structure, a local congregation, a religious tradition, or an ecclesiastical hierarchy, there is a spiritual reality—a reality corporate in nature and world-wide in its dimension—which we call by a classical Christian name, the *Church Universal*. This reality, the one Holy Catholic Church, here conceived as a world missionary Community, is the subject matter of the Science of Ecumenics and will, from this point onward, be the center of our thoughts.

The immense company of people who bear the Christian name and who are found today for the first time in history living in groups, large or small, in every representative area of the world, constitute, from the viewpoint of ecclesiastical affiliation, a most diversified family. It is not our purpose to describe or to classify, still less to appraise, the institutional claims or pretensions of the multiple Churches which constitute the Christian Church throughout the world. Our aim is to subject them, one and all, to the criterion by which all Christian Churches must be judged if they are to be "in very deed the Church." That criterion is that they should be, or aspire to be, a missionary Community of Christ.

Whatever may be the official status, outlook, or attitude of a given Christian communion, the thesis that inspires this book, and which we will now proceed to discuss, may be expressed thus: *The essence of the Christian Church is Community.* The Church, moreover, fulfills its destiny as the Community of Christ when it is *missionary* in character. Geographically universal for the first time in its history, the Christian Church needs to rethink its true nature, and face its worldwide missionary responsibility. This it must do by fulfilling its functions, by being "in very deed the Church" in all its relationships, and by developing, under the guidance of the Holy Spirit, a true strategy. This book is a humble attempt to open up a new field of study. It is hoped that the pages that follow may help the writer, and fellow Churchmen who read what is written, to fulfill the Church's mission.

CHRIST AND THE CHURCH

The center of the Christian Church, whatever be the Biblical figure used to describe it, or the ecclesiastical designation which distinguishes it from sister Churches, is Jesus Christ, whose name it bears. It can be said, without exaggeration, *Christianity is Christ*. He occupies a more basic place in the Christian religion than does Mohammed or Buddha in the religions which they founded. Christ and the Church, in its deepest reality, are inseparable. Looking forward to the future, He, Himself, said in pointed and unforgettable words, "Where two or three are gathered in my name, there am I in the midst of them" (Matthew 18:20). The sense of Christ's continuing presence as community-forming was so real in early Christian history that it gave birth to the classical saying, "Where Christ is, there is the Church."

No less significant is the fact that in the most varied types of Christian Community through the ages, individual Christians have given expression to their passionate devotion to Christ. The man from Tarsus set the pace and gave the tone to Christianity at the personal level. Said Paul in his letter to the Christians at Philippi, "To me to live is Christ" (Philippians 1:21a). Out of the Middle Ages come the words of that great Spanish philosopher, saint, and missionary, Raymond Lull, "I have one passion in life and it is He." Miguel de Unamuno, Spain's greatest man of letters since Cervantes, closes his poem, "The Christ of Velázquez," which is recognized as one of the most outstanding monuments of Hispanic verse, with these two lines:

> My eyes are fixed on Thine eyes, Christ.
> My gaze is lost in Thee, my Lord.[1]

When the Sadhu Sundar Singh, regarded by many as the most eminent of Indian Christians, was asked by old friends of his what it was he had found in the Christian religion that he could not

[1] "El Cristo de Velázquez."

have found in the great religions of his country, his reply was, "I have found Jesus Christ." When the Jerusalem Conference of 1928 endorsed a document that, drafted by William Temple, contained these words, "Our message is Jesus Christ," it showed itself heir of the Christian tradition at its best. Loyal to the centrality of Christ in the Bible and in individual Christian experience, the World Council of Churches made membership contingent upon the "acceptance of Jesus Christ as God and Saviour" on the part of its constituent denominations. It has also given Christ the preeminence in study themes for its world gatherings. He has been presented as the "Hope of the world" and as the "Light of the world." In the years immediately ahead, thought will be concentrated on Him as expressing "finality in an age of universal history." The far-reaching significance for Church thought and action of the centrality of Christ will be dealt with in subsequent chapters.

We pass now to consider the Church Universal, this spiritual reality which is inseparably related to Jesus Christ as being primarily and essentially *Community*, the Community of Christ.

THE CHURCH AS THE COMMUNITY OF CHRIST

In the spirit of what has just been said, the Church Universal may be defined as, "*The fellowship of all those for whom Jesus Christ is Lord.*" In an address delivered at the Amsterdam Assembly of the World Council of Churches, Karl Barth offered this definition of the Church. "The Church," said the eminent theologian, "is the living congregation of the living Lord, Jesus Christ." Barth had in mind primarily the local congregation. But the concept of the Church as a congregation, or Community, whose members are sensitive to the reality of Jesus Christ as a living Presence and who take His lordship seriously, may be extended to the Church as a spiritual reality around the globe. People in whom Christ is a living Presence and through whom He works, constitute the soul of the worldwide community of faith. These Christ-possessed men and women give true churchly reality to Christian congregations, denominations, and traditions as structured expressions of Christ's Church Universal.

This concept, which is basic to the present study, is difficult to express. There are, however, historical categories of theological and philosophical thought which may be helpful in enabling the reader to grasp what the writer is seeking to express. The thesis is this: Within the structure of the Church, as an organized society, exists the reality, in greater or lesser degree, of a community of people for whom Jesus Christ is truly Lord, men and women "in Christ," true members of the New Humanity. Here are some analogies. In his interpretation of the universe, Plato, with true intuition, sensed the reality of the Good behind all appearance in the empirical and phenomenal. Georg Hegel, in his quest of an ultimate society, spoke about "collective spirit" as underlying all manifestations of social organization. Karl Marx, inspired by Hegel, identified "collective spirit" not as a single nation, Germany, as Hegel and Nazi philosophers made it, but rather as a society constituted by the world proletariat. Whenever and wherever the Christian Church, as the supreme and ultimate society, is "in very deed the Church," its most visible, authentic, and potent feature is its spiritual reality as a Community *of Christ*. True churchly reality, from corporate worship and relations within a local congregation, to the life and witness of a Church whose organization extends to the frontiers of human habitation, is inseparably related to and will ultimately be judged by, the measure in which it constitutes a Community of which *Jesus Christ is Lord*.

We are now ready for the question, What is it that makes the Church as the Community *of Christ*, a true Community? What does "Community" mean?

The Christian Church, when true to its nature, is a *koinonia*, a fellowship. It was as a fellowship that it first came into being. Following the Ascension of Christ, a group of one hundred and twenty people who spoke of themselves as "brethren," and who were made up of the apostles, the mother and brothers of our Lord, and others who had been His friends and disciples were accustomed to meet together daily for prayer in anticipation of the Spirit's coming. To this first nucleus of the primitive Church three thousand more were soon added. The latter were converted after the Holy Spirit had descended at Pentecost time upon the original group of Christ's followers and inspired thereby Peter's famous sermon. This apostolic utterance led to the radical change in life and outlook that immediately became manifest among those who heard it.

Very important for the conception of Christian Community is the picture given in the Book of Acts of the spirit and attitude that were engendered in those new Christians. They were baptized, of course. After their public profession of faith in Christ, "they met constantly," we are told, "to hear the Apostles teach, and to share the common life, to break bread, and, to pray" (Acts 2:42).[2]

Not only, however, did they come together for instruction, social intercourse, and prayer, they became acutely sensitive to the individual needs of one another. In the most concrete and practical sense they were "one in Christ." According to the record, "All whose faith had drawn them together held everything in common: they would sell their property and possessions and make a general distribution as the need of each required" (Acts 2:44–45) N.E.B.

Here is Community at its holiest and best. The bond that binds all the members together is a common loyalty to Jesus Christ. There is a collective manifestation of the love of God and of one another, both in the home and in public, in worship and in service. There is mutual reverence for one another—no mere "star-friendship." There is joyous fellowship together, but the social contact goes far beyond "tavern friendship," for each "friend" continues to be part of the other's life and concern.

While the Community of Christ, the fellowship created by the Spirit, continued to grow, and its life and membership became more complex, while it became structured and organized in very diverse ways, while, in the course of ages, it had to give its witness in different cultures and had to confront the most varied human situations, one thing has remained constant. The image of the Pentecostal Community remains as the abiding prototype of true Christian Community. It enshrines the spirit and principles by which every organization which bears the name of "Church" must be judged and judge itself.

When it is stated that the theme or subject matter of the Science of Ecumenics is the "Church Universal conceived as a World

[2] *The New English Bible.* © 1961 by the Delegates of the Oxford University Press, and the Syndics of the Cambridge University Press.

Missionary *Community*," it is not being suggested that any Church as we know it is, or should aspire to be, an exact replica, sociologically speaking, of the first Christian Community. What I do suggest, however, is this. If the "Church" accepts as its goal to be "in very deed the Church," it can fulfill its true destiny, and achieve its churchly mission, only when it expresses in its common life the reality of true Community.

Laying aside for the moment all the things that distinguish or divide Christians from one another—things that will be dealt with in due course—there can be no substitute for a Christian society of friends, men and women who are friends of Christ and of one another. Whatever may be the institutional or theological questions that divide Christians, the manifestation of friendly, loving concern for persons on the part of Christians is more ultimate than their acceptance of an identical organization or the same system of ideas. In the Community of Christ, moreover, the fulfillment of responsibility is more basic than the insistence upon rights. The service, however costly, that Christians render must take precedence over the benefits they receive. And to be true to itself, and "in very deed the Church," the Community of Christ must constitute a fellowship that transcends race, class, culture, nationality, and ecclesiastical affiliation.

THE CHURCH AS A WORLD COMMUNITY

But where is this Community to be found? In germinal form, it is found in every place and in all groups where Jesus Christ is hailed as Lord. In perfect form, it is to be found in no place and in no group, whatever claim may be made to a superior relationship to Christ.

This Community, which constitutes the ultimate corporate reality in history, is today a microcosm of mankind. It is global in its geographical extension, and all-embracing in its human inclusiveness. Christians form today the largest, the most varied, and the most widely scattered religious fellowship that history has ever known.

The unique expansion of Christianity, as described by Dr. Kenneth Latourette, and the growth of the Christian Church until it has become "universal," that is, coextensive with the inhabited globe, have been due to an inherent sense of missionary responsibility. In every age and locality in which Christians have been sensitive to their vocation as followers of Christ, they have propagated their faith. This they have done as individuals, or as members of missionary societies, or as the representatives of established Churches that had won themselves a place in a nation or culture with which they became closely identified. In some instances, however, and to the shame of the empirical Church, the Christian religion was imposed upon the indigenous people to whom the Church came as the committed partner and agent of a political order. This is what happened to a lamentable extent in the coming of Hispanic Catholicism to Latin America.

The movement of Christianity in what Latourette calls the "Great Century," coincided with, and to a certain extent was influenced by, the spread of western civilization into Asia, Africa, and the islands of the Pacific. The same missionary passion that had marked the early centuries of Christian history was reborn. The result has been the establishment of Christian Churches, as an empirical fact, in every representative sector of the earth. The last political areas to grant Christians the right to establish congregations for worship, if not actually to carry on evangelistic activity, have been Nepal, Afghanistan, and Saudi Arabia. In the Communist world, Churches suffer many inhibitions. But while they lack complete religious freedom, they continue to grow in numbers, whether in Russia, China, or Cuba.

It is a significant and inspiring fact that in "the age of universal history," in the most revolutionary of all historical epochs, the Christian Churches of the world, both in their geographical dispersion and in their ecclesiastical diversity, have begun to yearn for the experience of *Community*. In manifold ways they express their desire to meet together, to talk together, to worship together, to serve Christ together. In a new, dynamic, and unsectarian sense, they want "to be the Church."

The Church as a Missionary Community

But Community at its best can never be an end in itself, whether it be the New Testament *Koinonia,* or as that mystic *Sobornost* which has been glorified in the Eastern Orthodox tradition, or as the form of ecumenical unity now being pursued among the Churches of the world. The Church conceived as a world Community of Christ must move beyond holy fellowship as its goal in history; it must not exist as a collective will merely to preserve "venerable truths," or "exalted moral principles," as Karl Barth would phrase it.

In its loyalty to the Bible and to Church tradition and doctrine, the Community of Christ must avoid the peril of glorifying these as mere library treasures that contain the wellsprings of orthodoxy and provide themes for "Faith and Order" discussion. The Church, to be "in very deed the Church," must be "missionary" by conviction and commitment, and must make abundantly clear that it *is* so by the policy and program it adopts.

This, therefore, is the subject matter of Ecumenics, and the theme of this book: The Church Universal as a world *missionary* Community. It will be ours to consider not only the *case* which the Church makes, or can make for itself, as a World Community; we will give thought, also, and very especially to the *cause* for which the Church lives, or should live. We shall seek to validate the assumption that it is the Church's glory, as the society of the redeemed, as Christ's friends, partners, and joyous servants, to fit into God's purpose for the world.

If, in the words of Henri-Frédéric Amiel, "action is the essence of life, as combustion is the essence of flame," missionary action, in the deepest and widest sense, can be predicated as belonging to the Church's essence. Conclusions must be followed by commitment, thought must originate action. Churches, Church leaders, and Church members are called by Christ to "follow Him" on the road to the "City which has foundations." Never must they be satisfied with being passive recipients of benefits, dedicated seekers of unity, or contemplative theorists of truth. They must be pilgrims, crusaders, pioneers on the way to the Kingdom. The Church's place as an essentially *missionary* Community is to live on the frontiers of life in every society and in every age. Its goal must be to fulfill God's purpose in Christ for mankind. Christians are called to make the Gospel known to all nations, and to live the Gospel in every sphere and phase of their earthly life.

God has willed that Christ should be known, loved, and obeyed throughout the whole world. It is His design that men everywhere may become sons of God and live as worthy citizens of His Kingdom. It is His will that barriers of separation should be broken down, that unworthy exclusiveness should come to an end, that humanity should be recreated in Christ.

What this means, and what it involves for the Church today, will, I hope, become clear in the chapters that follow.

The Church
in the Purpose of God

PART II

God's Design in History

chapter 4

The Christian Church is the special creation of God and the chief medium through which God operates in the life of the world. This is the foundational premise upon which the thought of this book is based and without which it has no consistency or meaning.

LOVE EVERLASTING

What do we understand by God? Over against the world's changing scene, civilizations that come and go, empires that rise and fall, stands God. Whatever be the name applied to the Reality that lies beyond man's transient life and nature's mysterious face, whether it be the Absolute, the Great First Cause, Ultimate Being, or Deity, the simple affirmation with which the Bible opens sets the context and the mood for all Christian thought and life: "In the beginning God. . . ." God, in the Christian Scriptures, is not the object of research or of apologetic defense, God *is*. His Being is accepted; His voice is heard; His movements are watched; His purpose unfolds; He grasps man in a grand design. The Word becomes flesh. The Eternal enters personally into the historical process to reshape man's nature and to weave the destiny of the "New Man."

Inasmuch as God is not a mere construct of man's mind, life has objective meaning and man has a spiritual Master. Because

God is not abstract Being but is the *living* God, who acts and plans in perfect wisdom, man becomes truly man when he joyously fits himself into God's great scheme of things, becoming thereby in a special sense, God's man.

The living God is also the *holy* God. He is the source and the guardian of all spiritual perfection. That being so, there are ultimate values and laws by which man should govern his life and relationships. These laws and values are not the creation of an aloof celestial Potentate who arbitrarily prescribes them to man for the direction of his terrestrial existence. God, the All-wise and the All-holy, is also God, the All-loving.

"God is Love." These three words are the basic theme of the New Testament, the perfected melody of chimes that began to sound in the Old. Because God loves, He *cares*. People, all sorts of people, bad people as well as good people, people who hate everything associated with the Everlasting Goodness, are objects of His compassionate concern.

With the advent of Christianity, love, which in Hellenic culture was known as *"eros,"* took on a new dimension. In Greek poetry and philosophy, *eros* was a longing desire to have something, whether sensuous or spiritual in kind, that one lacked and wished to possess. It was essentially egocentric; it could be predicated only of man and not of Deity. At its highest, it was a way of man to God and not a way of God to man. But in the Christian religion, *eros* became *agape*, the manifestation of a passionate concern on God's part for human beings and their welfare.[1] A new era began when it dawned upon people that there was a love movement from God to man, that "God loved the world so much that He *gave* to man and for man His Divine selfhood—His only son." And being All-mighty as well as All-loving, God guaranteed that the realization of the purpose that was the ultimate goal of His self-giving would not be frustrated.

THE ABRAHAMIC PRESUPPOSITION

This attitude towards the Absolute as more than an object of human admiration or longing, and as being essentially a subject of self-disclosure and concern, broke into history in the life of a

[1] See Anders Nygren, *Agape and Eros* (Philadelphia: Westminster Press, 1953).

people who traced their descent from a great nomad called Abraham. This man, already in his seventies, was living in retirement in an old ancestral home in the Euphrates Valley when suddenly he became conscious of a summons from Deity. The retired oldster felt a divine compulsion to leave the land of his ancestors and set out on a long journey towards a mountainous territory overlooking the Mediterranean seaboard. There he was to live a nomad's existence in a land that would in due course belong to his descendants, although as yet he had no son. He faced the future, however, in the firm faith that the mysterious Being who had called him to his great adventure would make him the father of a people whose life and destiny would be shaped by the God of Abraham, for the spiritual welfare of all mankind.

In due course, his wife, Sarah, bore Abraham a son, whom he named Isaac. Isaac became the father of Jacob, who in turn sired twelve sons. These became the fathers of twelve historic tribes. Thus was born the Hebrew people, the "children of Abraham" who became the "children of the covenant," the "chosen race." In the checkered history of this people, there appeared in successive generations the figures of Jacob and Moses, Joshua and David, Amos, Jeremiah, and a great prophet commonly called the Second Isaiah who lived in exile by the "waters of Babylon." After the "seed of Abraham" had gone through a full cycle of spiritual experiences, from the time their ancestor left the Euphrates Valley for Palestine to the time when they settled once again in their homeland, at the close of seventy years captivity in the land where Abraham had once lived, something happened. There appeared Abraham's greatest son, Jesus of Nazareth, who picked up and gave a new dimension to the Abrahamic adventure.

In recent years Biblical theologians and persons interested in the theology of mission have written so much admirable material regarding the missionary concept as embodied in the life and thought of the Hebrew people that I do not feel it necessary to deal in detail with the varied facets of this concept as found in the Old Testament. It is important, however, to set in high relief one or two elements of prime importance for our understanding of the Church in the purpose of God. These elements are enshrined in the figure of Abraham and in the prophetic view of Jerusalem as the Great Mother of Mankind.

It is impossible to think of Abraham and his personal encounter with Deity without being reminded that God is the God of persons. God *individualizes*. That is to say, He is interested in people as individuals, and not merely as members of a mass society, whether the society in question be a nation, a class, or a Church. This means that people grow up, become spiritually mature, and are able to fulfill their human vocation only when God becomes *their* God in a personal sense and they are able to say to Deity, "Thou art my God."

A contemporary thinker who has shown great insight into this matter is an Anglican layman, H. A. Hodges, Professor of Philosophy in the University of Reading, England. Himself the subject of a profound experience of Christian conversion when he was a young teacher in Balliol College, Oxford, this distinguished thinker has re-echoed in our time the strain that sounded in the rhapsodic utterance of that great French scientist, philosopher, and saint, Blaise Pascal. Pascal's words, written on a crumpled paper found after his death, sewed up in one of his garments, are these: "God of Abraham, God of Isaac, God of Jacob, not of philosophers and scholars, God of Jesus Christ, my God, and thy God. Thy God shall be my God."

Of first-rate significance for an understanding of the centrality of the individual in the Christian religion and of personal commitment on the part of individual people in everything relating to the Church's mission in history, are the following significant words of Professor Hodges. In a book, entitled, *Christianity and the Modern World View*, he writes as follows. Because of the importance of the issue involved and the extraordinary lucidity of the utterance, I venture to quote it at length. The professor says:

> I shall contend that Christian thinking proceeds on a presupposition of its own, which I shall call *the Abrahamic presupposition*, or *Abrahamic theism*. For the New Testament insists over and over again that Abraham is the model for Jew and Christian alike, and that the true Christian is the spiritual child of Abraham, that is, one whose relation to God is the same as Abraham's was. And here it does not matter whether the life story of Abraham as set forth in Genesis and interpreted in Romans and Hebrews is literal history or not. The point is that it gives us the standard by which our attitude to life is to be regulated, if it is to be a Christian attitude.
>
> Abraham is the story of a man who has committed himself

unconditionally into the hands of God; a man who does what God asks of him without hesitation, however paradoxical or self-contradictory it may seem, and who accepts God's promises, however mysterious and incredible they may appear. It is by virtue of this unconditional self-commitment to God that he has won the title of the friend of God. But such an attitude evidently presupposes a great deal. It presupposes not merely the existence of God, about which the philosophers have debated so lengthily, but that God is of a special character. It presupposes that God has complete control of the world and the course of events in it; that He exercises this control in a way that is purposeful; that human beings have a place in His designs; and that He communicates with them in ways which they can legitimately understand as commands and promises, and by which their lives can be guided. This is the presupposition of Jewish and Christian thinking, which I call Abrahamic theism. To work it out in detail, showing how it applies in actual life and thought, is the business of theology.

The Abrahamic presupposition differs in obvious ways from the scientific presupposition, but it has the same logical properties and status. It is not a self-evident truth, nor a piece of knowledge gathered from experience, but a presupposition made as a result of a basic acceptance.[2]

This viewpoint regarding the ultimacy of personal commitment to God, a viewpoint which is profoundly Biblical and classically Christian, is of crucial importance in considering the nature of the Church and its place in the purpose of God. Churchly reality and the efficacy of the Church's fulfillment of its mission are inseparably related to the seriousness with which each Christian takes his religion and his calling under God, as a member of the Covenant Community. For in the realm of the Spirit and in the Divine plan of the ages, committed individuals are the "Heartland" which, in the language of Geopolitics, is the "pivot of history."

INDIVIDUAL PERSONS AND UNIVERSAL COMMUNITY

Another classical passage in the Old Testament sets in equally bold relief the significance of individual persons, both for God

[2] H. A. Hodges, *Christianity and the Modern World View* (London: S.C.M. Press, and New York: The Macmillan Company, 1949), pp. 28–29.

Himself and for the world community which the God of Abraham purposes to establish. The passage in question is the Eighty-seventh Psalm. It was this great prophetic utterance that inspired John Newton's famous hymn,

> Glorious things of thee are spoken,
> Zion, City of our God.

The Psalm appears to have been written to cheer the drooping spirits of the Hebrew exiles after their return from Babylon. Sensitive as they must have been to the contrast between their insignificant little community in Jerusalem and the grandeur and glow of the description which prophets had given of the future greatness of Zion, their hearts would be consoled and their imagination fired by this prophetic poem. Its stanzas are so significant and brief that I quote them in full:

> On the holy mount stands the City He founded;
> the Lord loves the gates of Zion
> more than all the dwelling places of Jacob.
> Glorious things are spoken of you,
> O city of God.   Selah

> Among those who know me
> I mention Rahab and Babylon;
> behold, Philistia and Tyre, with Ethiopia—
> "This one was born there," they say.
> And of Zion it shall be said,
> "This one and that one were born in her";
> for the Most High Himself will establish her.
> The Lord records as He registers the peoples,
> "This one was born there."   Selah
> Singers and dancers alike say,
> "All my springs are in you."   (Psalm 87).

In this unique combination of poetry and prophecy, the Lord God of Israel is represented as standing upon Mount Zion. Around Him lies the Holy City. Holding in His hand a census roll, His eyes scan the far horizons where nations dwell that have had some historic relationship to Israel, His People. In His register, He inscribes the names of individual persons, this one and that one, who belong to nations that, as it happens, are representative of all mankind. God writes in His roll the names of Egyptians and of Babylonians, citizens of world empires that traditionally oppressed the Covenant Race. Here, too, are the names of war-like Philistines, the rural fellow citizens of Goliath of Gath. With them are the names of people from industrial Tyre on the Mediterranean seaboard and from distant, mountainous Ethiopia.

The prophetic vision of this bard of Israel represents a veritable "ecumenical" microcosm of the world's peoples. The persons listed in the divine census run the gamut of the human family and of civilization. Side by side, appear representatives of world-famous cultures, peasant folk, people engaged in industry and seamanship, primitive hillbillies—all are accounted by God as members of the Jerusalem community. The Lord God of Israel gives them the same status as the native-born sons of Zion.

Very luminous and true to the prophetic meaning of the words is the rendering given to verse five of the Psalm by the famous Biblical scholar, James Moffatt. Moffatt translates the verse in this form, "And Zion her name shall be Mother." Here is a prophetic image of the motherhood of the Christian Church, whose sons and daughters are individually written by God Himself into His "ecumenical" family. God calls people by their names. The Lord God Almighty, the All-wise and the All-loving, the God of Abraham and the God of Israel, the God of the whole earth, whose Kingdom shall embrace "all peoples and tongues," *individualizes*. But in His family there is no place for individualists. Each member of God's family, each citizen of Zion, must know who he is, whose he is, and what he is living for. He must also, however, fit himself into the over-all plan for the family unity, and the world mission of the Community of God.

In the fullness of time, the *kairos;* a Person appeared in history, who imparted new significance to the Abrahamic adventure. The promise made to Abraham entered upon a new phase on the road to its fulfillment. The ecumenical register that was described by the prophetic bard of Israel as replete with names of citizens belonging to all nations, became at Scripture's close the "Lamb's Book of Life." In the Eternal City whose light is God Himself, where stands the "throne of God and of the Lamb," into which shall enter everything of value in the life history of mankind (the "glory and honor of the nations"), the citizenry shall be made up of individual persons whose lives have been subject to the scrutiny of the Judge and whose names appear in the "Lamb's roll of the living" (Revelation 21:27) N.E.B.

The dynamic response to God, which is the "faith of Abraham"; the majestic scheme of God to embrace mankind in His future Kingdom in all the fullness of its diversity but as individual persons, as symbolized by the "Motherhood of Zion"; the figure of the Lamb, who continues to bear in Paradise the marks of the suffering it cost Him that human beings might be inscribed in the Book of Destiny—all find their meaning in the figure of Jesus of Nazareth. The God of Abraham and of his seed, the God of Moses and David, the God of Israel's poets and prophets, is, in a special sense, the "God and Father of our Lord Jesus Christ."

THE ECUMENICAL CENTRALITY OF JESUS CHRIST

God's self-disclosure achieved its fullness in the person of Christ; His grand design found fulfillment in the work of Christ. It can be said without exaggeration, "Christianity is Christ." Christ is the *core* of the Bible's message and the *clue* to the Bible's meaning. It is an inspiring feature of the World Council of Churches that, while there exists the greatest diversity of viewpoint among its member Churches as to the meaning of the Church, the status of the ministry, and the significance of the sacraments, there is no official discrepancy of judgment with regard to the place that belongs to Jesus Christ. In the council's constitution, He is hailed as "God and Saviour." In its world gatherings, He has been proclaimed the "Hope of the World" and the "Light of the World."

In the wider context of the Ecumenical Movement, Christ occupies the same central place in the faith of the nonhistorical Churches which belong to the Protestant tradition that He does in the faith of the great Churches of the Roman and Eastern Orthodox traditions. And, strangely enough, the figure of the Lord of the Church is the one Reality associated with the Christian religion for which eminent anti-Christian philosophers have felt an awesome reverence. It was Friedrich Nietzsche who said, "There was only one Christian and He died on a cross." In the last letter he ever wrote and after long years of mental agony, Nietzsche signed himself, "The Crucified." The famous Marxist professor of the Sorbonne, Henri Barbusse, who exercised a profound influence on the thinking of Cuban students studying in Paris after the dictator Machado had closed the University of Havana, wrote of Jesus Christ: "We, too, love Him; He belongs to us." So, too, it is in Latin America today. In the revolutionary southern continent with its secularized, anticlerical mood, the figure of the Nazarene is glimpsed with reverence and hopeful expectancy as He walks the billows of our time.

I have introduced this note on the contemporaneity of Jesus Christ in both the religious and the secular order for a very special purpose. I feel it important to draw attention to the fact that, as we explore the Biblical and theological setting of Christ's centrality in the Godhead and in God's scheme for a new humanity, no one can allege that such an exploration is irrelevant within the context of human sentiment today.

With this, we pass to consider the climactic manifestation of Deity in a native of Galilee, who twenty centuries ago founded a community called the Church, which God designed to fulfill His purpose in history. Our consideration of God's Son must necessarily be synthetic and brief, but I trust it will be luminous and basic.

Jesus Christ, born of Mary of Nazareth, is God in human flesh, truly God and truly man, the God-man. God *gave* Christ to the world as the supreme manifestation of His love for the world. Christ's life in the world was of such a kind as to reveal to men, by words and deeds, what God is *like*. To see the Son was to see the Father. To understand the Son was to understand the mystery of God's Being, and the meaning and goal of man's existence.

It is most important that stress be laid upon the true humanity of Christ. His historical life was much more than an "event" which inspired men in His time and continues to inspire men in our time to believe in the reality of God, and to learn about God's purpose in history. In many circles, where unhesitating, unequivocal assent is given to the Godhead of Christ, His true manhood is not taken seriously as an historical phenomenon, or regarded as the timeless pattern for human living. There is a present trend towards a new "Docetism." The man of Galilee tends to be regarded as one whose humanity was only phantasmic or apparential. He was truly God,

64 GOD'S DESIGN IN HISTORY

but not truly man. There has appeared, moreover, in circles that would be designated "liberal" or even "humanistic," a disposition not to take seriously the concrete pattern of Jesus's life as being essentially relevant to man's life today. The concrete historical life of Jesus has come to be regarded as dated, and as offering no meaningful justification, or cue, for a mid-Twentieth-Century *Imitation of Christ*.

But our contention is this. In loyalty to the New Testament portrait of Jesus, in the interests of dynamic Christian living, and for a true understanding by individual Christians and the Christian Church of what is meant by a sense of mission, it is essential to restore to current concern a forgotten mandate. This mandate is addressed to all who would take their Christianity seriously. Let them have their "eyes fixed on Jesus, on whom faith depends from start to finish" (Hebrews 12:2) N.E.B. The concentrated gaze here enjoined means much more than an absorbing interest in what Christ did as the Saviour of the world; it involves also a plea to be like Him, to follow "in His steps," to "let Christ Himself be your example as to what your attitude should be" (Philippians 2:5).[3]

Behold the Man! The Galilean showed that He was indeed Abraham's son and successor. He gave, in fact, a new dimension to the Abrahamic adventure. This He did when, in response to the call of God, He accepted His mission and had Himself baptized in the Jordan River. His identity and role were recognized by God when the Holy Spirit, as a Dove, descended upon His head. Jesus had now to show that He had what it takes to be a man, a real man, God's man. The same Holy Spirit who anointed Him for His office appointed Him to be tested by the Spirit of Evil, in order that He might show whether He had the spiritual stamina that was needed to give human history a fresh start. By refusing to recognize material well-being, dramatic showmanship, and opportunistic accommodation to circumstances as the three ultimates of human behavior, at the cost of loyalty to God and trust in His sovereign care, Jesus won a right to speak in God's name, and to die for man's sake. The manhood of Jesus of Naza-

[3] J. B. Phillips, *The New Testament in Modern English* (New York: The Macmillan Company, 1958).

reth as the supreme example and perfect prototype of humanity, occupies a central place in the Gospels. It has incalculable importance for our understanding of God's pattern for living. It provides the image of what men and women should be who take seriously Jesus Christ and His mission to the world. This is true, irrespective of what view be held of the origin and composition of the Gospel narrative. The God-like humanity of the narrative's central Figure shines through undimmed.

When we ask today, therefore, what it means to be a Christian, and to be involved in the world as a member of the Christian Community, the answer is: Look at Jesus, the "Pioneer and Perfecter of our faith." Look at Him in solitary communion with His Father. Look at Him in the hubbub of life, interpreting to people the meaning of *agape,* healing the sick, feeding the hungry, befriending the lonely, forgiving the penitent. Watch how His eyes become tearful with compassion in the presence of human sorrow, and how they blaze with fury at the sight of human injustice. Observe the Master Teacher, who simply and pictorially opens up the truth about God and life to thousands of common folk who hang upon His every utterance. Observe the same Teacher when He hurls anathemas at a religious elite who live masked lives, whose only interest in God is to become His patrons, whose only concern about people is to exploit them or to be objects of their acclaim. This man lived a quiet, dedicated life, without fanfare or bustle. He is history's most perfect image of a pilgrim. His home, as poetically depicted by one of His countless biographers, was "the road along which He walked with His friends in search of new friends."

The central message in Jesus's teachings was the Kingdom of God. That Kingdom had already come and was still to come. It was present as a force in His own person and ministry. It would finally be established by Him as a concrete reality in Divine-human relationships, by which God's purpose in history would be fulfilled. The citizens of that Kingdom will be persons "born again," as the expression is in the Fourth Gospel. Or, as they are described in the Synoptic Gospels, they will be persons who "believe the Gospel" of the Kingdom, persons who "come" to Him, who "follow" Him, and who, as His "friends," do what He commands them. Every burden of the spirit will become light when the burdened become "yoked" with Him. Life's deepest meaning will be fulfilled when His intimates are willing to become "servants of all," when they reproduce the servant image which He Himself bore and which He bequeathed to His followers as the true pattern for the advance guard of the New Humanity.

THE ROLE OF PETER AND OF THE CHURCH

Outstanding among the small group of specially chosen men, later to be known as "apostles," or "messengers," was a fisherman called Simon. To this man, who more than all his fellow apostles combined in superlative degree human weakness and spiritual insight, Jesus gave the name Peter (Petros, the Rock), after Simon had hailed his Master as "the Christ, the Son of the living God." Upon this confession, this foundational truth regarding Jesus Christ, a new Community called the Church was to be constituted, whose establishment in history would be linked to the name of a man called Peter.

Peter's great hour arrived in due course. Behind him was the dismal hour when he denied he ever knew the Galilean. The Crucified was now the Risen Christ. By a familiar lakeside, He restored the wayward disciple to full apostleship. After the Lord had given to His apostles the historic mandate to "disciple all nations," and had "ascended into heaven," He sent the Holy Spirit to empower them to discharge their "ecumenical" mission. It was then that Peter preached a sermon on the day called Pentecost. With the conversion to the new faith, as a result of that sermon, of three thousand people from every nation under heaven—representative, that is to say, of the whole Roman oikoumenē—the purpose of God in Christ, through the medium of the Church and by the power of the Spirit, began to be fulfilled. The Motherhood of Zion [4] began to be an historical reality; names began to be written in the Scroll of Destiny, in the "Lamb's Book of Life."

From redemptive fact and poetic figure we move to Paul's theological interpretation of the Church in the eternal purpose of God. The meaning of the Church and its role in God's design, are given comprehensive and climactic expression in the Letter to the

[4] See Psalm 87.

Ephesians. Let me briefly summarize what I have dealt with in detail in another volume.[5] In the great Ephesian Letter, written at the end of his career by the man from Tarsus, the apostle, "born out of due time" and chosen by God to carry the apostolic faith beyond the frontiers of Judaism, we have prophetic insight and poetic melody at their best. Here is "doctrine set to music." And this is as it should be, when so exciting a theme is treated as the historical and cosmic role of the Church in the purpose of God.

Paul is overwhelmed by what he calls the "mystery," the "unveiled secret of God." When he speaks of God's design to create "in Christ" a new cosmic unity, by joining together all things in "Him," things in heaven and things on earth (Ephesians 1:9, 10), he becomes literally rhapsodic. God wills fellowship, a transcendent community of love. Through Christ Crucified, Risen and Exalted, the great rift between the Divine and the Human, caused by the sin of man, is healed in the New Community of Christ. In this community, the age-long hatred between Jews and Gentiles, the traditional inequality between men and women, the inhuman relationship between masters and servants, will come to an end. In the new commonwealth called the Church, Christ's "fellowship of reconciliation," the bitter tensions associated with racial enmity, domestic strife, and social injustice, will find a solution. So epoch-making will be the composition and role of the Church in the purpose of God that by studying this novel community, this new creation of God, the "principalities and powers in the heavenly places" (Ephesians 3:10) will get their deepest insight into the manifold (many-colored) wisdom of God. This means, if we may speak in academic terms, that the study of the Church, a course in Ecumenics, will be prescribed by God as a graduate course for angels! Through this study, angelic spirits, unfallen and sinless, will learn things about God and man, about problems of mission and community, they could never otherwise have obtained. If that is so, as Paul suggests it to be, it is certainly a tremendous and exciting thing to have membership in the Community of Destiny, and the responsibility to participate in its mission.

[5] *God's Order: The Ephesian Letter and this Present Time* (New York: The Macmillan Company, 1953).

Biblical Images

of the Church

chapter 5

One of the marks of the Bible's authentic greatness as a monument of world literature is its use of images to convey truth. In the Hellenic tradition, when Plato reached frontiers of thought where philosophic concepts utterly failed him in his endeavor to interpret the secret of the universe, he had recourse to poetic images that might take the form of stories. Thus arose the platonic myth, the pictorial presentation of a great truth which eluded the conceptual. It can be said, indeed, that great poets like Homer, Dante, Shakespeare, and Milton have shown a deeper understanding of spiritual reality, especially of the suprahistorical, than the very greatest philosophers. And, after all, it is not the Head, not abstract reason, but the Heart, some cherished sentiment, that provides the philosopher with the axiom that becomes the basis of the system which he rears aloft by reason and consolidates by logic.

The Bible, both in the Old Testament and in the New, is a treasure house of great images. By means of these, men sensitive to God's revelation of Himself in nature, in the life history of the Hebrew people and in Jesus Christ, and inspired by the Holy Spirit, conveyed truths regarding God's relationship to the world, and especially regarding His New Creation, the Christian Church, the Community of Destiny. In addressing ourselves to a study of some of these images, it will be our endeavor not to transform images into allegories. The image is a poetic symbol designed to convey one central idea. In this it resembles the poetic description of a situation or the vivid story of an event, commonly called a parable. The parable was one of the favorite literary media which Jesus used to communicate important spiritual truths to His hearers. The allegory, on the other hand, is a literary device used by an author in which each detail of his description or tale is designed to have a significance of its own. Great care must be taken in Biblical interpretation not to allegorize the great images contained in the Book, as, alas, has oftentimes been done, with the most disastrous consequences for Christian thought.[1]

THE NEW ISRAEL

We begin with the image of the Church as the *Israel of God*. This designation is used by the Apostle Paul in his letter to the "Churches of Galatia." Affirming exultingly that for him as a Christian, the supreme object of adoration is the Cross of Christ in which was unveiled the very heart of God, proclaiming that the only thing that matters in the world of religion is not whether a man bears the bodily mark of circumcision but whether he has experienced spiritual change, becoming part, thereby, of a "new creation," he invokes God's "peace and mercy" upon those who stand where he stands. Such people are the ecumenical reality of which the Hebrew people were the national image. With their adoring eyes riveted on the Cross, as his eyes were, and their lives bearing witness to rebirth as his life did, all believers in Christ, whatever their racial background, were proclaimed by Paul to be members of a New Israel, the true Israel, the "Israel of God" (Galatians 6:14–16).

A study of this image supplies a number of important insights into the reality of the Church. These insights are not derived from an allegorical interpretation of separate facets of the image of Israel, but from Paul's identification of the Christian Church as Israel's successor. One such insight is the inseparable relationship

[1] See Paul S. Minear, *Images of the Church in the New Testament* (Philadelphia: Westminster Press, 1960).

between the history of the Hebrew people, from Abraham to John the Baptist, and the founding, world mission, and destiny of the New Israel. If the Church is to be "in very deed the Church," it must never cease to look at itself in the light of its ancient Palestinian prototype.

One of the profoundest prophetic insights into Israel's God-appointed role in history is that found in the utterances of the great Prophet of the Exile. The Second Isaiah puts these words into the lips of Israel's God: "You are my witnesses, and my servant whom I have chosen" (Isaiah 43:10). In another passage, the same prophet says: "You are my servant, Israel, in whom I will be glorified" (Isaiah 49:3) and "I will give you as a light to the nations, that my salvation may reach to the end of the earth" (Isaiah 49:61). The most tragic fact in Israel's history was that the people of the Covenant made with Abraham—who, like Abraham, were chosen by God to be His servant—refused to assume the servant role. Its religious hierarchy persecuted those who dared challenge their presumption that Israel was God's pampered darling, not His servant people, and that having "the temple of the Lord, the temple of the Lord, the temple of the Lord (Jeremiah 7:4)," the nation's destiny was assured.

With the passage of time, One who dared challenge the hierarchical interpretation of Israel's faith and status was crucified. But already a rugged ascetic, John the Baptizer, had arraigned the religious leaders of Israel beside the Jordan river. He told them squarely that they were not indispensable, that God demanded more than claims to pedigree; He demanded repentance (*meta-noia*), a total change of outlook and life, and active participation in His work. It was not enough to brag and substantiate the claim that they were sons of the great Abraham. "You brood of vipers," he said to them, "God is able from these stones to raise up children to Abraham" (Matthew 3:7, 9). He told them in effect that what mattered in religious leadership was not the substantiation of a claim to being in an historic succession. The important thing was to live a life of obedience to God, such as marked the career of Abraham and earned for him the title of "Friend of God." In the shadow of this encounter with the representatives of decadent traditionalism stands the Baptizer's encounter with another Figure who had also come for Baptism. With a profound sense of his own unworthiness in the presence of the Newcomer, he exclaims with a flash of insight, "Behold, the Lamb of God, who takes away the sin of the world" (John 1:29).

As regards the inseparable relationship between suffering and spiritual renewal in the creation of a New Israel, the prophetic and the apostolic traditions are both agreed. Referring to the "Israel of God" in his Letter to the Galatian Christians, Paul crystallizes the deepest thought in the Old Testament and in the New regarding the people that would be Israel's successor in history. It would be a people reborn through faith in Christ crucified, who were willing, as evidence of their commitment to Him and to God's purpose through Him, to bear, like Paul, on their bodies "the marks of Jesus." And this they would be able to do because their religion was not the legalistic expression of loyalty to an external code, as was the loyalty of Israel in the days of the "Old Covenant," but rather, the manifestation of a new life, a life centered in the Crucified and marked by spontaneous doing of what is right. The transition from the old order to the new, and the inner secret of the "Israel of God," which should mark the life of the Church Universal, is classically expounded in the Letter to the Hebrews. The writer enshrines in his epistolary classic the prophetic utterance of Jeremiah regarding a form of life whose concrete fulfillment he himself had witnessed. Here are the words, "This is the covenant that I will make with the house of Israel after those days, says the Lord: I will put my laws into their minds, and write them on their hearts, and I will be their God, and they shall be my people" (Hebrews 8:10).

This is the sense in which "subjectivity is truth." Here is the core of true Christianity, a norm whereby to measure the state of religion in the Church, an ideal to be pursued from the local congregation to the remotest frontiers of the Church ecumenical. There can be no substitute for personal religion, for a living relationship to Deity, for a buoyant response to God's call, for a contemporary version of Abrahamic and Pauline devotion.

THE FLOCK OF GOD

The image of the People of God as a *flock* is one which pervades the whole Bible. It serves as another link between the Old and the New in the fulfillment of God's purpose for the World.

One hears it said that the image of a flock of sheep in care of a shepherd is an image that means increasingly little in western civilization, and especially in urban and suburban areas. It is also contended that today flocks have become so vast and the means of exercising supervision over them so impersonal and mechanical, that this ancient, and essentially rural image, conveys little meaning to contemporary man.

In response to these contentions, several observations are in order. In the first place, if it is true that the intimate relationship between God and persons, whether as individuals or in groups, cannot be meaningfully conveyed by this Biblical image, it is imperative that some other image, which more adequately communicates the truth it enshrines and challenges the thinking of men today, should be created to replace it. In the second place, however, the chief problem, and the most revolutionary in the world of our time, has its center in the vast rural areas of Asia, Africa, and Latin America. In these areas, vast millions of people are today living in hunger and dereliction, where the shepherd-flock image is very real. The approach that must be made to those people should embody understanding, sympathy, and effective aid. It should either restore to currency the ancient image of abandoned sheep and irresponsible shepherds or create a challenging new image. In the third place, it is important, so far as responsible Christians are concerned, that they learn, as all students of great literature must learn, to cultivate an intelligent sensitivity to the classic imagery of their faith.

The fact is, however, that the more we reflect on this image of divine-human relations, the more exciting is the truth it conveys. Said the Hebrew author of the Twenty-third Psalm, that most familiar and loved jewel of Biblical verse: "The Lord is my Shepherd, I shall not want; He makes me lie down in green pastures. He leads me beside still waters; He restores my soul. He leads me in paths of righteousness for His name's sake.

Even though I walk through the valley of the shadow of death, I fear no evil; for Thou art with me; Thy rod and Thy staff, they comfort me."

Here is that personalism, which is not individualism, that awareness of Deity in personal relationship to human selfhood which is the glory of the Christian religion. My Hegelian professor of philosophy, J. B. Baillie, who was himself not a Christian when I sat at his feet in Aberdeen was accustomed to draw the attention of his class to the unique personalism that marks the relationship between God and man in the Hebrew Psalms. "Thou art *my God* —Thou art *my son.*" It does not mean that the sacred bard was a pure individualist, and that he was unaware of being but one member of the "flock of God." What it does mean is that in the Twenty-third Psalm, the author speaks as the representative of a community of people who in varying degrees recognize the reality of God and their personal indebtedness to Him in daily living.

The sensitivity and loyalty of the sheep to the individual they regard as their shepherd is referred to by Him who called Himself the "Good Shepherd." "My sheep," said Jesus on one occasion, "know my voice . . . and they follow me" (John 10:27). This sensitivity towards their leader produces a unity and integrity on the part of all members of the flock. "A stranger," said the shepherd, "they will not follow, but they will flee from him, for they do not know the voice of strangers" (John 10:5). The implication is that a "flock" can never be converted into a mere collectivity; it is and must ever remain a group of individuals knit together in a common loyalty to one to whom they are individually sensitive. God individualizes, Christ individualizes; Christians as members of the "flock of God" must in turn cultivate an individual, personal response to their Shepherd. This form of mutuality and reciprocity between God and man in the community called the Church is of supreme significance and is timeless in its relevancy.

In the context of the Bible, the image of the flock is inseparably related to the existence and responsibility of a shepherd. To emphasize this fact is in no sense to allegorize the image with which we are dealing, but rather, to draw attention to the shepherd role in everything pertaining to the "flock of God." While in the Bible the "servant" is the image used to designate what God was willing to become, and what a Christian man taking seriously Him who took the "form of a servant" should always strive to be, the image of the "shepherd" is used to depict in concrete vocational terms the precise form that the service should take. This is true both as regards man and as regards God. God has revealed Himself as a shepherd. He is dramatically depicted as a Being who possesses the qualities and concerns which are associated with an oriental shepherd at his best.

Our Lord Jesus Christ, who gloried in the fact that He had come
to "serve," used the "shepherd" image to designate the supreme
form of service to which He was committed. "The Good Shepherd," said the Servant of God and man, "gives his life for the
sheep." He who claimed to be, and in the apostolic age was regarded as being, the "Great Shepherd of the Sheep," invested
Peter, when restored to apostleship, with the pastoral vocation.
It would not be enough that the fallen and restored disciple
should have an orthodox view of the Person of Christ, or be able
to witness to the Resurrection of Christ. Christ, the "Son of the
living God," risen again from the dead, was interested in people.
So He said to Peter three times, "Feed my lambs"; "Tend my
sheep"; "Feed my sheep" (John 21:15–17). The crown and glory
of apostolicity was thus set forth as the possession of a shepherd's
heart and the exercise of a pastoral ministry.

The importance attached to pastoral concern on the part of
both clergy and laity in the early years of the Christian era becomes abundantly plain in the apostolic writings. Very striking
and significant is the injunction given by Paul to the elders of the
Church in Ephesus when on his voyage to Jerusalem he met them
during a stopover at the seaport of Miletus. To those lay leaders
of the Church, whom he had specially requested to come to see
him, he made clear their responsibility for the rank and file of the
local congregation. "Keep watch over yourselves," he said to
them, "and over all the flock of which the Holy Spirit has given
you charge, as shepherds of the Church of the Lord, which He
won for Himself by His own blood. I know that when I am gone,
savage wolves will come in among you and will not spare the
flock . . . So be on the alert" (Acts 20:28, 29, 31) N.E.B.

This injunction involved several things. It involved, of course,
pastoral care in the form of spiritual nurture and tender concern
for the development of the Church's membership. But it would
also be the responsibility of those Ephesian elders, in loyalty to
the shepherd tradition established by the "Head Shepherd," who
won the flock "by His own blood," and to Him who had been their
Shepherd for three years, to exercise eternal vigilance lest "savage
wolves" enter the fold and disrupt the flock. It is a timeless obligation of "shepherds" not only to perform duties expressive of the
Shepherd-heart, but also to assume militant opposition to every

attempt designed to confuse the flock and lead the sheep astray. For today in America, as in First-Century Asia, there are people who bear the name of Christ and extol the Bible, whose God is a demonic negativism, and who live to malign and shatter the growing unity of the flock of Christ throughout the *oikoumenē*.

No less timely, and in the shepherd tradition at its best, is the classical plea of Peter. Addressing himself not to the officers of a local congregation but to those of "God's scattered people" in many communities, he says: "I appeal to the elders of your community as a fellow elder and a witness of Christ's suffering, and also a partaker in the splendor that is to be revealed. Tend that flock of God whose shepherds you are, and do it not under compulsion, but of your own free will, as God would have it; not for gain, but out of sheer devotion; not tyrannizing over those who are allotted to your care, but setting an example to the flock. And then when the Head Shepherd appears, you will receive for your own the unfading garland of glory" (I Peter 5:1–4) N.E.B. Here we have a marvelous description of the spirit that should animate all "under-shepherds" of the ecumenical "flock." Here is struck the central note of authentic Christianity, a note which should be re-echoed today in the lives of all who occupy a position of leadership in the Church. Church leaders must be motivated by a spirit of "sheer devotion" to Christ and to the welfare of people. They should not be controlled by any external compulsion nor by a love of pecuniary gain, nor by an internal craving to lord it over others in order to achieve status. Let all God's "shepherds" live, said Peter, as he himself sought to live, by the significance of "Christ's sufferings" and the hope of participation in His eventual triumph.

THE BUILDING

There are in the New Testament three images of the Church which constitute a unique trinity. They convey insights into three distinct facets of the Church and its role in history which because of their complementary character must be studied in close relationship to one another. The images in question are the Building, the Bride, and the Body. The symbolism that inspires them is derived in turn from the physical order, the biological order, and the summit of human affection, the love between man and woman.

All three images are found in the climactic Letter to the Ephesians, although as individual images they occur also in other books of the New Testament.

The particular type of building used to symbolize the Church is the temple. The center of Israel's worship in Jerusalem, the great shrine first erected by Solomon, with its Holy of Holies, and restored by Ezra and rebuilt by King Herod, became the image of a spiritual edifice, the "Household of God" (Ephesians 2:19). This particular image was used and consecrated by Jesus Himself. Peter's great affirmation identifying his Master as the "Christ, the Son of the living God," would be the "Rock" upon which Christ would build His Church" (Matthew 16:18, 19). This spiritual edifice would prove to be unshatterable, and, according to the Lord Himself, would outlive the assault of demonic forces. "The forces of death," said Jesus, "shall never overpower it" (Matthew 16:18) N.E.B.

In the apostolic image of the Church which subsequently emerged, Christ Himself, meaning His total reality, human and divine, all that He was and all that He did, with His massive significance for thought and life, would be the "chief cornerstone," that is, the "keystone." In the architectural design of that epoch, a large and solid monolith gave stability, unity, and cohesiveness to the whole structure. Thus, we sing in the words of a great hymn, so familiar in ecumenical gatherings, "The Church's one foundation is Jesus Christ, her Lord."

It is significant that the imagination of Peter, the "Rock," glowed with the figure of Christ, the "Cornerstone." Writing to the "exiles of the dispersion," he thus quoted Isaiah's striking allusion to the foundation God would lay in Zion (Isaiah 28:16). "Behold, I am laying in Zion a stone, a cornerstone chosen and precious, and he who believes in Him will not be put to shame" (I Peter 2:6). He then re-echoes words of a famous psalm that were much in Jesus's own thoughts towards the close of His life. "The very stone which the builders rejected has become the head of the corner" (I Peter 2:7b). No image could convey more pointedly the foundational centrality of Christ in the Church and the dramatic movement from the old Israel to the new.

The relationship of the Church to history and, at the same time, the foundational importance for Christianity of the witness of the prophets of the Old Testament and the apostles of the New are significantly set forth by the affirmation that these constitute part of the foundation of which Christ is the cornerstone. A cornerstone needs other stones in order that they may constitute together a foundation. Christ as the "keystone" could have no abiding significance for Christian thought and life apart from the place occupied in the design of God by those who, centuries before, spoke with profound insight into His coming and Kingdom. It was the apostles who interpreted in due course to their own generation, and to all generations to come, what Christ and His coming signified for God and man. By so doing, they laid the foundation of a new society, which is imaged in terms of a building. This imagery gives to Holy Scripture, which is basically formed by the writings of prophets and apostles, and by history and poetry which were inspired by their spirit and insights, a massive and unique foundational status in the Christian religion.

Erected upon this foundation rise the walls of the Building which is composed of "living stones." The whole structure joined together in Christ Jesus the Cornerstone "grows into a holy temple in the Lord" (Ephesians 2:21). Into this structure, Christians are built "for a dwelling place of God in the Spirit" (Ephesians 2:22). Big stones and little stones all have their places and are needed. The grand design is, that He who dwells not in "temples made with hands" should have a spiritual temple, a human collectivity, redeemed by the Holy Spirit from the general mass of humanity, in which the Real Presence may abide forever.

Here is an image which affirms the reality of the Church. This spiritual Community which historically is inseparably related to Jesus Christ, to His apostles and to the Hebrew prophets, and is indwelt by the Living and Eternal God, shall outlive all historical change, whether it be evolutionary or revolutionary. The Church, so conceived, though not necessarily any one of its institutional structures, shall be marked by stability and permanency to history's close.

> Built on the rock the Church doth stand,
> Even when steeples are falling.
>
> Surely in temples made with hands,
> God, the most High, is not dwelling,

High above earth His temple stands,
All earthly temples excelling;
Yet He whom heavens cannot contain
Chose to abide on earth with men,
Built in our bodies His temple.*

Two things are true, and will be true, till traveling days are done, and time shall be no more. One, God shall dwell in a special manner in the midst of the Christian Community. Two, God shall also dwell in the inmost being of each Christian believer.

THE BRIDE

Just as the Church imaged as a Building emphasizes the stability, continuity, and eventual triumph of the Church in history, because of its objective relationship to Christ, the Church's image as a Bride emphasizes its subjective relationship to Christ the royal Bridegroom. We now move into the realm of passionate Christian love and devotion of which Christ Himself is the object. This is the realm where Christian selfhood, both in its collective and personal aspects, cultivates purity, enjoys transitory communion, develops ardent expectancy, and awaits the day of spiritual union.

We find in the Old Testament, especially in the writing of the Eighth-Century prophet, Hosea, a moving allusion to the symbolic nuptial relationship between God and His people, Israel. Israel is an unfaithful spouse, who has left her first and true lover. But God does not abandon her. He allows her to suffer the consequences of her lewd behavior with other lovers, the pagan Baalim who had lured her away. But in her new wilderness dereliction, He woos her to Himself again. How moving are the words, "In that day, says the Lord, you will call me, 'My husband,' and no longer will you call me, 'My Baal' [my owner]. . . . And I will betroth you to me forever; I will betroth you to me in righteousness and in justice, in steadfast love, and in mercy. I will betroth you to me in faithfulness; and you shall know the Lord" (Hosea 2:16, 19, 20).

This passage has profoundly influenced the evangelical accent in Christian thought. The divine love passion that glows in the

* (Verses one and two) Nicholai F. S. Grundrig (1783–1872).

decision, "I will betroth you to me forever," supplied the text for
many a sermon in the great awakening of the Eighteenth and
Nineteenth Centuries, sermons that changed the lives of thousands. It spoke to a concrete situation in the life of the Church at a
time when religion had ceased to stir the lives of people. It laid
bare with poetic glow the inmost heart of God, and aroused an
excited response in the hearts of men.

The image of the bridal tie between the New Israel and her
Divine Redeemer is given classical expression in the writings of
St. Paul. Feeling himself to have been the object of passionate
affection on the part of the Risen Christ, at a time when he was
engaged in wild escapades to destroy the Galilean's memory, and
having made Christ his very life, he depicts the bond between the
Church and her Lord. This bond resembles the sacred tie between
a betrothed bride and her lover, who enter into the relationship
of marriage. The courtship has been dramatic. Christ proved
Himself a passionate suitor, who plighted His troth by an act of
supreme sacrifice for the one He loved. "Christ loved the Church,"
says Paul in the Ephesian Letter, "and gave Himself up for her,
that He might sanctify her, having cleansed her by the washing
of water with the word, that the Church might be presented before Him in splendor without spot or wrinkle or any such thing,
that she might be holy and without blemish" (Ephesians 5:25-27).

In this imagery, several things stand out. Particularly worthy of
observation is the fact that the Divine Lover makes a supreme
sacrifice in order to be able to cleanse the life and lift the lot of
one who possessed no personal worthiness to be the object of so
great a love. But she, transformed by that love of His, became so
closely related to Him as to be henceforth part of His very being.
Lover and Bride, Christ and the Church, become one forever. The
Bride, redeemed and wedded, is henceforth Christ's very Body
which He "nourishes and cherishes." This relationship of "spiritual
marriage," admitted by Paul to be a "great mystery," is conceived
by him as offering a pattern for what human matrimony should be
at its highest and best. Moving and significant in this connection
are his words: "Even so [in view of Christ's relationship to the
Church] husbands should love their wives as their own bodies.
He who loves his wife loves himself. For no man ever hates his
own flesh, but nourishes and cherishes it, as Christ does the

Church, because we are members of His Body. 'For this reason, a man shall leave his father and mother and be joined to his wife, and the two shall become one.' This is a great mystery, and I take it to mean Christ and the Church" (Ephesians 5:28–32).

In the Book of Revelation, the image of the Church as a Bride takes on eschatological significance. The marriage bond is not presented in terms of an event realized within history, but as one which will be consummated at history's close. The Church lives on earth in a state of expectancy against the day of her espousal. Maintaining herself pure, living in loyal devotion to her one Lover, she looks forward to eternal union with Him beyond the bourne of Time. The apocalyptic seer hears from "beside the Throne" what appeared to him to be "the voice of a great multitude, like the sound of many waters and like the sound of mighty thunderpeals, crying 'Hallelujah! For the Lord our God the Almighty reigns. Let us rejoice and exult and give Him the glory, for the marriage of the Lamb has come, and His Bride has made herself ready; it was granted her to be clothed with fine linen, bright and pure'—for the fine linen is the righteous deeds of the Saints" (Revelation 19:5–8). In a later vision, "the Bride, the wife of the Lamb," is "the holy city Jerusalem," which the seer, having been taken by an angel to a great high mountain, sees "coming down out of heaven from God" (Revelation 21:9–10). While the symbolism varies, the idea conveyed by the image is clear. There will be consummated an everlasting union between the Church and Christ. This union shall fulfill all that was implicit in the historic events that took place in Jerusalem, and all that is involved in the true concept of human matrimony.

At intervals in the course of the ages, the image of the Church as the Bride of Christ exercised a profound influence upon Christian thought and devotion. This is equally true in the Roman Catholic and the Protestant traditions. In both traditions, and very specially during periods when the official Church became cold and institutional and developed a persecuting trend toward all nonconformists, many outstanding Christians became inspired by the image of the Church Bride. Isolated and lonely, in the midst of a loveless formalistic Church, in which any idea or expression of personal religious emotion not recognized by the Church was looked at askance, and might involve the subject in reprisals, they moved inward. They sought communion with Christ in the inner Shekinah of their being.

An outstanding example in the Roman tradition of this type of Christian was Theresa of Avila. After more than twenty years as a nun in a Carmelite convent, Theresa passed through a profound religious experience. For the first time in her life, Jesus Christ became personally real to her and unspeakably dear to her, as a living Presence. He became the object of her passionate devotion, the Lover of her soul, a Being whom she adored and to whose service she gave herself in loyal obedience. Here was a woman who knew in the intimacy of her personal life what it was to become ecstatic, but who, on the other hand, was the most practical of women in the application of her ideas and experiences. She devoted herself to the reformation of the Carmelite Order. Though weak and sickly, Theresa of Avila traveled incessantly throughout Spain under difficult circumstances, to see that life and activity in the houses belonging to the religious community to which she belonged were worthy of Christ. "The Lord wants works," [2] she said, works which were not a means of salvation, but the fruit of salvation. And when the young women of her order would sometimes complain of the monotony of their work, she would reply, "My daughters, the Lord moves among the pots and pans." [3] The classical symbol of Theresa in Christian art is that of a female figure in mystic rapture, whose heart is pierced by a love dart from a Seraph's bow.

The age of Theresa was a time when the Spanish Church frowned upon religious subjectivity or mysticism. It violently opposed any claim on the part of the faithful to a personal relationship to God apart from the rites and ceremonies of the Church and the control of the Church's ministers. Theresa's younger friend and fellow Carmelite, John of the Cross, one of the greatest Christian mystics of all time, was put in prison by the Inquisition because of what were regarded as his heretical ideas and practices in the realm of Christian experience. It was in prison in the city of Toledo that he wrote the great literary and religious classics with which his name is associated. Theresa, too, would have been

[2] *Obras quiere el Señor.*
[3] *Entre los pucheros anda el Señor.*

sent to prison, were she not a woman and a person who had some influential friends in Rome. The Council of Trent was soon to put a total ban on claims to personal communion with Jesus Christ, apart from the modes and practices prescribed by the Church. The result was disastrous as far as the Roman Catholic tradition is concerned. Trent marked the close of the era in which were produced the greatest masterpieces of devotional literature, and of Christian mysticism at its best and purest. This is admitted by distinguished Catholic thinkers. It is an equally significant and admitted fact that in the post-Tridentine era, a greater wealth of outstanding devotional literature was produced by Protestants than by Roman Catholics.

As the representative within Protestantism of the large number of devout men and women who were captivated by the image of the Church as the Bride of Christ and tended to personalize it in their own devotional life, I select Samuel Rutherford. Rutherford, a Scottish churchman who lived in the first half of the Seventeenth Century, occupied successively the positions of pastor, professor of theology, and the principalship of the University of St. Andrews. He was a writer of distinction, and is best known among the learned by his famous book, *Lex Rex*. This book was publicly burned during a stormy epoch in Scottish history by a government controlled by Church prelates and institutionalists.

Imprisoned two years in Aberdeen for his determined stand against ecclesiastical tyranny, Samuel Rutherford wrote some five hundred letters to friends and acquaintances. Those letters were subsequently published in a volume destined to become one of the great monuments of Christian devotion. Central in the Rutherford letters is the expression of a passionate, adoring devotion for Jesus Christ the Kingly Lover, together with suggestions as to what the love of Christ should mean for Christian life and witness. The letters are penned in the rich poetic imagery of the Bible, especially of the "Song of Solomon" and the Forty-fifth Psalm. Rutherford calls his prison "Christ's Palace in Aberdeen." In a complete edition of the *Letters,* edited by Alexander Duff, the pioneer Scottish missionary to India, who subsequently became an ecumenical pioneer, Duff makes remarks about the glowing imagery and the rapturous utterance that mark the famous letters from "Christ's Palace in Aberdeen." Says the man who convened the first united missionary conference ever held by the Churches, "In the case of one of a hard, dry, logical metaphysical, or mathematical temperament, even if religiously disposed, but deficient in, or wholly destitute of, the poetic, aesthetic, or deeply emotional element, he will be apt to regard them [the Rutherford letters] with shrinking aversion, if not positive disfavor and disrelish." [4]

Yet metaphysicians, too, have been Christ-lovers in the evangelical mystic tradition. In the same class as Rutherford might be put Jonathan Edwards. Edwards, who is recognized as the profoundest metaphysician in the history of American philosophy, was one of the first presidents of Princeton University. This man "in whom," to use Duff's words, "the ratiocinative faculties so marvellously predominated over the aesthetic," referred thus to his early religious experience: "I felt an ardency of soul to be, what I know not otherwise to express, emptied and annihilated, to lie in the dust, and to be full of Christ alone; to love Him with a holy and pure love; to trust in Him; to live upon Him; to serve and follow Him; and to be perfectly sanctified and made pure, with a divine and heavenly purity. . . . The sense I had of divine things, often would, on a sudden, kindle up an ardor in my soul that I knew not how to express." [5]

What is the point of these allusions to Saint Theresa of Avila, to Principal Rutherford of St. Andrews, and to President Edwards of Princeton? Simply this. They are representatives of a classical and creative spiritual tradition, profoundly Biblical in background and evangelical in inspiration. In this tradition are men and women who, while being intensely intellectual, practical, and creative, were passionate lovers of Jesus Christ. They were not cranks or neurotics. They were transfigured humans. Their love for Christ is the closest approximation in Christian history to the concrete fulfillment of the Bride image. Their spirit has abiding relevancy for the life of the Church. For let it be quite clear that the passionate love of Christ and all that it involves, is of the essence of Christian devotion. It, moreover, provides a norm for the valuation of the Church in every epoch and in every place. The image

---

[4] *Preface to Letters of Samuel Rutherford* (Edinburgh and London: Oliphant, Andrews and Ferrier, 1875).
[5] *Ibid.*, pp. 17, 18.

of the Church as Christ's Bride symbolizes the fact that it can be and should be an exciting thing to be a Christian, whether the designation be applied to individuals, congregations, denominations, or the Church Universal.

THE BODY

The most meaningful and dynamic of all the metaphors used in the Bible to designate the Church is the image of the *Body*. The Church is the *Body* of Christ. Between the physical image of a Building, which symbolizes the Church's continuity throughout history, and the spiritual image of a Bride, which symbolizes its terrestrial loyalty and eschatological triumph, is the image which symbolizes its *functional activity* within history.

What is a body? What is the biological organism which we associate with human beings? When is a body truly a body? When does it function in such a way as to be true to its nature and role? It is important that we become clear as to the essential status of a body in the daily life of people.

A body fulfills the idea of a body; it plays its role in the economy of nature when it actively responds to the mandate of the head and to the impulse of the heart. In doing so, it becomes the medium whereby an individual person expresses his will or desire. A man's body, to have real significance, engages in movement of some kind, movement that is climaxed by definite action. Now, action at its highest is physical motion that takes place in the fulfillment of a purpose, whatever that purpose may be. The higher the purpose, the more significant is the physical activity by which it is carried out. In a word, our body is the instrument, or servant, whereby, under normal conditions, we give objective expression to our desires and ideals. That is to say, the biological organism called a body fulfills its role in the natural order when it is the *subject of action* and not merely when it is the *object of attention,* or an organ of pretentious claims.

This does not mean, of course, that it is illicit for the body to become an object of attention. Quite the contrary. It is natural, and at times, imperative, that the body should even be an *object of concern.* This is particularly true where the health of the body is concerned. The reason is obvious. While it is a fact that some of the most dedicated and creative personalities who ever lived did not enjoy robust health, and that some of them were physically handicapped, it is equally true that their physical condition was often an agonizing concern for themselves and others, as it was in the life of St. Paul.

On the other hand, the achievement and maintenance of perfect health as the supreme goal of existence cannot be regarded as being in itself a worthy motivation for living. The reason for this is clear. To receive from the doctor, after a thorough physical examination, a perfect bill of health, should never become an occasion for boasting. For if a biological prodigy of this kind will stop vaunting and listen, he will hear a voice which says, "Health for what? What are you doing with your body? What are you living for? Tonight you may have a call."

So, too, with other concerns about one's body. It is an exciting experience to become famed for physical loveliness, to be acclaimed as "Miss America" or "Miss Universe." But what woman would feel happy in the course of the years if her claim to recognition by others should be totally unrelated to those qualities that are the true glory of womanhood, and she were linked exclusively to an aesthetic judgment pronounced by jurors long ago? It is natural that a young man should aspire to a degree of physical strength and prowess that would win him national or world renown as an athlete. He would not be happy, however, if the passage of time were to condemn him to be a mere relic of a glamorous physical achievement of years gone by. A real man is satisfied only if bodily development and strength fit him to put his life at the service of a great idea or a great cause. The truth is that never have physical health, beauty, and strength fulfilled their destiny more truly than when all of them were set aside as ends to live for, and when the human personality who possessed one or all of these qualities sacrificed his body in suffering and death for a spiritual goal—for God or country, for Truth or Justice. A body is never so truly a body, the servant of the head and of the heart, as when it is sacrificed for something greater than itself—a great thought or a great affection. That is to say, it is of the very essence and genius of the human body to be the instrument of something that transcends the purely corporeal.

In the New Testament, the image of the body, as applied to the

Church, takes on what might be described as a psychic character. Neither in Hebrew nor Greek thought is the body at any time anything more than a physical organism. We find no instance in the Old Testament in which the body is used as an image of Israel. In this respect it does not have the status of the images of the Flock and the Bride. Moreover, in Greek philosophy and religion, the body, the *soma*, is never employed as a metaphor to depict a human collectivity of any kind. In the apostolic writings, however, those belonging to the Christian Church are imaged as members of the Body of Christ. They are represented as being related to a reality which transcends in significance and intimacy any relationship that can possibly be symbolized by a biological structure called a body. This is due to the fact that, in a very real sense, the Community of Christ in the world fulfills the function of Christ's Resurrection Body. In this Community, as the organ of Christ's activity, though in no sense the only organ, the Lord is abidingly present. I say, *not the only organ* of Christ's activity. Let it be clear that the activity of the Risen Christ through the Holy Spirit is not limited to a particular community or organization, which in any place or time is called, or calls itself, the Church. This said, let us consider the New Testament image of the Church as the Body of Christ.

The moment we explore the Body image as applied to the Church as a corporate entity, we become aware of the basic importance attached to the individual Church member, whose own *body* is a "temple of the Holy Spirit" (I Corinthians 6:19). The Christian's body, his whole physical being, is "for the Lord" (I Corinthians 6:13), and not for the expression of sensuality. The body must undergo strict discipline, after the pattern followed by St. Paul himself, who, aspiring to be a spiritual athlete and calling upon fellow Christians in Corinth to be athletes, too, exclaimed, "I pommel my body and subdue it" (I Corinthians 9:27). Christians must be careful also how they talk, because the "tongue" can conduct itself in such an irresponsible manner as to be comparable to fire that gets out of control. "The tongue," said St. James, "is in effect a fire. It represents among our members the world with all its wickedness; it pollutes our whole being; it keeps the wheel of our existence red-hot, and its flames are fed by Hell" (James 3:6) N.E.B.

Christians, however, who struggle daily by deed and by word to live a life worthy of Christ, have the assurance that in the end they will triumph through Christ. Says Christianity's greatest athlete, crusader, and saint, "Brethren, join in imitating me, and . . . await a Savior, the Lord Jesus Christ, who will change our lowly body to be like His glorious Body, by the power which enables Him even to subject all things to Himself" (Philippians 3:17, 20, 21). Here, as in the images of the "Israel of God," the "flock of God," and the divine Register, God individualizes. People become members of His Everlasting Kingdom and live their Christian lives as individual persons and not purely as members of a group. The ultimate evidence that they belong to this spiritual Kingdom is not that they make the utmost human sacrifice to attain it, delivering their "body to be burned," but that they "have love" (I Corinthians 13:3). This Biblical emphasis upon the basic significance and role of the "body" of the individual Christian, conceived as being a reality in which Christ dwells by His spirit and molds to His likeness, must never cease to be the background for all discussion of the Church as the Body of Christ.

To catch the glow, and begin to discern the majestic significance, of the apostolic vision of the Church as the Body of Christ, it is important to start from the rhapsodic affirmation with which Paul concludes the first of his two great prayers in the Letter to the Ephesians. Christ, Crucified and Risen, whom the Apostle glories in depicting as the "Head" of the "Church which is His Body," has been constituted by God as supreme Ruler of the Cosmos. But God's ultimate design in putting all things under His feet is that the Christ so exalted should be the "head over all things for the Church, which is His Body, the fullness of Him Who fills all in all" (Ephesians 1:22–23). Here, the development and mission of the Community, in which Deity dwells in His fullness, is made the supreme object of God's cosmic concern. The Head of this Body is also Head of all that exists. Such is the status in human and cosmic history of the Church as the Body of Christ.

Who are members of the Body? The membership is representative of all mankind, of the "uncircumcised" as well as the "circumcised." The Gentiles are "fellow heirs, members of the same body, and partakers of the promise of Christ Jesus through the Gospels" (Ephesians 3:6). Besides people belonging to the Greek and Roman *oikoumenē*, whether they be "slaves or free," there will be in the Body the greatest diversity of human beings, knit together by a relationship of common allegiance to Christ who "is all, and in all" (Colossians 3:11).

How do people become members of this "Body" to which all human beings have a right to belong? By Baptism. But the "Baptism" which, in the apostolic writings makes people members of the Body of Christ is something much more vital than the formalistic sacramental act which has come to be regarded as automatically relating baptized persons to the Church as Christ's Body. In the apostolic era, as it continues to be today in some parts of the *oikoumenē*, it was a very decisive, exciting, and even costly thing to become a Christian through Baptism and so become related to the community which is the Body of Christ. Then, as now, there were hypocrites in the Church, people who led masked lives, who were not what they appeared to be. There were people who violated their solemn commitment to live a life "worthy of the vocation to which they were called."

It is of crucial importance for our understanding of the New Testament conception of membership in the Body of Christ, and its implications for Christianity in our time, to grasp what Paul, the creator and chief user of the Body image, meant by Christians being members of the Body. "By one Spirit," said he in his first letter to the Corinthian Christians, "we are all baptized into one body—Jews or Greeks, slaves or free—and all were made to drink of one Spirit. . . . Now you are the body of Christ and individually members of it" (I Corinthians 12:13–27).

Two things become clear. First, for Paul, a local congregation can be and should be a microcosm of the Body of Christ as an ecumenical, a suprahistorical, and even as a cosmic reality. But in every instance when the "Body is in very deed the Body"—to adapt a now familiar allusion—there is involved a dynamic mutual interdependence between all the members and a vital relationship of each member to Christ Himself. Second, however diversified the Body may be as regards the variety, the status and the role of its individual members, *all* the members are necessary. In the interests of the Body, they should, therefore, function harmoniously, manifesting a mutual concern for one another, and participating all together in the sorrow or joy of each. For what makes the Body a true body is the presence of a community spirit among all members.

But community, however real and inspiring both as regards the individual members and the body corporate, can never be an end in itself. There is a goal beyond unity; the community must act together; the body exists for action. Paul stresses this fact in a vivid, dramatic way. He designates the diverse roles to be played by individual members of the Body of Christ as God-appointed officers of the Church. Such officers are, in his own words (having in mind the First-Century Church), "first apostles, second prophets, third teachers, then workers of miracles, then healers, helpers, administrators, speakers in various kinds of tongues" (I Corinthians 12:28). Each of these officers has his specific God-given task within the unity of the whole, and having regard to the total task of the Body.

What is this total corporate task? It is expressed in a striking way in the Letter to the Ephesians. The role of the leaders, Christ's "gifts" to the Body, is that of "building up the body of Christ," so that the Church may the better achieve full maturity, true manhood, "the measure of the stature of the fullness of Christ" (Ephesians 4:13b). How significant are Paul's words, and how relevant to the Church today! "These were His gifts: some to be apostles, some prophets, some evangelists, some pastors and teachers, *to equip God's people for work in His service, to the building up of the body of Christ*" (Ephesians 4:11-12) N.E.B. Church leaders fulfill their function, the Church as the Body of Christ is built up and fitted to "be in very deed the Church," when the laity, the "saints," "God's people," are equipped to be themselves "ministers," that is, prepared "for ministering," for work in His service. It may, therefore, be affirmed: The Church is made up of all its members; its task is the corporate and the individual task of all; the effectiveness of a Church's leadership will be measured by the seriousness with which the rank and file of "God's people" take their membership in the Body of Christ.

But for what is all this in God's design? What shall be the ultimate goal of the Church, the Body of Christ, when blessed with effective leadership, and manned by a dedicated laity, it comes to maturity, growing up in every way into Christ, the Head, and "upbuilds itself in love"? The Church, as the Body of Christ, is

worthy of its Head and fulfills its mission as His Body, when it
incarnates in its life, and transmits by word and deed, Christ's love
passion for the world. Maturity in Christ must become manifest
not merely in a mystic unity marked by the love of Christ and of
one another, but in a unity which is the prelude to dynamic missionary action under the leadership of Christ, the Head of the
Church.

The image of the Church as the Body of Christ fulfills the meaning of a human body at its best, and fits into the scheme of apostolic thought, when all that the Body is, together with all its
attributes, healthful unity, appealing beauty, perfect functioning,
proven strength, are subject to the Head and responsive to His
command. It is not allegorization to contend that both the natural
image of the body and the Biblical use of that image to symbolize
the Church as the Body of Christ, rule out the legitimacy of exalt-
ing that image into a position where it would become a pure object of admiration or a recognized center of power. The Body of
Christ exists for action in some form, for action consonant with
its nature, for action inspired by the Head.

What form does that action take? How significant and thrilling
it is that Paul the Apostle, after he has descanted on the Body of
Christ and described its members and the gifts they should
"earnestly desire," exclaims, "And I will show you a still more
excellent way" (I Corinthians 12:31), or, as his words might be
rendered, "a still higher path" (Moffatt). That path is the way
of love. After he has enshrined that "way" in one of the Bible's
most loved and challenging prose poems (I Corinthians 13), he
says to the Body, its officers and its members: "Make love your
aim." For Paul, love is greater and more basic than "faith" or
"hope."

Make love your aim. The Hellenic *eros,* whose glories Corinthian and Philippian Christians were accustomed to hear sung,
could be fulfilled by becoming ecstatic over objects that stirred
their admiration. But commitment to the Christian *agape* as their
"aim" and goal meant the awakening within them of a love passion like that of Christ's. By this love passion, Paul himself had
been "constrained." It had led to his involvement in a human situation that called not for admiration, but for compassion and concern. He found, and he gloried in the fact, that the acceptance of

"love" in this sense was costly business. It cost him personally the "marks of the Lord Jesus" in his own body. But in this he rejoiced. For it was God's way for advancing the interests of the Body of Christ. Writing from a Roman prison to the members of the Church in Colossae, he said, in the same spirit, "I rejoice in my sufferings for your sake, and in my flesh I complete what remains of Christ's afflictions for the sake of His body, that is the Church, of which I became a minister" (Colossians 1:24). And this Church, the Body of Christ, for whose welfare he sacrificed his own body, Paul did not think of as a static, ingrown corporation in quest of admiration. He thought of it, rather, as a mobile community, a community ready to bear the "marks of the Lord Jesus," and committed to proclaim and to live the Gospel of the Cross in the midst of their society. And this they would do in order that the Body might be enlarged and reach the uttermost bounds of the *oikoumenē*.

Possessed by the *agape*, which is inseparable from a sense of indebtedness to Christ, and which manifests itself in Christ-like concern for people in every phase of their lives, the man born in Tarsus, who was executed in Rome, bequeathed this injunction to all fellow members of the Body of Christ: "Follow me as I follow Christ."

The Church
as a Fellowship of the Road

chapter 6

We come now to the climactic designation of the Church. The Christian Church as a Fellowship of the Road, a Community on the march, expresses the inmost nature and genius of the Church in the context of the Bible. This is, moreover, the image of the Church which is most relevant to the present human situation and which offers the greatest challenge to Christian thought and imagination.

The Church is ultimately Community, and true Community it must remain to the end. But only as a mobile, dynamic community, a fellowship on the march in every land and culture can the Christian Church fulfill its destiny and achieve its God-given mission. Only thus can it be truly ecumenical, and be "in very deed the Church." This is the thesis of the present chapter. It is also the thesis which shall govern thought in the chapters that will follow.

THE IMAGE OF THE ROAD

The context of our time offers an unusual setting for the Biblical concept of the Church as an itinerant fellowship. We live in an epoch of dramatic change. To a degree unparalleled in human history, humanity is on the march. New nations, recently come to birth, demand recognition and status. Movements into outer space are matched by movements into inner space, to expose the heart of the atom and the bosom of the earth. Cultured imperialists and uncouth guerrillas are equally on the move. Crisis and tragedy have taken on fresh meaning. Frontiers have increased in number and have acquired new significance. Peasants in countrysides around the globe, who have lived for millennia in a state of fatalistic resignation, are now standing with heads erect in revolutionary mood. Their emergence on the world scene gives revolution an imminent volcanic dimension. Some concerned people speak of the need for involvement in the problems of the masses; others begin to grasp the significance of the *incarnational* approach to the human problem. New fellowships of dedicated people of all ages (the Peace Corps, for example) are coming into being. Groups of campaigners to end racial discrimination, to "ban the bomb," to achieve world peace, not to speak of millions of disciplined Marxists, are on the march.

This situation serves to remind the Christian Church that it, too, was born as a Fellowship of the Road, the "Fellowship of the Spirit." The Church came into being as a Community redeemed by the divine *agape*, a Community responsive to the mandate of Jesus Christ to disciple the nations and dedicated to express His concern for mankind. Having this in mind, and seeking to be sensitive both to human reality in our time and to God's purpose for the Church in all time, let us examine what is meant by calling the Church a "Fellowship of the Road."

It is abundantly clear that God has willed fellowship. It is no less clear that the Community called the Church is the fellowship He willed. It is sadly forgotten, however, that Christ charged this fellowship with a world mission which can be fulfilled only if the Church is willing to be a Fellowship of the Road. This does not mean that a pilgrim Church can be itself, and fulfill its mission, only if everything and everybody associated with its life are everlastingly on the march in a purely physical, ambulatory sense. The "Road" is an image, a metaphor, a figure expressive of movement towards a destination, which may be perchance a distant frontier. But a "frontier" is not necessarily geographical in character, but can signify an object or goal that is reached by dynamic action. So, too, with the "Road." It envisions an attitude which runs counter to complacent self-satisfaction with achievement, whatever the achievement may be. For the fellowship called the Church, the "Road" means a sense of beyondness. This involves calm, dedicated movement in the direction of being and doing what the Holy Spirit would have the Church be and do, in every movement of its own life and the life of the world.

It is not the purpose of this study to raise the ecclesiological question as to which communal or institutional form expresses most adequately the nature of the Christian Church. It is nonetheless imperative to establish norms whereby, in full consonance with the genius of the community which Christ founded, every historical manifestation of the Church must be judged. Such norms are provided by reflecting upon the Church as being essentially a fellowship of the Road.

A COMMUNITY ON THE MARCH

Any Church, whether local congregation, national denomination, or world community, approximates to churchly reality in the measure in which a spirit of fellowship prevails among all who are its members. The members, knit together by a common loyalty to Jesus Christ as Lord, will love God and one another. They will be committed persons who know what they believe and what they stand for. They will not constitute an elite whose members owe their place in the fellowship to considerations relating to money, race, culture, social status, or nationality. Their friendship will not be of the Nietzschean star variety, already alluded to, where the protocol of social relationship is correctly but coldly observed; nor of the "tavern" type, where group hilarity and a good time together are substituted for intimate personal encounter. They will be successors of those who in New Testament times were known as the "saints," persons who responded to the Christian Gospel and abandoned their former way of living in order to follow Him who was called the Way, becoming thereby "Christ's men and women." Each member, according to his age, ability, and the judgment of fellow members, will play a part in the life and work of the fellowship. Speaking collectively, they will never say, "we and only we constitute the Church," or "we and we alone possess the truth." In selecting a place of meeting, or a center for service, or when they erect a sanctuary for corporate worship, they will be guided by a spirit of Christian reverence and a desire for effective witness. They will not be inspired by a craving for fame nor succumb to a delirious desire for recognition. In their concern about the physical, the material, and the aesthetic, they will not spend time and money which had better be expended in meeting the spiritual and temporal needs of people.

As regards those members of the fellowship who are its recognized and responsible leaders, whatever may have been the particular method of their election to office, it will be theirs to take their role seriously. Their concern will not be to court the applause of their fellow members. They will not cultivate pompous airs nor live parasitical lives. In the particular situation in which the fellowship is found, whether it be in the inner city or suburbia, in a rural area, an industrial center, or on a university campus, they will play the part of those chieftains in the turbulent days of Israel's history—the role so graphically described in the "Song of Deborah" (Judges 5). This valiant, poetic, female bard was enraptured by the fact and blessed the Lord for it, that "the leaders took the lead in Israel," and that "the people offered themselves willingly." The timeless principle that is extolled in this ancient melody should mark the behavior of "leaders" in the fellowship called the "Church." *Let the leaders take the lead.*

When "the mountains quake," and "the earth trembles," and "war is in the gates" (Judges 5:4, 5, 8), let Christian leaders not waste time in efforts to establish their descent from ancient "apostolic" warriors. Let them be concerned rather to show by their own devotion to Christ and by deeds of apostolic mold that they are true successors of the "apostles." Let them prove their participation in the mission to which the Founder of the fellowship called the first apostolic band, by summoning and mobilizing the "saints" for proclamation and action on the contemporary Road.

The Community of Christ—there is no escaping the fact—must live everlastingly on the Road. The image of the "Road" in turn must be interpreted in terms of the Church's life and witness in the age and environment in which its lot is cast. Inasmuch as the Church exists in God's design to "prepare the way of the Lord," the Lord, "whose it is and whom it serves," and who will come again to establish His Kingdom, the Church must never allow itself to become so integrated into any nation, civilization, or culture as to become no more than a representative expression of its life. Aware of the fact that they belong to a fellowship which is a "colony of heaven," Christians will never cease, in the spirit of the Abrahamic adventure, to "look forward to the city with firm foundations, whose architect and builder is God" (Hebrews 11:10) N.E.B. With the pattern of the "city" engraven on their spirit, and with their "eyes fixed on Jesus, on whom faith depends from start to finish" (Hebrews 12:2) N.E.B., they will endeavor to imprint that pattern upon every form of human relationship in which members of the fellowship may be involved. They will also seek to make the Lordship of Christ a dynamic factor in human relations whithersoever they go.

As this journey is not one in which the travelers take to the highway primarily in quest of truth, but under the leadership of Him who is the Truth, their attitude and demeanor will reflect a mood of quiet determination. They will not be obsessed with the necessity of wearing the chief symbol of the Truth as a distinguishing badge on their lapels or around their necks, but as a cross engraven in their hearts. Being committed to action, Truth will be to them a belt (Ephesians 6:14) with which they gird themselves, as they take each morning to the Road. It will resemble an unfurled banner (Psalm 60:4) which goes before them on the march. Flowers from the wayside they will savor for their fragrance. They will pluck them to be inspired by their beauty, but not for the sake of mere adornment. Like those figurative crusaders in search of the tomb of the Knight of the Mancha, whose journey is described by Miguel de Unamuno in his essay "The Sepulchre of Don Quixote," they will be frank and forthright in their witness. They will call a thief a "thief," and a liar a "liar," and will be ready to take all the consequences of their stand.

FROM MOTION TO MEDITATION

From time to time, the pilgrims will stop by the wayside for a period longer than that prescribed by the necessities of food and rest. Following the example of their Leader in the "days of His flesh," and in the great prophetic and apostolic tradition of their faith, they will time and again leave the highway in quest of a lakeside haven, or a woodland or mountain solitude. There they will commune uninterruptedly with God and with one another. They will retire from the world in order to be more relevant to its needs when they return. Through study of the Word and prayer, through meditation on the Faith and on the state of the world, through confrontation with themselves and the nature of their task, through reflection upon the unity and mission of the Church and their own specific role in "preparing the way of the Lord," they will ready themselves for a renewal of the march.

Times will come, however, when the sojourners will be barred by circumstances from taking to the Road. Political change, military might, internal dissension, physical weakness, economic necessity, or even spiritual declension may interrupt the journey for a period long or short. But the dawn will break again. The Leader's voice will sound. New lessons will have been learned; old ways will have been reformed. New problems will meanwhile face the travelers; but a new vision will also inspire them, and new strength will carry them forward. They will leave their caves; they will come down from the clouds; they will take to the Road again. Once more they will tread the "highways to Zion," which during the time of their frustrating "captivity" never ceased to "dwell in their hearts" (Psalm 84:5).

Let me repeat it. In the life of the Christian Church there can be no substitute for dynamic movement toward its God-appointed goal. Rest by the wayside, spiritual retreats, mystic contemplation, theological study and debate, organizational reform, the merging of Christian communities, enforced cessation of the march for a season by the secular power, are all for the sake of a return to the highways or byways. Recognition by all the Churches that it is of the very essence of the one Church to be in missionary motion becomes particularly important at a time when a new historical era is being born and crusading forces, who know exactly what they want, are on the march. I will conclude this analysis of the Church as a *fellowship of the Road,* an image which I profoundly believe symbolizes the Church's essential reality, by referring to three contemporary illustrations of what is meant by dynamic united action in pursuit of a goal.

CHALLENGES TO THE CHURCH

THE SEARCH FOR A TOMB

I have already made reference to Miguel de Unamuno's essay, "The Sepulchre of Don Quixote." This essay, which constitutes the Prologue to the Spanish writer's greatest work, his *Commentary on the Life of Don Quixote and Sancho, by Miguel de Cervantes,* is one of the least known but most significant masterpieces of Twentieth-Century literature. Unamuno describes the spirit and fortunes of a group of crusaders. They set out in search of the tomb, whose whereabouts are unknown, of the Castilian knight who regarded himself as the "Arm of the Lord" to restore the Age of Chivalry. The crusaders have no map of the route, nor any clear-cut program for their journey. But they have faith that they will be guided aright. So onward they struggle, braving ridicule and righting wrongs as they go. They are willing to be dubbed "fanatics" and are inspired by the "abysmatic poetry of fanaticism."[1] "Mad but not stupid,"[2] they at length give up their lives in death. Where the crusaders die, there is the tomb, and there a shining star comes down from Heaven. But there, too, beside the star, the tomb, and the dead crusaders, is the "cradle," the "nest" where new life is born. And from that spot, the star, "flashing and sonorous," rises again towards Heaven.

Influenced in the first decade of the present century by the writings of Sören Kierkegaard and by Ibsen's *Brand,* Unamuno here enshrines the basic idea which he subsequently developed in *The Tragic Sense of Life, The Christ of Velázquez,* and *The Agony of Christianity,* namely, that the essence of life is struggle. Struggle there must ever be to pierce the mystery of existence, struggle to overcome life's paradoxical contradictions and to serve a great positive idea or cause, struggle to tread in the steps of the Crucified, and like Paul, to bear His "marks." From a study of this man who was the first writer in the Western World to sense the reality of tragedy, at a time when his fellow men of letters were still living in the quiet evolutionary atmosphere of the Victorian

---

[1] *la abismática poesía del fanatismo.*
[2] *Locos mas no tontos.*

era, Christians today can learn much that is relevant to the nature and mission of the Christian Church. Unamuno's thought is a needed antidote to the dialectical pragmatism whose God is ambivalence—a pragmatism which threatens to sterilize Christian thought and action.

MYSTIC GUERRILLAS

The second challenge to contemporary Churchmen to rediscover that the Church can be "in very deed" the Church only in terms of dynamic movement, comes from a quite unexpected quarter. It comes from the spirit and discipline of guerrilla bands in Asia and Latin America.

A book entitled *Violence in Colombia,*[3] recently published by the Faculty of Sociology of the National University of Colombia, describes the most tragic decade in that nation's history, the years 1948–58 when approximately three hundred thousand people lost their lives in the Colombian countryside. Reacting against the indignities to which they and their ancestors have been traditionally subjected, and reflecting the new spirit of revolt against feudalism and oppression that has gripped the peasant folk in many Latin American lands, the rural inhabitants in many provinces in Colombia organized themselves into guerrilla bands. Although guilty of the most indescribable cruelty in their retaliatory campaigns, the guerrillas were knit together in quiet disciplined unity in the achievement of revenge. In a section of this book, under the caption "Guerrilla Mysticism,"[4] the writer, German Guzmán, a distinguished Roman Catholic monsignor and sociologist, describes how completely and trustfully knit together are the members of these guerrilla bands with one another and with their leader. The members of the band choose their own leader, they follow him with blind obedience, in admiration of his courage and capacity. They carry on their campaign with a mystic sublimation of motives.

Another Colombian writer who has made a special study of guerrilla psychology is cited by Monsignor Guzmán. He heard these words from the mouth of a guerrilla, "We would fight

[3] *La Violencia en Colombia,* 1962.
[4] "La Mística Guerrillera."

against everything," said this crusader, "even against our own selves. There is where the battle begins. The foundation of that great edifice which is called revolution is the victory which we achieve over ourselves by conquering our flesh, our fear, our hunger, our sleep, our passions, and impulses. We seek to conquer our egotism, and to sacrifice it entirely for the sake of a cause."

These words, from a strange but representative sector in the revolutionary world of our time, are genuinely Christian in tone. Any effort on the part of the Christian Church that, in defining its nature and confronting its mission, fails to give centrality to this dedicated, disciplined spirit, will be less than Christian. It will fall short in theological interpretation, and it will be foredoomed to failure in witness and service.

THE QUEST OF UNITY FOR MISSION

The third challenge to the Church to take to the Road comes from the deliverance of one of the great Protestant denominations of America. When it came into being through the union of two Presbyterian Churches in 1958, the new United Presbyterian Church in the United States of America, was made profoundly aware, in the first hours of its life, of the issues with which this chapter deals. The first action taken by the Uniting General Assembly was the endorsement, as its own, of a message entitled, "In Unity—For Mission." From the closing section of this message, which the General Assembly ordered sent down for study and action to the ten thousand congregations of the Church, I cull the following paragraphs:

> God summons us to pilgrimage, to life on the missionary road. We must journey not only along desert paths and jungle trails, but in the teeming alleys of our cities. God commands us to be missionaries not only in the community where we live, not alone in the national environment of our home church, but to the ends of the earth. The Church's place is the frontier. But for the Church in the discharge of its God-given mission, the frontier is more than a location. It is wherever any sector of thought or life has to be occupied in the name of Jesus Christ.
>
> Only as church members become Christ's missionaries in their several vocations, in government and diplomacy, in in-

dustry and commerce, in the home and in the classroom, in the clinic and on the farm, will men perceive that Christ is *the* Way, *the* Truth and *the* Life.

The world is not better than it is primarily because we Christians are no better than we are, and for the same reason, the Church is no better than it is. . . . Let the Church demonstrate by the consistency of its life the validity of its claims.

This we call upon our churches to do. Every congregation should be a reflection of the holy, catholic Church. 'There is neither Jew nor Greek, there is neither slave nor free, there is neither male nor female; for you are all one in Christ Jesus.' In Christ, racial, cultural, social, economic, and sex distinctions become meaningless and are erased. As the Church is commissioned to make disciples of all nations, so each congregation is called upon to evangelize, and to welcome into its membership, all the unchurched people of its community without regard to their racial, economic, or cultural background and condition. To fail at this point is to deny the efficacy of the Atonement in our own lives and to betray the very Gospel we seek to proclaim. . . . Let us be so constrained by the love of Christ that we shall show our love for Him by becoming channels of His love to others. Jesus promised His followers that He would be with them in holy companionship to the end of the road, to the close of the Age. As we gird ourselves for our pilgrimage, our courage is in His pledge. And, as we journey, our strength is in the imperishable hope that the kingdoms of this world shall become the Kingdom of our Lord and of His Christ.

The grace of our Lord Jesus Christ be with us all.[5]

[5] *In Unity—For Mission. A Message to All Congregations from the Uniting General Assembly of The United Presbyterian Church in the United States of America*, May 30, 1958. Issued through the Office of the General Assembly, Witherspoon Building, Philadelphia 7, Pennsylvania.

The Functions
of the Church Universal

PART III

The Church's
Worshipping Function

chapter 7

Having defined the nature of Ecumenics, and considered the significance and contemporary challenge of the classical images of the Christian Church, we are now ready for what forms the main part of this study. We move to a consideration of the Church's functions. These functions are four in number, constituting together the principal dimension of the Science of Ecumenics.

In our study of the Biblical images of the Church, and in the general perspective of the Bible and the human situation, we have seen that the Christian Church is designed by God to be the chief medium through which He shall operate in the world to reconcile men to Himself and to one another, and to fulfill His purpose in history. That being so, it is not as an end in itself, but as an instrument whereby God may achieve His end, His grand design, that the Church should exist in every place and time. For God has willed that the Church shall live to unveil in its own life the glory of His divine character, and be the instrument whereby, through the Holy Spirit, He may carry forward the work of Christ in history. By so doing, and only by so doing, shall the Church enjoy the Eternal Presence to the end of the Road.

For the Church is *essentially* and must become *existentially*, a dynamic Community. It must manifest in its historical existence what it is in its spiritual essence. To use an abidingly relevant term from the thought of ancient Greece, the Church must fulfill its *telos*, that is, the *end*, the God-given objective, for which it has its being. Inasmuch as it owes its being to God, the Church will develop its full potentiality, and achieve its true destiny, only when it pursues and fulfills its *telos*. For this *telos* is the *wherefore*, the *final cause* of the Church's being. In its movement towards fulfillment, the Church must, therefore, exercise functions which are native to its reality as the New Humanity.

There are four specific functions which the Church must fulfill, four spiritual operations in which it must engage, in order to be "in very deed" the Church. There is, first, the Church's *worshipping* function; second, the Church's *prophetic* function; third, the Church's *redemptive* function; fourth, the Church's *unitive* function. These four functions, taken together, constitute what might be termed the Functional Quadrilateral of the Christian Church.

THE MEANING OF WORSHIP

Worship as a general religious concept is the expression of veneration for what is conceived as being in some sense Divine. In the Bible, "worship" and "service" are inseparably related. It has been stated by a recognized authority that "In the Old Testament, the 'worship of God' and the 'service of God' are practically synonymous terms." [1] Worship in the New Testament involves, as in the Old, the most absolute response of the worshipper to God's claims upon him. It becomes progressively centered, however, in Jesus Christ, God manifest in the flesh, in whom God meets man and man meets God. As was natural, the kind of "worship" or "service" which was rendered to Deity depended upon the concept of Deity and of the will of Deity that was entertained by the worshipper. It was one of the tragedies of Israel's history that, time and again, the form of worship in which priests and people engaged reflected the influence of pagan cults.

It was the glory of the Hebrew religion at its purest and best, that the worship of God was inspired by a profound conviction equally shared by lawmakers, priests, kings, prophets, and psalm-

[1] Alan Richardson, ed., *A Theological Word Book of the Bible* (New York: The Macmillan Company, 1951), J. S. McEwen articles, pp. 169–71 and 287–89.

ists. All were convinced that the Living and Eternal God, the God of Abraham, had chosen Israel to be His Covenant people, disclosing to them His character, His will, and the form of true worship. We discover in consequence a note of exultation, resounding very especially in the Psalms: "The Lord reigns; let the earth rejoice" (Psalm 97:1). "The Lord reigns; let the peoples tremble! He sits enthroned upon the Cherubim; let the earth quake! The Lord is great in Zion; He is exalted over all the peoples" (Psalm 99:1, 2). "Make a joyful noise to the Lord, all the lands! Serve the Lord with gladness! Come into His presence with singing!" (Psalm 100:1-2). Mingled with strains in which are echoed triumphantly God's majesty, His presence in "His holy temple," in the "city of the great King," and His universal dominion, are other stirring notes. It is sounded forth that the Lord God of Israel, the God of the whole earth, is a "forgiving God," a God who "loves justice," and who upholds by His "steadfast love" those who "trust Him and who walk in the light of His countenance," a God who "delivers the needy when he calls, the poor and him who has no helper."

What could be more thrilling than the outburst with which a sacred bard concludes one of the greatest poetic treasures in the Psalter, "Blessed be the Lord, the God of Israel, who alone does wondrous things. Blessed be His glorious Name for ever; may His glory fill the whole earth!" (Psalm 72:18-19). No less in the spirit of Israel's worship was the soft melody of deep personal devotion which falls on the ear in words like these: "Bless the Lord, O my soul; and all that is within me, bless His holy Name! Bless the Lord, O my soul, and forget not all His benefits" (Psalm 103:1-2). Consonant with the spirit and implications of a type of worship which related Deity to people corporately and individually, which centered in a God who reigned in heaven, and over all the earth, in human hearts, and in a temple shrine, are the words of one of the later prophets, "Be silent, all flesh, before the Lord; for He has roused Himself from His holy dwelling" (Zechariah 2:13).

In the New Testament, the rapturous cadences of Israel's worship continue to make music in Christian hearts and wherever Christians gather together, but they do it in a new perspective and with a fresh emphasis. The presence of Deity is no longer associated with, still less confined to, a given geographical spot or a special physical structure. What essentially matters is no longer the place where worship takes place, but the frame of mind of the worshipper. In the course of one of His journeys, Jesus Christ unveiled this revolutionary truth to a simple woman, a Samaritan Magdalene. This embarrassed woman posed to Him a religious problem, in an endeavor to divert His attention from a moral problem in her own life. She wanted to know the precise identity of the spot, whether it was a sacred mountain solitude or an urban shrine, where man could reckon on God's Presence and worship Him. Jesus replied thus to her query, "Woman, believe me, the hour is coming when neither on this mountain nor in Jerusalem will you worship the Father—But the hour is coming, and now is, when the true worshippers will worship the Father in spirit and truth, for such the Father seeks to worship Him. God is Spirit, and those who worship Him must worship in spirit and truth" (John 4:21, 22, 23).

THE SOUL OF CHRISTIAN WORSHIP

Taking due account of the meaning of worship in Holy Scripture, how should Christian worship be defined? In a book entitled, *The Church and Its Functions in Society*, which was issued by W. A. Visser 't Hooft and J. H. Oldham in connection with the Oxford Conference on *Church Community and State*, Oldham offers a remarkably basic and luminous definition of worship. In the section "The Functions of the Church," he defines worship in these terms: *"Worship is the response of believing men in adoration and joyous self-dedication to God's revelation of Himself and to His redeeming grace."* [2] Remembering that J. H. Oldham was the man who organized the Edinburgh Conference of 1910, the gathering which gave birth to the Ecumenical Movement, and that he was also the organizer and moving spirit at the Oxford Conference of 1937, which restored to currency the term "ecumenical," and made the Christian Church and its role in human society the main theme of discussion, this definition has profound significance. We listen to the words of a Christian saint who has

---

[2] *The Church and Its Function in Society* (Chicago: Willett, Clark & Company, 1938), p. 143.

been a prophetic thinker and an ecumenical statesman. Oldham's definition of worship is, moreover, so basic and impressive that it merits special analysis.

Christian worship is a *"response"* made to God. Its essence is not an effort to create emotion or to awaken religious sentiment or to put oneself in a religious mood. Feeling is inseparable from worship, but worship does not consist in the promotion of feeling, or in making the possession of feeling the chief end of worship. Worship is the response, feeble or decisive, to another Reality than ourselves, who has come to the world, who comes to us, who seeks us, who calls us. To respond to God, who has taken the initiative, to be sensitive to God's approach, to be receptive to His Presence, is to cross the threshold of the House where God dwells. This responsive, outward movement across the threshold of the soul is much more than the cultivation of a sense of the Infinite. It goes beyond an awareness of man's dependence upon Deity. It is a motion God-ward, a motion beyond absorption in religious sentiment.

They who thus respond are *"believing men."* Their response to God in an act of worship is not produced by any combination of phenomena which stir the senses or entrance the imagination, or otherwise produce a reaction which may be designated aesthetic. Things there may be in the environment of the worshipper that fascinate his eye or his ear, or that produce in him a feeling of mystery or awe. But he truly engages in Christian worship only when his response is that of one who, being aware of who God is, and of what He has done to merit the devotion of persons like himself, gives to Deity the homage of which He is worthy. And this the worshipper does with an enlightened mind and a glowing heart, saying to God, from the depths of his responsive spirit, "Thou art my God."

A striking illustration of the difference between worship as response to pageantry, and worship as response to a simple affirmation regarding God's concern for man, is found in the religious history of Chile. Many years ago, one of Chile's most distinguished educators told me of the extraordinary effect the pageantry that marked the religious services conducted by the early Spanish missionaries had upon the aboriginal population of that South American land. They were thrilled by it; they wanted to belong to the religion whose culture could captivate their spirit and transport them above the sordid realities of their daily existence. But the aesthetic pageantry had no influence whatever upon their lives. The time came when it ceased even to appeal to their senses. Their successors down the centuries sank deeper and deeper into social misery. The simple peasant folk had never been given an intelligible understanding of the Christian faith, nor had God and religion ever been made relevant to human welfare.

The generations passed. In the early years of the present century, there was born in Chile, under the influence of a Methodist missionary, a religious movement of a "Pentecostal" character. Simple men and women whose lives had been changed by the Gospel of Christ began to travel in small groups through the Chilean countryside. Their kindly dispositions and the help they rendered wherever they found special need won the affection of the people they visited. Having gained the confidence of the simple folk, they would very informally gather groups together for a Christian service. A speaker would say to those squatting around, "God loves you." "Impossible," would be the response, "No one has ever loved us." Repeating the affirmation, "God loves you," their visiting friend would open up to his incredulous, but soon enraptured, hearers, the story of the love of God for men, giving them the core of the Gospel story. The Evangel was understood and accepted. The moment the people believed that their abject lives had significance for Deity, they responded in simple evangelical faith to God's love in Christ. A new sense of human dignity engendered within them began to be reflected in their homes, in their relations with one another and with other people, and in their determination to better their lot.

Today there are more than half a million "Pentecostals" in the Republic of Chile. Hundreds upon hundreds of their boys and girls are in Chilean institutions of higher learning. Some years ago the Chilean government went on record with a declaration that never in the history of the country had a movement done so much for the welfare of the people.

Why have I told this story? Because here is an instance of the "response of *believing men.*" Pentecostal worship in Chile and elsewhere may be associated with phenomena that raise questions and cause concern in the minds of Christians in the classical Chris tian tradition. But let this be remembered. True Christian worship involves "believing men," who respond to a God whom they come to love and desire to serve. Aesthetic thrill can have its place, but let it never become a substitute for evangelical faith in anything that presumes to be Christian worship. This is specially important because of a most sobering fact. A very large proportion, perchance a majority, of Christians belonging to the Roman, Orthodox, and Protestant traditions of Christianity participate from time to time in Christian worship but do not participate in any real sense as "believing men."

Oldham is right in making "adoration" the initial expression of Christian worship. This is in accord with the true Biblical and classical tradition concerning the spirit in which man should approach his Maker. Adoration in the worship of Israel has its peak example in Isaiah's vision of God in the temple, where he saw the "Lord high and lifted up." Christian worshippers today continue to chant the words of the song which the seraphim sang to Him "whose train filled the temple." The song sounded in the prophet's ear at the same time that the vision of the "Lord sitting upon His throne" dazzled his eye: "Holy, holy, holy is the Lord of Hosts; the whole earth is full of His glory" (Isaiah 6:3), were the words he heard. The essence of this experience, and the mood of adoration which it inspired, are still real in worship—sometimes in temples made with hands, sometimes as Jesus promised, "wherever two or three are met together in my name." Whatever the place may be, provided "believing men" "wait for the Lord," listen for His voice, long for a sense of His Presence, they will now as always "renew their strength." That is, they will "change their strength for God's strength," and begin to "mount up with wings like eagles" (Isaiah 40:31).

Spiritual rapture can still be real in the sanctuary and outside it, and it need have nothing to do with external sensuous devices designed to promote devotion. We have witnessed in recent years a resurgence of the ecstatic in Christian worship. Not confined to Pentecostal gatherings it has appeared also in congregations belonging to the historical Churches. Glossolalia ("speaking with tongues") must be taken seriously by Christian traditionalists and aestheticists who view with suspicion any outward manifestation of religious emotion and who give their sanction only to such orderly and controllable feelings as are fostered by the sights, sounds, and odors regarded as appropriate concomitants or stimulants of Christian worship.

But whatever opinions be held regarding the status of the rapturous and ecstatic when God is being adored, Christians may become equally "lost in wonder, love, and praise," when they express their adoration of God in a quieter, but nonetheless real manner. What can be more expressive of the adoration of "believing men" than many moving stanzas in the ancient Psalms? How often have the cadences of the One Hundred and Third Psalm risen adoringly from the hearts and lips of worshippers met together on a Scottish hillside to celebrate the Sacrament of the Lord's Supper. As the communicants moved forward to take their place at the Holy Table, they sang:

> O Thou my soul, bless God the Lord;
> And all that in me is
> Be stirred up his Holy Name
> To magnify and bless.

Nowhere in Scripture is there a more moving ascription of adoration and praise to God than in that rhapsody with which the poet-Apostle who wrote the Letter to the Ephesians began his great Epistle: "Blessed be the God and Father of our Lord Jesus Christ, who has blessed us in Christ with every spiritual blessing in the heavenly places" (Ephesians 1:3). And how fully can "believing men," in all the Christian traditions, join with Cardinal Newman in expressing adoration:

> Praise to the Holiest in the height,
> And in the depths be praise;
> In all His words most wonderful,
> Most sure in all His ways.[3]

The adoration of God in an act of worship is accomplished by the commitment to God in *joyous self-dedication* on the part of the worshipper. He does not worship God from a sense of religious obligation, nor as part of a required ritual, nor in order to get God's

[3] John Henry Newman (1801–90).

sanction and strength for the achievement of his personal plans. With entire spontaneity and with a sense of privilege he puts himself at God's disposal, surrendering to Him his entire selfhood. He desires that God may keep him from all evil and may use his personality and his possessions for the fulfillment of His own purposes. In this dedication of himself to God, whereby he rejoices in being God's son, God's friend, God's servant, the worshipper experiences that sense of freedom which comes to the spirit of man when it becomes a willing, joyous captive of the Spirit of God. Spirit meets spirit. "God is Spirit," said Jesus, "and those who worship Him must worship in spirit and truth" (John 4:24).

The spirit of man is the chief place of encounter between the Divine and the human. To worship God "in spirit" is to allow God, who also is spirit, and not the mere totality of all things, but active, purposive, loving spirit, to become the controlling reality in our human spirit. To worship God *"in truth"* is to have a true image of God, and in full awareness of the fact that He is worthy of our devotion, to give ourselves to Him in utter sincerity. In Jesus's view, moreover, true worship, worship that is sincere in the fullest sense, is necessarily preceded by an act of reconciliation with any other human spirit whom the worshipper may have wronged. "First be reconciled to your brother, and then come and offer your gift" (Matthew 5:24b), said Jesus. With still greater reason, if the gift he offers to God is the gift of his own selfhood, a Christian worshipper must see to it that his selfhood is not haunted by the memory of a misdemeanor towards a fellow human being, for which amends were never made, nor forgiveness sought. Only a forgiven self can truly dedicate itself to God in worship.

The climactic expression of the New Testament viewpoint that "joyous self-dedication" to God lies at the heart of Christian worship and gives it true meaning, is found in Paul's Letter to the Romans. Having descanted on the grandeur of God's character and redemptive work, and His worthiness to be the object of man's unqualified allegiance, the Apostle says, "I appeal to you, therefore, brethren, by the mercies of God to *present your bodies as a living sacrifice,* holy and acceptable to God, which is *your spiritual worship*" (Romans 12:1). In the King James version, the designation "your spiritual worship" appears as "your reasonable service."

In the New English Bible, the phrase is rendered as the "worship offered by heart and mind," or, as suggested in a footnote, "for such is the worship which you as rational creatures should offer."

The significance of this passage for the Christian conception of worship cannot be exaggerated. The "worship of God" and the "service of God" are inseparably related. The supreme act of Christian worship is, in the words of the New English Bible, "to offer your very selves to Him: a living sacrifice, dedicated and fit for His acceptance, the worship offered by mind and heart." This is the sacrificial *offering*, the *service*, the *worship*, which God asks *of* us in view of all that He has done *for* us. Such self-giving, in turn, in which heart and mind are in full accord, enables a man to fulfill his true humanity. For he dedicates his entire selfhood to a Divinity that became manifest in humanity. Those who thus offer themselves to God become, in virtue of that act, the spiritual successors of the priests of ancient Israel who brought animal sacrifices to the altar. In the words of St. Peter, they approach Deity, as "a holy priesthood, to offer spiritual sacrifices acceptable to God through Jesus Christ" (I Peter 2:5). In this way, "believing men" exercise in worship a priestly function. They not only take advantage of their inherent, God-given right of free access into the Holy of Holies of God's presence; they take seriously the priestly obligation to bring to God an offering, which, in their case, is their own selves, that is, all that they are and all that they have. It is precisely this phase of the glorious doctrine of the "priesthood of all believers," the phase that stresses the priestly *responsibility* as being equal in importance to the priestly *privilege* of "believing men," that stands in need of restoration in the Christian Church today. However impressive may be the external forms of worship, unless the worshippers fulfill this primary requisite, unless subjectivity accompanies objectivity, there is no true Christian worship.

But why should a Christian hesitate to "respond" to God in the radical way which true worship involves, when he considers God's radical approach to his own personal need and to the need of all men? How appropriately does Oldham affirm that the "joyous self-dedication" of "believing men" in Christian worship is "response" to a God who has *revealed Himself!* Just as man is never so truly man as when he joyously declares himself "God's man" in worship, God was never so truly God as when He became "Man's

God," unveiling His character and design in human history and eventually becoming man for man's salvation. For Christian worship has meaning and vitality only in the measure in which the worshippers have an understanding of and are inspired by the heritage of faith that is enshrined in Holy Scripture whose center is Jesus Christ, the Reconciler. The story of God's self-giving love —in Christ's Incarnation and Life, in His Death and Resurrection, in His Ascension, His continuing Intercession, and His Coming Again—constitutes the core of the Christian religion and is the chief inspiration for Christian worship. The more, therefore, that the Evangel, the "Gospel of Jesus Christ, the Son of God," is studied by Christians and inspires their life, the more their lives are immersed in the devotional riches of the Bible and of literature which owes its inspiration to the Bible, the more they struggle where their lot is cast to live their faith, the more meaningfully will they approach God in praise and prayer.

"And to His redeeming grace." It is God's loving movement towards man in quest of man's love, and the continuing operation of the Holy Spirit within man, that provides the spiritual energy whereby a Christian is enabled to overcome all that holds him back from responding to God's call, or that prevents him giving himself to God afresh in the "secret place of the most High."

The fountain of God's "redeeming grace" is Christ Crucified, who is both the crowning manifestation of His reconciling love and the eternal wellspring from which divine grace flows into the soiled and withered lives of men. With good reason is the Cross the abiding and undisputed symbol of the Christian religion in all the great traditions of the Faith. This is true, however much the use made of the symbol of the Cross may vary from one tradition to another, and even among the diverse Churches in the Protestant family. But all Christians unite in thought and devotion in acclaiming the Crucified as being in very truth the "Lord high and lifted up," the Christian fulfillment of Isaiah's sublime vision in the Temple. It was natural that the prophet's immediate reaction was an acute awareness of his own sinfulness. From his inmost being comes the exclamation, "Woe is me! For I am lost; for I am a man of unclean lips, and I dwell in the midst of a people of unclean lips; for my eyes have seen the King, the Lord of hosts!" (Isaiah 6:5). It was then that a seraph took a "burning coal" from the altar, and with it touched the mouth of the stricken prophet, saying, "Behold, this has touched your lips; your guilt is taken away, and your sin forgiven" (Isaiah 6:7).

The image of the Crucified as One who continues to reign from the Cross, the slain Lamb of the apocalyptic vision who occupies a throne while continuing to bear the marks of His suffering, is the image that spells forgiveness for the Christian soul and offers the assurance that he, too, at whatever cost, shall, like Christ, triumph at the last. The Crucified-Risen Christ provides also the "marks" which a forgiven man like Paul wishes to reproduce in his own life of Christian discipleship. It is the altar from which comes the glowing ember that set his lips aflame with a love passion to proclaim the Gospel of Christ and to live it. For the man from Tarsus to "know Christ, to experience the power of His resurrection, and to share His sufferings, in growing conformity with His death" (Philippians 3:10), meant something poles removed from maudlin sentimentality. It gave him rather an abiding pattern and a dynamic source of strength, for his own life as a Christian crusader. In the tradition of Christian life and worship at their classical best, are the words of Isaac Watts, in that hymn which more than any other has expressed the "adoration and joyous self-dedication of believing men."

> When I survey the wondrous cross,
> On which the Prince of glory died,
> My richest gain I count but loss,
> And pour contempt on all my pride.
>
> Were the whole realm of nature mine,
> That were a present far too small;
> Love so amazing, so divine,
> Demands my soul, my life, my all.*

This was the spirit that gave birth to the Church Universal. This is the spirit that is the soul of Christian worship. The rebirth of this spirit is what the frontiers of the Kingdom need. It is the one and only spirit that can make the Church a pilgrim "fellowship of the Road," to match the resurgence of militant, pilgrim forces in our time.

* Verses one and four. Isaac Watts (1674–1748).

In this context, how significant and timely are the words of God and man with which Israel's dramatic temple experience ends! That worship was concluded thus: "I heard the voice of the Lord saying, 'Whom shall I send, and who will go for us?' Then I said, 'Here am I! Send me'" (Isaiah 6:8).

THE FORMS OF WORSHIP

While worship is less than Christian unless the worshippers as individuals give their own selves in "joyous self-dedication" to the God whom they worship, Christian worship has an external aspect which is an integral part of its nature. This is particularly true insofar as the corporate life of the Christian Community is concerned.

We have been witnessing in recent years a great liturgical revival in all the Churches, especially in the Churches of the West. Diverse motives inspire a movement which seeks to provide impressive, symbolical form for man's yearning for objectivity, the craving for a meaningful relationship to the Ultimate.

The Liturgical Movement at its best is an attempt to get back to the spirit and ideas that inspired worship in the primitive Christian Community. There is, unfortunately, little documentary evidence as to the precise forms of worship that prevailed in the first three centuries of Christian history. This is itself significant. In those years of great spiritual vitality in the Church, Christians were more concerned about their wholehearted participation in worship than in talking or writing about it. What is certain is this. Each Christian congregation, taking seriously the promise of Christ, considered itself to be the living vehicle of His Presence. The members felt themselves to constitute the Body of Christ and they assembled together with a sense of being possessed by the Spirit of Christ. Their worship was thus marked by a note of jubilation. They were literally children of joy, for salvation through Christ was a reality in their experience. They knew the meaning of pneumatic enthusiasm. Amid an air of mystery, and with the holy supper at the very center of their worship, there was, among the worshippers, a spirit of great spontaneity. As has been said by that outstanding authority on Christian worship down the ages, Dr. Friedrich Heiler, "The life (of those early Christians) had not been confined by the rigidity of outward forms, nor subtilized by intellectual reflection." [4]

It is for historians to trace the course of the Church's life, including its liturgical life, from the early centuries to the present time. In the present study our sole concern in dealing with the worshipping function of the Church, is to determine what constitutes the essence of Christian worship in the dual perspective of the Church's nature and mission as the community of Christ, and of representative forms of worship that have marked the course of the Church's history. The crucial, but also very delicate, question is: When is the Church "in very deed the Church" in its liturgical life?

THE EASTERN ORTHODOX AT WORSHIP

Worship in Eastern Orthodoxy, which claims unbroken continuity from the apostles and represents today a single Christian Communion under fourteen distinct Patriarchs, is of the type which might be designated *mystery-drama*. With an ornateness and pageantry unparalleled in the history of religion, and in which choral singing plays an important part, the mystery of the Incarnation, Death, and Resurrection of Jesus Christ is displayed before the assembled worshippers. These gaze in a spirit of adoring wonder at the unveiling, in successive symbolic acts, of the mystery of God manifest in human form. They hear in their own tongue the chants and songs that accompany the ritualistic acts. They gaze and listen, and even understand, but they do not participate in the service in any way that is reminiscent of a worship service in the primitive Church. For the role of the people even though they experience a unique sense of togetherness *(koinonia)*, is to be purely receptive.

It is the glory of Eastern Orthodoxy, let it be said with appreciation, that it enshrines in matchless liturgical symbols the reality of Christian forgiveness and sanctification, as climaxed in the Resurrection from the dead of Jesus Christ, the Crucified Savior. Christ's rising from the tomb, and all that is associated with Easter

[4] *The Spirit of Worship* (Garden City, N. Y.: Doubleday & Company Inc., 1927), p. 42.

Sunday, constitutes the center and chief inspiration of Orthodox
worship. "Christ is risen!"; that has been, and continues to be, the
watchword of the oriental Churches, which since the birth of the
Ecumenical Movement, are in close contact with the non-Roman
Churches of the world.

"Christ is risen!" But for what? To be the center of a marvellous
liturgy? To be the Head of a Christian Communion which claims
to stand alone in unbroken and orthodox succession from the
apostles of the Risen One, and whose mission consists in substanti-
ating this claim? I speak with deep feeling and concern. I do so
because contact with beloved friends in this historic Church has
awakened within me the feeling that the Eastern Orthodox
Churches have tended to cultivate a mood of unwarranted complacency with regard to their ecclesiastical status and its implications.

Let me explain my concern. That saintly man, now alas no more,
Archbishop Germanos of the Greek Orthodox Church, was a
member of the Commission on "The Universal Church and the
World of Nations" of the Oxford Conference of 1937. From time
to time, members of the commission would give expression to
severe indictments of the Church Universal for its failure to witness adequately in human situations, charging it with attitudes
which could only be characterized as its "sinfulness." On two
occasions when this kind of discussion was in progress, the venerable Archbishop, who was seated in the front row, just beneath
the chairman's desk, slipped into my hand a note which said, "The
Church cannot sin." This precisely has been the historic problem
of the Churches belonging to the Orthodox Communion—their
incapacity for serious self-criticism, their failure to recognize that
the Body of Christ can sin, and does sin, when it fails to be
responsive and obedient to its Head.

A similarly revealing incident took place in 1949 at a meeting
of the Faith and Order Committee of the World Council of
Churches. Discussion turned upon the question of Truth, and of
the relation of the Church to Truth. A distinguished Orthodox
Churchman, who was a warm personal friend, made the statement
that the discussion of Truth as a problem was not a concern for
the Orthodox Church because the Church *had* the Truth. I
asked if Christ's great commission to His disciples was part of the

Christian Truth. "Of course," was the reply. Then I said, quietly, "Can a Christian Church say that it *has* the Truth, if it does not *do* the Truth? For Christian Truth," I continued, "is not something that we *possess*, but something that *possesses* us, something by which we are *possessed*." What concerned me was the fact, to which I alluded at the meeting in question, that the Eastern Orthodox Church had ceased to be a missionary Church, in obedience to the command of Christ. My remarks were received in the spirit in which they were made. It is cause for sincere rejoicing that the members of the Orthodox family of Churches begin to manifest missionary concern after long centuries of complacency and stagnation.

But one thing is still lacking. The timeless principle which is enshrined in the historical Incarnation of Christ awaits expression in the relationship of this great Communion to the world of contemporary man. It is truly cause for rejoicing that the Eastern Church possesses in its liturgy the treasure of the Gospel. But this treasure must be shown in "earthen vessels," as well as in liturgical drama. It would then be revealed in all its splendor outside the sanctuary. Friedrich Heiler envisions the happening that would make it "in very deed the Church." Says in effect this sympathetic student of Eastern Orthodoxy: "It only awaits a great evangelical awakening, so that the Evangel, so gloriously enshrined in the Liturgy, may become manifest in the rhythm of Life." These are prophetic words that should be heeded by the Churches in all the Christian traditions.

ROMAN CATHOLIC WORSHIP

Largest among the Christian Communions, if the basis of judgment be the number of baptized persons, whether or not they have continued a visible relationship to the Body of Christ, is the Roman Catholic Church. This great Communion, claiming even more than do the Eastern Churches to be the "Catholic" Church, the *Una Sancta*, the empirical synonym of the Body of Christ, has made the *drama of Christ's death* the center of its service of worship. The Roman liturgy covers, in the course of the calendar year, the whole drama of the story of salvation. Attention is focused, however, in a unique manner and degree, upon Christ's Oblation, whereas the Eastern Churches give liturgical centrality to His Resurrection.

The most sacred and culminating moment in the daily act of worship is the elevation of the Host (the *Hostia* or divine Victim). Christ, in the form of a wafer of bread, is offered afresh to God by priestly hands in the Sacrifice of the Mass, in such wise that His sacrificial death on Golgotha is re-enacted continuously, not merely symbolically, but actually. He, who twenty centuries ago died for the sins of the world, continues to die for mankind day by day. And this, in the context of liturgical celebration carried on by a worldwide Church, means hour by hour, minute by minute. When worshippers are present at the time of the Sacrifice of the Mass—for the rite is valid even when the sanctuary is empty—the re-enactment of Christ's death is followed by Communion. The worshippers partake of the consecrated wafer, which is the very Body of our Lord Jesus Christ.

Roman Catholic theologians stress the fact that the Church's liturgy is "dogma set to prayer." [5] As the official worship of the Church takes place "under the unerring guidance of the Holy Spirit, the Spirit of Truth," the liturgy occupies a place of authority in the faith of the Church second only to the Scriptures, and above that of the Fathers. This fact is of first-rate importance. It implies that the worship of the Church is inseparably related to dogmatic presuppositions, not only regarding the person and work of Jesus Christ, but regarding the status and authority of the Roman Church in relation to Christ Crucified and Risen.

Most illuminating for our understanding of the Church's view of its own absolute primacy as an historical institution are some affirmations of a leading Roman Catholic scholar, Dom Virgil Michel, S.B., S.J. In a book entitled, *The Liturgy of the Church,* issued the same year as the Oxford Conference, the author cites a variety of recognized authorities on the subject with which he deals. Here are some significant citations from that volume:

> It is through the Church, says Michel, that Christ comes to full maturity. The Church is Christ Himself. The Church is the plenitude, the accomplishment of Christ, His body and His real

5 Dom Virgil George Michel, *The Liturgy of the Church* (New York: The Macmillan Company, 1937), p. 16.

and mystical development and is Christ in His totality and plenitude.[6] Thus, among the works of God, the Church occupies the very place of Christ; the Church and Christ, they are the same work of God. . . . The Mass is the sublimest function the Church is capable of, for it is the continued oblation of Christ Himself to the heavenly Father.[7] . . . The same proportion that exists between the Father and the Son, exists analogously between the Son and the Church. . . . Since Christ, as the sole means of all sanctification and salvation, performs His mission through the liturgy of His Church, and since the Holy Ghost gives the efficacy to the powers of Christ, the liturgy must finally receive its efficacy through the operations of the Holy Ghost, of the Spirit of Christ and the Father. The liturgical action of the Church, being the fulfillment of Christ's missionary work, and the plenitude of Christ coming through the Holy Spirit, the two must converge. And in truth, the liturgy of the Church effects her divine mission through the divine Spirit. . . . Christ continues to live here on earth in His Church, and He continues the exercise of His salutary mission in the official actions of this Church, in her liturgy.[8] . . .

Since it is in the liturgy of the Church that the sacrifice of the Church is repeated day by day and that the fruitful activity of the Redeemer is perpetuated, it is by association with the liturgical action of the Church's sacrifice that the individual can find Christ. Hence, by virtue of her liturgy the Church has become, in a subordinate sense, our way, our truth, our life, for she conducts us to Christ, for in her teaching she dispenses unto us the word of Christ, for in her sacraments and sacramentals she communicates to us the divine sap of Christ.[9] The Mass is truly a liturgical drama. As such, it is pre-eminent fulfillment of the aim of all liturgy, of the mission of Christ, which is the glorification of God and the sanctification of men.[10]

Our final quotations will be from another authoritative source, *The Churches and the Church: A Study of Ecumenism,* by an eminent Roman Catholic theologian, Bernard Leeming, S.J., who

[6] *Ibid.,* p. 22.
[7] *Ibid.,* p. 30.
[8] *Ibid.,* p. 44.
[9] *Ibid.,* p. 45.
[10] *Ibid.,* p. 209.

in recent years has been close to the Ecumenical Movement. Father Leeming in the chapter, "The Catholic Attitude towards Ecumenism," makes these very significant statements:

> The Catholic commits himself to Christ *in the Church*, and makes that self-committal as absolutely and finally as a non-Catholic makes his self-committal to Christ as God and Savior.[11] . . . For those outside the Roman Catholic Church, to doubt the Gospel would be to doubt and betray Christ; for a Catholic to doubt the teaching of the Church would be to doubt or betray Christ. For any Christian, face to face with non-Christians, even to appear to doubt the Gospel would be to betray Christ; for a Catholic, even to appear to doubt the Church would be to betray Christ.[12]

This is a point at which reflection is called for. It is claimed that an inseparable relationship exists between Jesus Christ and the Roman Catholic Church and that the Church's liturgy, in which its infallible dogma is enshrined, has essentially a missionary role to perform. Confronted with the liturgy, Christians and non-Christians alike are summoned to commit themselves to the Church, which is the visible manifestation of Christ, the place where He dwells and the sole medium of His continuing activity. And the Church, according to this claim, is constituted by its hierarchy, who belong to the Church and so to Christ, in a manner and to a degree that cannot be affirmed of the Christian rank and file. Christ is the Church, and the Church is the hierarchy. And this is so, according to the premise, because God willed that it should be so and made it so.

This premise, needless to say, is utterly unacceptable to non-Roman Christians. It is not the purpose of this study, however, to engage in matters relating to the theological presuppositions upon which the diverse Churches seek to establish their ecclesiastical claims. Starting from the classical New Testament affirmations of Christian faith regarding Christ and the Church, which transcend confessional boundaries, the one presupposition which constitutes the foundation of this study and serves to provide it with per-

[11] Westminster, Maryland: The Newman Press, 1960, p. 170.
[12] *Ibid.*, p. 171.

spective and standards of judgment is this: *The Christian Church was designed by God to be a missionary community.* Only in the measure in which it fulfills God's design in the exercise of its diverse functions and relations can it be in the profoundest sense the Church. Therefore, the Church's worship, the Church's liturgy, the exercise of the Church's worshipping function must ultimately be judged in each instance by the measure in which a Church, including the great Roman Communion, gives dynamic expression to the Church's mission.

I have considered it important to pause at this point, and by way of an interlude, to emphasize afresh the main thesis of this book. I do so for this reason. The thesis as restated will serve as a norm for appraising the historical witness of the Roman Catholic Church in a region in which the Church gave the most absolute, concrete, and uninhibited expression to the theological doctrines, the administrative procedures and the liturgical practices, which constitute its ecclesiastical selfhood. I refer to Hispanic Catholicism, the phase of the Christian religion that has been historically associated with Spain, Portugal, and Latin America.

No Church in Christian history has been so indisputably Roman, or so consistently loyal to the Roman See, as the Church that Christianized Hispania and her ancient colonies. And yet this Church, according to the informed and dispassionate judgment of many loyal Roman Catholic Churchmen in the United States and Europe, failed in its essential Christian mission. Their criticism is that it lacked the incarnational quality; it controlled life, but it did not relate itself to life in such a way as to transform life.

Very briefly, let me state the facts. Let me describe what can happen when a Church interprets the promotion of Christianity as being chiefly the advancement of its own institutional power, and in so doing identifies people's acceptance of Christ Crucified with their absorption in liturgical rites in which He is the center.

1. *The Hispanic Church assumed the role of being Christ's master and overlord.* The lordship of the Church over Christ took some very extreme forms. Christ's reality became so identified with a dead Figure and a Sacramental Wafer that the Risen Christ played no part in the official religion of the Iberian Peninsula and Latin America. There is no painting of the Resurrection by any

great Spanish artist. So secondary and irrelevant has been the
Resurrection in Hispanic Catholicism that in the traditional religious ceremonies held during Holy Week in the City of Seville,
no special service was held to mark the advent of Easter morning.
On Saturday at noon, the veil that covered the high altar in the
great cathedral was "rent." On Sunday was celebrated not the
Resurrection of Christ, but the first bullfight of the season, when
blood began again to flow. The concentration of the public mind
upon the fact and implications of Christ's Resurrection was viewed
as theologically irrelevant; ecclesiastically, such concentration
could be embarrassing for hierarchical authority. Only quite recently, and as an expression of concern in high Vatican circles,
has Easter Sunday begun to be stressed religiously in the historic
ceremonies at Seville.

The great Russian novelist, Dostoevsky, a true son of Eastern
Orthodoxy, penetrated to the heart of Hispanic Catholicism in
his "Legend of the Grand Inquisitor." The Cardinal became
alarmed when he saw a Figure, who seemed to be the Nazarene
risen from the dead, being acclaimed with joy by the common
people of Seville, because of His gracious personality and healing
works. Ordering Christ to be arrested and jailed, the Hierarch
came to the prison cell at midnight and thus addressed the
Prisoner: "Why hast Thou come to molest us; we will finish Thy
work in Thy name." Was the Grand Inquisitor unorthodox? Was
he not giving expression to sound Church doctrine, namely, that
Jesus Christ related Himself so absolutely to the visible Church
that He gave up the right to exercise authority outside its structure?
This Grand Inquisitor was really giving crude expression to the
contemporary claim of the Roman Catholic Church as interpreted
by Father Leeming in words already quoted, and which I repeat:
"among the works of God, the Church occupies the very place of
Christ; the Church and Christ, they are the same work of God."

2. *In the Sixteenth Century when Hispanic Catholicism was
at the zenith of its glory, some of the Church's loyal sons and
daughters claimed to have personal communion with Jesus Christ
that was unrelated to liturgical rites, affirming at the same time
that Christ's presence was not confined to a holy shrine.* The great
Spanish mystics, St. Theresa of Avila, St. John of the Cross, Fray
Luis of Granada, and Fray Luis of León, were all persecuted by

the official Church. The fact has already been mentioned that
Theresa, one of the greatest and most practical Christian women
of all time, passed through a profound spiritual conversion some
twenty years after she became a nun in a Carmelite convent. Her
conversion gave the Saint of Avila an awareness that the living
reality of Christ could be experienced independently of any
liturgical ceremony. Her books are a witness to this fact. In that
great classic, *The Mansions of the Soul*,[13] the devout Christian's
culminating encounter with the Beloved is in the inmost recess of
the human spirit. The reader will recall in this connection the
memorable and significant words she once wrote to a group of
young nuns who complained of the drudgery of their daily chores.
"My daughters," she said to them, "the Lord moves among the
pots and pans."

So it was, too, with that great Augustinian scholar and saint,
Luis de León, who was imprisoned by the Spanish Inquisition for
having translated a book of the Bible into the Spanish vernacular.
In that monument of literature and Christian theology, *The Names
of Christ*,[14] Fray Luis gives expression to a thought which carries
Christ beyond the bounds of Church and liturgy. "Christ lives in
the fields," says the poet-theologian. His words were spoken in
full loyalty to the New Testament and to Christian experience.
For Jesus Christ, the Lord of the Church and the Lord of Life,
lives as truly at the grass roots of human existence as He does in
"temples made with hands," or where episodes of His passion are
re-enacted in liturgical ceremony.

3. *The Church's opposition to claims that Christ could be
met in spiritual encounter at times and in situations not directly
controlled by the Church's ministers dominated the Council of
Trent.* This attitude towards subjectivity became responsible for
the fact, already mentioned, that in the post-Tridentine era the
quality of devotional literature declined in Roman Catholic circles, whereas among Protestants, literature of this type enjoyed
a rich florescence.

This particular phenomenon begins to be recognized by concerned Roman Catholic scholars. We witness today a resurgence of
interest among Catholic clergy and laity in the great classics of

[13] *Las Moradas*.
[14] *Los nombres de Cristo*.

the spiritual life. This is happening at a time when, paradoxically, interest in the inner life tends to decline in institutionalized Protestantism. A distinguished theologian, the head of a Roman Catholic seminary in the United States, and a personal friend, has been awarded a Fulbright Fellowship in order to study John of the Cross and compare the thought of this great Spanish mystic with that of his peers in the Protestant tradition of English Protestantism.

4. *The promotion of Christianity in the Western Hemisphere by the representatives of Hispanic Catholicism took the form of imposing upon the aboriginal peoples the ceremonies of a religious establishment which demanded their unqualified allegiance, or else that they suffer the consequences of their refusal.* Even when Spanish and Portuguese colonialism came to an end, the Church of the new republics continued to make liturgical ceremonial the principal basis of appeal to the people. Acceptance by the people of baptism and the designation "Catholic," coupled with their material contributions to the Church and loyalty to it, became regarded as the supreme objective of the Church's task.

This interpretation of the Church's mission, with its exclusive concentration upon the liturgical and the institutional as instruments of Christian advance, produced disastrous consequences in the life of Latin America. Religion came to be regarded as irrelevant to culture and morals. Its abuses produced violent reactions. Today, this region, until recently regarded as the most vast and uniformly Catholic in the world, is being described by informed and deeply concerned Roman Catholic Churchmen, as a "disaster area" for the Church. They recognize, and have so stated, that, despite statistics provided in the *World Almanac* and the *Statesmen's Yearbook*, the immense majority of Latin Americans are Catholic in name only. Latin America has, therefore, become the leading mission field for Roman Catholic missionaries, especially from the United States and Canada. It is recognized that a totally new Christian approach, one which runs counter to the predominantly liturgical approach of Hispanic Catholicism, must be made while there is still time.

The concern in Roman Catholic circles regarding Hispanic Catholicism and the missionary approach now being made to the Latin American situation are described in a number of important works that have been issued in recent years by eminent Roman Catholic clergymen. I would draw special attention to the works of that most distinguished Maryknoll cleric, Father John J. Considine. Invaluable also is the volume entitled, *Latin American Catholicism: A Self-Evaluation*, the author of which is another Maryknoll scholar, William J. Coleman, M.M. Published in 1958, this book (which bears the imprimatur of Cardinal Francis Spellman) is a study of what was said at a now famous Inter-American Catholic Action Conference. The conference in question took place in 1953 in the Peruvian town of Chimbote.

Most significant and revealing are some sentences which occur in the Preface to this volume. The sentences in question read as follows:

> Here we have for the first time an objective and realistic self-evaluation of that Catholicism which is such a great enigma to even the well-informed Catholics in the United States. The Chimbote analysis, however, does not pretend to be a formal study of Latin American Catholicism. It is primarily a symposium on how best to carry on a modern lay apostolate within a Church whose traditional position in Latin American society has radically changed within the past generation. Hence, the Chimbote approach is broadly sociological and psychological; it is not theological, much less historical.[15]

It would be obviously inappropriate and unorthodox for the men of Chimbote to offer a critique, based on theological considerations and citing historical facts, of the approach to a human situation conducted by Hispanic Catholicism. For the Hispanic Church represented history's most authentic, most potent, and least inhibited expression of the faith of the Roman Catholic Church, as that faith was formulated afresh by the Council of Trent. Had it been permissible for the Catholic Churchmen at Chimbote to set the religious situation in Latin America in the perspective of theology and history, it would have been necessary to resuscitate the memory and ideas of that great Catholic missionary to Latin America, Fray Bartolomé de las Casas, who was

[15] *World Horizon Reports* (Maryknoll, New York: Maryknoll Publication, 1958), p. v.

the learned and ceaseless critic of his Church's missionary policy. We proceed therefore, to this other reflection.

5. *Bartolomé de las Casas, one of the great Christian missionaries of all time, and, next to Columbus, the greatest westerner ever to come to Latin America, was severely critical of the official policy of his Church towards the indigenous people.* He advocated that people should be confronted with Christ in their homes and at their tasks, by men and women who bore Christ's likeness and possessed His spirit, before they were invited to confront Him in a sacred spot or a liturgical act. This man who first came to the Americas as a young colonist in Columbus's second voyage, passed through a profound experience of evangelical conversion in Cuba. He joined the Dominican Order, became an evangelist and was elected Bishop of Chiapas in Mexico. Las Casas, in the course of a dedicated missionary career, which lasted until he was past eighty, became a writer of outstanding merit. In addition to a voluminous work, *The History of the Indies,* recognized as an historical classic, he wrote a book entitled, *The Only Way to Attract All Peoples to the True Religion.*[16]

In this recently discovered and still little-known work, the Sixteenth-Century Dominican missionary and scholar, embodies his views on the true Christian approach to non-Christians. With marvellous insight and acumen, he shows from the Scriptures and the writings of the Fathers how Christians who take the Scriptures, Jesus Christ, and their Christian calling seriously should relate themselves to people in such a way as to win their right to be heard on behalf of Christ. This right they could win only by being the kind of people, and doing the kind of things, that made them attractive to the people to whom they went. The faith and life of Las Casas were eminently Christ-centered. Jesus Christ was more than the Church. His living Presence, moreover, as was emphasized by the missionary bishop's contemporaries, Theresa of Avila, John of the Cross, and Luis de León, could not be controlled by the Church. Nor was that holy Presence confined to the liturgy of the Church. Christ lived supremely in His Word, in the Christian heart, in the places where Christians met or toiled, and

---

[16] *Del Único Modo de atraer a todos los Pueblos a la Verdadera Religión* (Mexico: Fondo de Cultura Económica, 1942).

where people yearned for a new life. Had the viewpoint represented by Las Casas prevailed with the authorities of his Church in the years of Iberia's glory, the situation in Spain, Portugal, and Latin America would be very different today from what it actually is, both in the Church and in society.

The control of Christ by the Church, which is implicit in the Roman Catholic doctrine of its own status, and the status of its liturgy and priesthood, and the restriction of Christ's Presence to shrines and liturgy, produced a profound psychological effect upon worshippers who yearned for a Christ who was more human and more directly relevant to their daily living and concerns. Not being encouraged, however, to seek the Christ who lives in His Word, and "where two or three are met together in His name," who "dwells among the pots and pans," and "in the fields," who is found on the "summit of Mount Carmel," and in the "heart's secret chamber," people sought substitutes for the Real Presence in daily life. Hence the development of a situation which I describe in this final reflection.

6. *Hispanic Catholicism, because of the manner in which it removed all sense of the Living Christ from the religious thought and life of the people, became noted for the special devotion accorded to the saints and the Virgin Mary.* It is not too much to say that the cult of the saints, in their great number and diversity, culminating in the cult of the Mother of our Lord, had much more reality in the popular mind and exercised a much greater influence in the lives of men and women, than Christ Crucified and Sacramentalized. Christ spoke to their need when they were gripped by the fear of death; Mary and the Saints inspired them as they faced life. The Virgin became, moreover, a potent instrument of the hierarchical Church to control the masses. The Virgin of Guadalupe, a dark-hued figure, who allegedly appeared to a Mexican Indian, has become the symbol in the Western Hemisphere that Mary belongs to the aboriginal world of Aztecs and Mayas, and it to her. The Virgin of Fatima, who allegedly appeared to three children on a Portuguese Plateau in 1917, is portrayed in impressive symbols as the controller of human destiny. She who made herself known at a spot called Fatima, so named for the daughter of Mahomet, and the same year that the Communist Revolution broke out in Russia, is represented above the

portals of her shrine in the act of being crowned by the Holy Trinity. Above the high altar within the sanctuary, Mary appears in solitary splendor as the Queen of Heaven and Earth. The symbolism, geographic, historic, and artistic is clear. The Church's most dynamic creation, raised from the dead and ascended into heaven, has been constituted the Executive Director of Deity in order to control the life of humanity and to assure the triumph of Christ and the Church over their chief contemporary rivals, Communism and Islam.

Why have I ranged so far afield in this discussion of worship in the Roman Catholic tradition and in Hispanic Catholicism in particular? Because I believe that what has been said involves issues that are of supreme importance for the Ecumenical Movement and indispensable in a study of Ecumenics as the "Science of the Church Universal, conceived as a World Missionary Community." The main issues are these. One: What may happen when, as in Hispanic Catholicism, historical circumstances make it possible for a Church to give uninhibited expression to a theological premise that it is so integrally one with Christ as to become institutionally Christ Himself in the maturity of its being? Two: What is the relationship between the assumption that the activity of Christ is circumscribed and controlled by the Church, and the evangelical affirmation, which is rooted in the New Testament and has been proclaimed by eminent Christians in the Roman Catholic, Eastern Orthodox, and Protestant traditions, that Jesus Christ is the Sovereign Lord of the Church and of history? Three: How far does a Church fulfill its God-given mission as the Church of Christ when it devotes preponderant attention to the presentation of Christ in liturgical ritual, and less attention to proclaiming Him as God and Savior in evangelical speech?

PROTESTANTS AT WORSHIP

From the mystery service which has marked worship in the Eastern and Roman Churches, we pass to the type of worship which may be designated the Word-of-God service. This is the type of worship service which has characterized the corporate approach to Deity in the Churches that trace their descent from the Protestant Reformation.

Central in the assemblies for worship of Sixteenth-Century Protestants was the Bible, freshly discovered, and the Bible's central theme, the Gospel of Jesus Christ. The Bible was publicly read in the vernacular of the worshippers, in which also the good news of salvation and the new life in Christ was proclaimed. The congregation joined in praise to God. Prayer was offered by a minister duly set apart by the Church for the exercise of "divine service"; and from time to time, with varying degrees of frequency, the sacraments of Baptism and of the Lord's Supper were administered. While the Word of God, read and preached, marked every service of worship, there was, from the beginning, considerable variation (which increased as the years passed) with regard to the forms of prayer, praise, and the celebration of the sacraments in Protestant worship.

LUTHERAN WORSHIP

Foremost among Protestant Churches, both as regards the date of their birth and the number of members they officially claim, are the Lutheran Churches. Lutheran worship has manifested from the beginning the influence of the experience and insights of Martin Luther. The rapturous joy which Luther experienced when the words, "the just shall live by faith," solaced his anguished spirit and a strange new world opened up to his gaze, became reflected in the "divine service" of those who rallied to the Gospel banner he unfurled. The circumstances surrounding Luther's conversion, his own emotional nature and love of music, his view of Christian freedom, together with the musical temperament of the German people, all contributed to the spontaneity and enthusiasm that marked worship in the early Lutheran Community. For those men and women, the Gospel had become a transforming reality and the Bible a living Book. They were active participants in the worship of a living Deity, whose power they had experienced and whose presence they felt. They were not merely entranced spectators of a dramatic representation of what God had once done for men in Christ, and of what a man, duly authorized by the Church, could continue to do with Christ. Christ, proclaimed in the Word, was present in the pews and in their hearts and was not confined to an altar and a wafer.

Lutheran worship, in the course of the years, underwent a very considerable liturgical development. This it was free to do, provided the Word of God was its Alpha and Omega. But the Bible was not regarded as prescribing any set patterns for the conduct of Christian worship, as it did for the formulation of Christian belief. In European lands today, due to a variety of reasons, Lutheran worship has lost much of its vitality. The liturgy has undergone a process of petrification, becoming, as one authority has described it, "an outward almost legalistic Church institution, from which the freshness of life had departed." [17]

This is particularly true in the Scandinavian countries, where Lutheranism is the state religion and where the state subsidizes and, to a large extent (as in Sweden), controls the Church. The total result has been a loss of vitality in the services of worship and a tragic decline in Church attendance—matters which arouse deep concern in Lutheran circles and among Christians in general. In Denmark, for example, more than 90 percent of the population would be regarded as being Lutheran. Some years ago, in Copenhagen, Denmark, a survey was made of the number of people who attended worship in the city's churches on a Sunday morning. It was found that in one of the great Lutheran capitals of the world, 1 percent of the people, that is, ten thousand out of a population of one million, went to church. Of these, the study revealed, seven thousand, or .7 percent, attended worship in Lutheran churches; the remaining three thousand were in places of worship belonging to the so-called "sects." I mention this fact, of which I was informed while attending a meeting of the Central Committee of the World Council of Churches in Nyborg, Denmark, because it has significance for the present study. "Disaster areas" for traditional state religion in our time are not confined to the countries of Latin America. Ecumenical realism is essential in the interests of the Church Universal and its mission to the world.

REFORMED WORSHIP

No less representative of Protestant Christianity is the Christian tradition associated with the name of the Genevan theologian and Churchman, John Calvin. This tradition is embodied

[17] Heiler, *op. cit.*, p. 92.

ecclesiastically in those Churches known as "Presbyterian" or "Reformed." Theologically, however, Calvinism has played a decisive role in shaping the religious thought of Churches that bear the denominational names of "Anglican," "Baptist," "Congregationalist," "Disciples of Christ." In each of these, certain so-called "Reformed" or "Calvinistic" ideas are deeply ingrained. What concerns us here, however, is not the history or the structure of those Churches, or the differences between them. Our concern is rather to consider worship in theory and practice as it is conducted by Churches that regard themselves heirs of the Reformed tradition, and to examine the worship of these Churches in relation to the world mission of the Holy Catholic Church.

Reformed worship was traditionally marked by a certain austerity, with a total absence of aesthetic frills. This was due to the overwhelming sense of the majesty of God, which John Calvin infused into the thought and life of the Church. The brilliant young humanist who, shortly after he had written a book on Seneca the Stoic, felt himself grasped by the hand of Deity, derived from that experience a sense of the sovereign greatness and the gracious condescension of God. As Luther's wounded spirit was healed, Calvin's proud spirit was subdued, by the coming of God. Conquered in a Divine-human encounter, to which he alludes but once in his writings, the future author of the *Institutes of the Christian Religion* surrendered his life to God and undertook to live for Him. His response, his life and theology, and the genius of Reformed worship, are enshrined in a famous emblem known as Calvin's Crest. This emblem which takes the form of a flaming heart, held in a hand outstretched towards Deity, is interpreted by the words, "My heart I give Thee, Lord, eagerly and sincerely." These words of unreserved commitment to God, in response to what God is and has done for men, echo the music that has resounded through the centuries in Reformed worship, when the worshippers have been sensitive to God's sovereign grace, *"Soli Deo Gloria"* ("Glory to God alone"). The spirit of this motto has inspired the homage to God that has marked the worship of the Reformed Churches at their truest and best.

The somberness and sobriety that characterized Reformed worship until quite recent years were due to Calvin's view that the form of the Church's worship, as well as its thought and organization, should be rigidly based upon the Scriptures. Luther had felt free to allow Christian worship to be inspired not only by the Biblical Revelation of God in Christ and by man's experience of the grace of Christ, but also by the natural response of redeemed men, who were free to make use of their musical and artistic talents in the external expression of their worship. Calvin, on the other hand, considered that the form of worship should be rigidly patterned upon the worship of the early Christian community as described, or alluded to, in apostolic writings. The consequence of this was that in Reformed worship for several centuries singing was limited to metrical versions of the ancient Psalms, unaccompanied by instrumental music and without the use of any liturgical manual. There are today some Presbyterian Churches that continue to put a ban upon the inclusion of "uninspired hymns" and instrumental music in the public worship of God.

On the other hand, Reformed worship, especially in Scottish Presbyterianism, has continued to emphasize the community spirit that should mark the celebration of the Lord's Supper. Those who partake of the sacred emblems of the Body and Blood of Christ do so while seated together at specially prepared tables, or in pews which have been draped with white cloths to give them the semblance of tables. The bread and wine are blessed and distributed not from the altar, but from a communion table at which are seated the ministers who officiate at the service. In the tradition of Scottish Presbyterianism, Communion Sunday, which in some rural districts came only once a year, was the chief day in the Christian calendar. The celebration of the Lord's Supper, held frequently in the open air, for lack of room in any available building, was the culminating act in a series of prayer meetings and preaching services. These were attended by thousands of people from neighboring and remote districts, and lasted several days. Among the worshippers was a profound sense of the Real Presence of Christ as a concrete Living Reality. The Crucified and Risen Lord was not only believed, but was also *felt* to be personally present, communicating Himself to those who worthily partook of the sacred symbols. These communion services, conducted in the countryside for people who often endured ribaldry, scorn, and persecution for their faith, could not be ex-

celled for spiritual insight, deep emotion, and consecration of
life by any eucharistic service held in the loftiest liturgical tradition. These were the eucharistic encounters of a pilgrim people
with the Christ of the Road in "temples not made with hands,"
encounters that will increase in significance in a revolutionary era
in which structures totter and fall.

Preceding the celebration of the Communion, and central in
every service of worship in Reformed and Presbyterian Churches,
is the preaching of the Word of God. It must be freely admitted,
however, that in Reformed worship today, the sermon does not
in general have the quality, or the significance it once had. It is
true that the preacher has many more competitors for the attention of Church members and the general public than he did
before the coming of radio and television and the development
of popular literature. Nevertheless, at a time when there is a
growing craving among the laity for spiritual direction and nourishment, and among youth for something genuinely exciting that
can challenge their devotion, this must be said: The proclamation
of the Gospel as a healing balm for the wounds of the human
spirit, that was given prophetic utterance by Luther, and its
proclamation as a summons to total surrender to God, that inspired the equally prophetic spirit of Calvin, are less articulate
than formerly. Christ Crucified and Risen, moreover, is presented
in such a way as to make Him less relevant to the needs of contemporary man than the situation demands. Worship services in
an increasing number of Presbyterian, Reformed, and Protestant
Churches in general run the peril of providing escape experiences
from reality and of becoming theatrical substitutes for the "response of believing men in adoration and joyous self-dedication
to God."

This is not written in a pessimistic mood. Far from it. Signs of
promise are not lacking in all the Christian traditions and denominations. Save in the most congealed hierarchical circles, and
among religious leaders who exalt ideas, feelings, personages,
and structures into the place of the Deity, there are signs of promise, signs of a coming springtime in the life of the Church Universal. The reality of the Holy Spirit in doctrine and in the
common life is being rediscovered. The historical Churches are
directing a fresh and sympathetic look towards the so-called

"sects," who in some parts of the world are growing faster, and are doing more effective work, than they are. The phenomena of "glossolalia" and healing have appeared within the precincts of the traditional Church bodies and are being examined. Small groups of concerned and committed people, who are loyal members of the churches to which they belong, meet together privately for prayer and Bible study. An increasing number of Church men and women give their support to and participate in movements designed to reach the vast multitude of the unchurched of diverse types and ages. The awareness grows that the most authentic form of Christian worship is that in which all who claim to belong to the universal priesthood of believers should, in the words and spirit of St. Paul, offer to God their "very selves as a living sacrifice." The worshippers should also "in the priestly service . . . of the Gospel of God" offer to God others still ignorant of Him "as an acceptable sacrifice consecrated by the Holy Spirit" (Romans 15:16) N.E.B.

Let the central affirmation of this chapter be repeated. In both the primitive and the Biblical concept of worship, the worship of God is inseparably related to the service of God. Therefore, Christian worship at its highest consists in the offering up to God of one's own self as a living sacrifice, and thereafter, of others, whose lives have been set aflame by the love of God through the Gospel. Our concern was not to discuss forms of worship or liturgical questions as such. Our sole objective in this chapter has been to explore the nature of Christian worship and to establish the norm by which the Church may judge whether in the exercise of its worshipping function it is "in very deed the Church."

The Church's

Prophetic Function

chapter 8

The Christian Church as a missionary Community has also a *prophetic* function to perform.

Christian worship at its highest, even when it gives expression to the sincere offering up to God of the Church's selfhood in the liturgical setting which the worshippers consider most appropriate for their response to Deity, cannot be regarded as the ultimate end for which the Church exists in history. The worshipping Community must also be a prophetic Community if it would fulfill its role in God's design. The Church's exercise of its priestly function, even in a way that would do full justice to the affirmation that all Christians are called to be priests, is not enough. The spiritual vitality of the Church of Christ, and its relevancy to the world's need and to God's purpose, cannot be judged by the multitudes who may attend its services of worship. It is incumbent upon the Church not only to respond to the love of God, but also to radiate the light of God. It is an essential part of its role to make clear to men what God is saying to them, not only as human beings, but also as citizens of a particular country and as contemporaries in a particular era. In a word, the Church must be *prophetic*. It must be responsive to the Word of God, sensitive to the voice of God, and obedient to the will of God. That is to say, it must set the whole life of man in the light of God.

To affirm the prophetic role of the Church is to call upon Christians to take seriously the implications of God's revelation of Himself in Holy Scripture and in Jesus Christ, and His promise of the Holy Spirit as an abiding Presence in the Community of faith. "Would that all the Lord's people were prophets, that the Lord would put His Spirit upon them" (Numbers 11:29), said Moses to Joshua, his chosen successor, when the latter complained that two men who were prophesying had not fulfilled official regulations. It was an early warning that the Spirit could not be confined within purely institutional boundaries. The distinction of Israel's prophets was that they gave expression to insights and warnings which they proclaimed to have received from God and which ran counter to current ideas among the rulers, the priests, and the official prophets.

PROPHETIC PERSPECTIVE

Very striking and significant were the words which Jesus addressed on a memorable occasion to the religious leaders of His time. "You hypocrites," He said to them, "you know how to decipher the look of the earth and sky; how is it you cannot decipher the meaning of this era?" (Luke 12:56) Moffatt. They were excellent meteorologists, but they were blind and insensitive to the hand of God in contemporary history. In like vein, Christ spoke to Peter when the latter challenged affirmations which the Master had just made regarding His own impending death and Resurrection. "Get behind me, you Satan!" He said to him, "You are a hindrance to me! *Your outlook is not God's, but man's*" (Matthew 16:23, Moffatt).

To be able, under the guidance of the Holy Spirit, to "decipher the meaning of this era," and to bring "God's outlook" to a study of the human situation is an abiding responsibility of the Christian Church. When the question at issue is wisdom and understanding, as distinguished from mere empirical knowledge, the Christian Church must, in the great prophetic tradition, "turn away from man" (Isaiah 2:22). It must look at man and his world in the light of God, God's purpose in Christ and His sovereign sway over the events of history. For that reason, it is of paramount importance that the Church, and Christians in general, in loyalty to God, in love for people, and in concern about their mission in the world, should make every effort to study the realities of their time with insight and spiritual understanding. It is equally important that the results of such study should be made available for "all whom it may concern."

Let me offer a pictorial description, through the use of some simple images, of what is involved in the achievement of prophetic perspective.

Prophetic perspective involves, first of all, *height*. What our Lord called "God's outlook" can only be attained when one soars aloft into the realm of the Transcendent and the Eternal, the Absolute and the Real. In Biblical imagery, this signifies the view obtained from a mountain summit, from an eagle's flight above its rocky eyrie or from a mystic experience like Paul's, in the "third heaven." In contemporary imagery, it is the view of an airplane passenger looking serenely downward from miles above the ground. In a word, it is a bird's view of the world, as distinguished from a frog's view. The frog in its puddle cannot see beyond the rushes at the water's edge. But the bird can see the frog and his puddle. Beyond the rushes, it can also see the plain, the hills, the rivers, and on the far horizon, the great ocean. A bird's view of the world, a view of man and history from the standpoint of the Eternal God, from the perspective of Ultimate Reality and meaning—that, in poetic language, is the "outlook" which Christians claim to be possible. Over against the two-dimensional world of naturalism, they set the third dimension of the Eternal and the perspective derived from height. They look at things in terms of the now unpopular, but classical tradition of human thought, *"sub specie aeternitis"* ("under the form of Eternity").

Involved also in prophetic perspective is *light*, that is, true visibility. A bird's view of the world, to be truly meaningful, must also be a day view. For an adequate world view, light is as necessary as height. In the light of the moon and stars and city lamps at midnight, the contours of the ground are visible. But only in the gleam of sunlight do colors and shapes and roadways become clear to the downward gaze of the observer; only then do things visible fall into true perspective so that their identity can be discerned. Thus it was that out of Eternal Being came the Eternal

Light, in the person of Jesus Christ, the Light of the World. For Christ, as stated in a previous chapter, is the core of the Bible's message and the clue to the Bible's meaning. Applicable to Him in a supreme sense is that prophetic utterance of one of the great bards of Israel, "In Thy light do we see light" (Psalm 36:9). It is in the light of Christ that God and man, life, and history can be adequately studied, and not in the gorgeous moonlight of Reason, nor by the flares of the most luminous ideological flashlight Reason can create.

But height and light must be followed by *insight*. A photo taken above the earth under the most favorable conditions, and by the most powerful camera, must be interpreted by people. The picture must be studied by persons competent through experience to judge what it represents, whether it shows the erection of a new factory or a missile installation.

So, too, the student of things human and terrestrial must bring to his study an intimate personal acquaintance with the problems of man and his environment. He must become, in the fullest sense, incarnationally identified with the objects of his concern and concretely involved in their life. His knowledge must include more than can be provided by belief in God and by an intelligent understanding of God's revelation in Christ, with all that these signify. His concern for people and for the human situation in any given place and time must be accompanied by two things. There must, first, be a strong conviction on his part as to what Almighty God can do for every man, because of what He did for himself personally. That is to say, theological dogma needs to be illumined and verified by personal experience. Second, the student of human affairs must have a sensitive awareness of the real issues involved in the lives of persons, and in the environment, sociological and historical, in which their lot is cast. When these conditions are met, when people interested in the tragic problem of man, are not merely informed spectators but transformed crusaders, insight becomes real. And when insight into the human situation as the fruit of divine Revelation is validated by personal experience and produces concern for spiritual change, it becomes incumbent upon Christians and the Church to become prophetic, to give contemporary relevancy to "God's outlook."

THIS "DAY OF THE LORD"

How should "this time" be deciphered? Evidence increases that civilization has entered upon another "Day of the Lord," in which darkness and light both alternate and commingle. In the course of this study, we have had occasion more than once to use images for the interpretation of the divine and the human. Our time is one of God's springtimes, albeit one of His terrible springtimes.

If the suggestion be made that it is a contradiction in terms to attach the epithet "terrible" to any of nature's springtimes, the suggestion is belied by the course of events in many an American springtime. In this northern clime, the bloom and fragrance of myriads of flowers in gardens, woods, and countryside make spring's return a season of loveliness and thrill. But the loveliness of forsythia and dogwood may be matched by the ravages of tornadoes that cut swathes of destruction through towns and villages, and by rivers in flood that spread desolation where the swirling waters overflow their banks. All this takes place in the springtime and by reason of conditions created in the natural order by the coming of spring. The unsinkable ship *Titanic* was ripped and sunk in northern waters on her first voyage by an iceberg that was loosened from its static mass by the warmth of returning springtime.

Jeremiah's first prophetic vision, which came to him in the early days of youth, was a vision of springtime on the Judean plateau. What he saw was a symbolic picture of God's working in his own time and country. The young man of Anathoth, called by God to be a "prophet to the nations," saw on the plateau near his home "the branch of an almond tree" (Jeremiah 1:11). The Hebrew word for "almond tree" means *awakeness* or *watchfulness*. This shrub in bloom is the first token of spring at the close of a Palestinian winter.[1] To the young prophet, the first blossom on the wintry fields spoke of God's awakeness. It gave him the assurance that the God of Abraham was awake and ready to get into action. Said God to His new prophet, "I am awake over my word to perform it."

[1] See George Adam Smith's *Jeremiah* (New York: Harper & Row, Publishers, 1940), pp. 84–88.

But in the background of the almond blossom there was another, a very different sight. Jeremiah, in response to God's question as to what he saw, replied, "I see a cauldron boiling and its face is turned northward." God responded: "Out of the North shall evil boil forth on all that dwell in the land; for behold, I am calling all the kingdoms of the North. They shall come and each set his throne in the openings of the gates of Jerusalem, on all of her walls round about, and every township of Judah. And my judgments by them shall I utter on the evil of those who have left Me, who have burned to other gods and bowed to the works of their hands" (Jeremiah 1:13-16) G. A. Smith's translation. The seething cauldron, whose embers were fanned by northern winds, represented the northern kingdoms, Assyria and Babylon, that were destined to spell Israel's doom—to begin in Jeremiah's time.

God's springtime! The blossoming almond and the boiling pot both belonged to it. God was awake and His springtime awakeness was to be made manifest in mercy and in judgment in the fall of old Jerusalem and in the making of a new Covenant, both events to take place in a single historical epoch and in the lifetime of one man. Just as Jeremiah is the man who more than any other Old Testament prophet, speaks to our time, the springtime, God's terrible springtime, which the Anathoth boy discerned in vision, and in which it was his lot to live, is a vivid representation of the mid-Twentieth Century. It is important, therefore, that we should take a glance, brief but basic, at the situation in which the world-wide Community of Christ must carry on its work today.

GOD'S SPRINGTIME

It gives cause for rejoicing that in the "almond blossom" many things in today's world find a prophetic symbol of God's springtime awakeness. In the natural order are to be noted the technological achievements of man in the course of the present century, whereby, to use once again Keyserling's terms, the world has become an "ecumenical organism" and all its inhabitants live in an "ecumenical era." They are neighbors and contemporaries for the first time in history. From the viewpoint of physical proximity, no time in history has offered mankind a greater opportunity to cultivate ecumenical brotherhood and to make scientific technology the servant of spiritual unity. It is cause for rejoicing that among many men of science there appears an increasing attitude of reverence towards the universe. They manifest a deepening appreciation of mystery, as the secrets of the atom and of the stellar spaces are explored together. There is a disposition to take seriously the reality of a Supreme Creator and Sustainer, who is "awake," who is to be sought and must be found. Man himself becomes garbed once again in mystery; he can no longer be regarded as a mere part of nature. The intellectual insight that came to the great Danish thinker, Sören Kierkegaard—that man can fulfill his human destiny and can achieve true existence only when he makes a decision to become God's man—is challenging, in diverse manners, traditional forms of Idealism and Humanism. Existentialism, at its truest and best, as represented by Kierkegaard, and such recent thinkers as the Spaniard, Unamuno, and the German, Bonhoeffer, calls upon man to wake up, to respond to the awakeness of God, and to live for something bigger than himself.

Evidence also of a spiritual springtime is the reawakened interest in the Bible, in Jesus Christ, and in the Church. The Bible has been translated into more than a thousand tongues, and enjoys a phenomenal and ever growing circulation throughout the world. It is also being studied with deepened insight. Important in this regard, and very creative, is the study of Biblical theology, which has rediscovered and set in perspective for contemporary study such natively Biblical concepts as "Covenant" and "People of God." The figure of Jesus Christ, moreover, stands out as does no other, and not merely as a liturgical symbol or a theological foundation, but as one who awakens the interest of men of letters and even of Marxist philosophers such as Henri Barbusse. And what shall be said of the rediscovery of the Church in our time, and its status as a world Community? This book has no meaning except as an attempt to make the Church the subject and dynamic center of a new science that its ecumenical development has made imperative.

Worthy, however, of special mention is the springtime change, the impressive symbol of God's awakeness, that has taken place in the Roman Catholic Church during the past decade. This will be dealt with in its appropriate place as our discussion develops.

But, at this point, let us hail with springtime joy the abounding signs around the globe that the great Roman Communion is abandoning its traditional attitude of overt hostility to Protestants and to Protestant Christianity. Who could have thought, even a few years ago, that Protestants would be designated "separated brethren" and that Protestant Churches would be invited to send observers to the Second Vatican Council? How can Christians everywhere fail to rejoice at the new status being given to the study of the Bible by clergy and laity, at the revived interest in evangelism, at the stimulation of dialogue between Catholics and Protestants, at the rediscovery and study of a forgotten evangelical stream in Roman Catholicism, and the growing appreciation of evangelical classics. In a few brief years, the late Pope John XXIII became the most loved and admired personality in the world. There is springtime balm and freshness in the ecclesiastical air. Once again the almond tree is in blossom.

But God's new springtime in the Sixties of our century is also a time of troubles. There is darkness as well as light, tornadoes as well as flowers, judgment as well as mercy, a boiling pot in the shadow of a blossoming shrub. Our time is a time of trouble that embraces the globe, the whole "ecumenical organism." It is indispensable that Christians, and Christian Churches who would take their calling seriously, should be realistically aware of the seething cauldron that meets our gaze in this Day of the Lord.

How tragic and ironic it is that a world which, physically speaking, was never so much one as today, is, spiritually speaking, more globally divided than at any previous time in the history of mankind. Whatever formula may be used to interpret the present situation, calling it an instance of the "dialectic of history," or affirming that "every advance creates its opposite," and that "world history is world judgment," the sombre fact remains. We face today a world that is abysmally rifted. What is more, the smoke and steam that ascended from the pot in Jeremiah's vision ascend today from volcanic craters that belch out along the sordid boundaries that separate men and nations. This is not the kind of world that Christians faced in the First Century, or that their missionary successors faced in the Nineteenth Century and the early decades of the Twentieth.

Today, Christian witness has to be carried on in the atmosphere of a global propaganda phenomenon called "Cold War" between "East" and "West," at a time when the spiritual ultimate has become the dread of atomic war. There are ancient cities and new nations that are geographically rent asunder, because of rival ideologies; their separation is maintained by military might. There are leading countries that call themselves Christian whose inhabitants are engaged in bitter, and often bloody, racial strife. There are "Christians" who legitimatize, and even canonize, hate when it is directed against "Communists." These facts cannot be ignored by the Christian Church in the fulfillment of its world mission. They must be presented with prophetic accent. At the same time, the implications of these tragic phenomena must be taken into due account, in the kind of approach which is made, in the name of Christ and the Church, to human situations where they influence the public mind. Alabama, Mississippi, and South Africa are names that create problems for all Protestant Christians, and very special problems for those who are dedicated to the conversion of Africans to "Jesus Christ as God and Savior."

A crisis confronts mankind. To affirm this is to do more than repeat a shibboleth or re-echo a wearying cliché. It is to face a sober fact. The white man's stocks are down. An era is coming to an end. Traditional structures tremble. Seismic revolution, which has shaken society horizontally, is being succeeded by volcanic revolution, which shatters its vertical structure. Asia, Africa, and Latin America are becoming a "rosary of craters in activity." What has happened? What is happening?

The great fountains that have watered western civilization through many ages are being shut off, and the spirit of man in many western lands is becoming dry. God and the Christian religion have ceased to provide the inspiration for living and the principles for human behavior and relationships that they once did. Policies are shaped and programs are carried on, not under the aegis of principles, but in the interests of what is conceived to be individual or national security. Values no longer have the status or significance that was theirs in a former period. Righteousness has become an almost forgotten or meaningless word. Its heirs, or rather its substitutes, are prestige, power, propaganda value. Our situation is closely akin to that of Israel in Jeremiah's time, which the prophet described thus: "They went after empty idols and became empty themselves" (Jeremiah 2:5) G. A. Smith. There is still meaning and contemporary relevance in the words of the poet, T. S. Eliot, who won fame after World War I with his poems, *The Waste Land* and *The Hollow Men.*

> We are the hollow men
> We are the stuffed men
> Leaning together
> Headpiece filled with straw. Alas! [2]

Still more applicable are the words of Jesus: "What does a man— gain—by winning the whole world—at the cost of his true self?" (Mark 8:36) N.E.B. The same is true of a nation. Imperialistic egotism, personal or national, does not eventually work in God's world.

FROM THE GLORY OF GOD
TO THE GLORY OF MAN

It is cause for concern that the place of God in the current world-view of western countries is being taken by man. Because of the decisive part that the Christian Churches in the United States of North America have played in the effort to carry the Gospel to the whole world and to promote ecumenical unity, many Christians view with disquiet the increasing naturalistic trend in the American philosophy of life. It is a phenomenon of a very peculiar type, and affects both Church and society. This nation, in recent years, has begun to reproduce traits and to adopt unwittingly the philosophy of life which predominated in the Hispanic world for more than four centuries and which has been responsible for the tragic problems that today afflict Latin America, not to mention the mother lands of Spain and Portugal and their present-day colonies in Africa.

Let me make clear what I mean. And let me do it, not as a prejudiced person, but as one who owes to certain phases of Hispanic culture and religion more than pen can tell or life repay. The treatment of this issue must necessarily be very brief and

[2] "The Hollow Men," *Collected Poems 1909–1962* (New York: Harcourt Brace & World, Inc., 1963), p. 77.

succinct. It is mainly designed, moreover, to raise questions which I believe to be important for Christian understanding and the Church's prophetic witness at the present time.

It has been rightly maintained that Hispania, the ancient name for Spain and Portugal, has been the mother of men, not of ideas. Hispanic history has been shaped by personalities, tremendous personalities, and not primarily by clearly defined ideas. Sons of Hispania have not been marked by a capacity to evolve systems of thought. They have been marked rather by an extraordinary capacity to give expression to the "natural man," that is, to human nature in its most pristine reality, unconquered by reason and unredeemed by religion. Both reason and religion became servants of the "natural man," who in a manner and to a degree unprecedented in history, became the "measure of all things."

This phenomenon produced far-reaching consequences. It came about that Latin American political history has been chiefly dominated by personalities and not by principles. Hence, the phenomenal number of dictators. The untamed sons of the "natural man" have been characterized by an extraordinary acquisitiveness. In the Western Hemisphere, they acquired billions of acres of land. This land they came to regard, and also the people upon it, whom they made their servants, as part of their own being, which their pride, called "honor," would not allow them to give up. For them, the ideal form of government was one which would not challenge their property rights, their business procedures, or their labor relations. They claimed freedom and insisted it be given to them. But freedom they interpreted in anarchic terms. It meant freedom to do anything they took into their heads to do, that is, anything they had the whim to desire or the power to achieve. But the hour of reckoning is near.

In the realm of relations between the sexes, to be a real man (hombre) was to excel in the conquest of women, to be a "Don Juan." In the sphere of culture, the important thing for a student was to acquire the knowledge necessary to enable him to enter a desired profession. It was not his concern to be equipped to fulfill a vocation. Unamuno, who more than any other man diagnosed the basic problem of Hispanic civilization, charged that many sons of Hispania in the Old World and the New, who boasted of their encyclopedic knowledge, treated great ideas as if they were just so many intellectual mistresses, and not the life partners of a home.

In the sphere of religion, the tragedy of Hispanic civilization in Europe and the Americas was that the official Church, as distinguished from some individual Churchmen, never succeeded in taming, restraining or redeeming the "natural man." It can be said, indeed, that Hispanic Catholicism was, in a unique sense, the creation of the Hispanic spirit. After eight hundred years of Moorish domination, the Spanish people united and broke the power of Islam. The Moorish power was vanquished in the spring of the same year that Columbus discovered America. The Vatican granted authority to the Spanish monarchs to control the affairs of the Church during the conquest of Hispanic America and throughout the colonial period of its history. A theocracy was thus constituted; the Emperor Ferdinand became "The Patriarch of the Indies." The Church now served directly the interests of the state, using secular, imperialistic methods to Christianize the indigenous people. As the supreme servant of the state, it sanctified the actions of the conquerors, whatever these might be. Stirred by the "Natural man," the Church developed "a delirium of grandeur." * It was seized by a passion for greatness. Jesus Christ was not set forth as the Lord of the Church; He was presented, rather, as One who became the Church's Servant for the fulfillment of its mission. The "grand design" was the Church through Christ, not Christ through the Church.

Disturbing developments took place. The Church would suffer no challenge to its ideas or its procedures: The Spanish Inquisition was created. The Church gave expression to Hispanic acquisitiveness by becoming the greatest property owner in Latin America: The Mexican Revolution broke out. The Church established its exclusive right to be recognized as the soul and mentor of the Spanish people: The doctrine of *Hispanidad* was developed. Racial integrity was equated with ecclesiastical fidelity, and a concordat that validated the equation was established between the Roman See and a Spanish despot who claimed to incarnate the Eternal Spain. The truth is, however, that Franco's Spain is the Spain of the "natural man" at its historic worst, and on the

* "un delirio de grandeza."

eve of its demise. Hispania, in the Old World and in the New, awaits a new Day of the Lord. It awaits one of God's springtimes, when the almond spray, whose fragrance began to fill the air in the witness of Theresa of Avila, Juan de Valdés, and the apostolic companion of Columbus, Bartolomé de las Casas, will bloom again, and the fumes of the "boiling pot" will subside.

It is a tragic irony, but a fact that must be squarely faced by all who are concerned about Christianity in our time, that North American history in recent years shows evidence of reproducing the spiritual rhythm that was the bane of historical development in the Hispanic world. The ground of concern may be stated thus. The founders of this nation were men and women who had become captives to a sense of Deity and to principles of behavior prescribed by Deity, and who sought to regulate their lives and relationships by what they believed to be God-given standards. From the beginning, the "natural man" was subjected to what was conceived to be a divine moral order. This order was to be found in the Bible, a book that was banned in the Hispanic world. Man could not do whatever he felt inclined to do by way of satisfying his instincts or achieving status. He was free to do whatever he conscientiously believed to be right, provided his conscience was subject to God and to what God had revealed regarding the proprieties of human action. True men were men who took God and principle seriously in every sphere and relationship of life. Life for the individual and for the nation began and ended not with the "natural man," but with the order that God had revealed in His Word and in natural law. It was proclaimed in due course that, under God, all men have a right to life, liberty, and the pursuit of happiness. While the "natural man" was never absent in American life and succeeded in frustrating in a subtle way many accepted principles of behavior, he was present not as an acknowledged Deity but as a ghostly tempter.

A change has come about. This is not the place to describe the process or to define the causes. Our purpose is simply to draw attention to the nature of the change and to the likeness between its several facets and the old Hispanic way. There is being reproduced in North American life today, in a different guise and setting, some of the traditional features of the Hispanic way. And this is happening at the very time when Latin Americans are becoming increasingly self-critical and are in quest of a "new way."

To begin with, personality is taking the place of principle in many areas of American life. The really important thing, it is maintained, is not whether a man is a good man and committed to what is right, but whether he has glamour, prestige, power, or propaganda value that can make him a good promoter of a project, even though the project be inspired by no more than human egotism. As in the old Hispanic tradition, freedom has come to signify freedom to do whatever a person or members of a group may take into their heads to do, if only it is in their interests to do it. It is not important whether what they do is strictly in accord with the law or with the truth, or in the best interests of society. What matters is that those who engage in an undertaking should be successful, provided they do not create a scandal. The supreme freedom, the freedom which must be insisted upon at all times, is the freedom to make money and to own property. Yet, it is frankly acknowledged that, because of economic oligarchies, "Free Enterprise" in the traditional sense is dead. In the realm of sex, Don Juan has become a popular hero. His message is this. Be as voluptuous, as immoral as you like, if only you can sin charmingly and avoid embarrassing consequences.

The chief national absolute has come to be *security*. To security, which Shakespeare described as "mortals' chiefest enemy," all else must be subordinated. Toward achieving security, all policy and program must be directed. Security's greatest foe in thought and life, at home and abroad, is considered to be Communism. To be anti-Communist has thus become, in influential circles, the badge of what is truly American. Inspired by the same kind of dread that, in the Hispanic tradition of the Sixteenth Century, created the Spanish Inquisition to eliminate every trace of Protestant influence, there emerged in contemporary America the Un-American Activities Committee. This committee was charged with the task of scouring every nook and cranny of American life for evidence of Communistic influence or infiltration. The objectives, spirit, procedures, and fruits of this organization reproduce the image of an historic body which today is the object of universal reprobation in the Hispanic world and in all Roman Catholic circles. History has repeated itself in an unexpected place and manner. At the very time when a beloved Roman Catholic Pontiff issues an encyclical in which he pleads for the betterment of relations between Communists and non-Communists, nationally and internationally, an official committee, whose spirit is the most un-American in American history, resuscitates the terrors of the Spanish Inquisition. The living God and the American spirit have thus been betrayed.

It has been one of the glories of the United States of America that the Christian Churches within its borders have played a truly creative role in the life of the nation. They have been foremost, moreover, among the Churches of the world in their dedication to the Christian missionary task and to the pursuit of Christian unity. They exert today a major influence in the Ecumenical Movement.

Although this is true, the Protestant Churches in America have reached a moment of crisis. They run the danger of reproducing the features that marked the history of the Hispanic Church in its internal development and in its relations to government and the Hispanic way. It is important that attention be drawn to a startling parallel and to a real peril.

The Hispanic Catholic Church was the most highly institutionalized Church in Christian history. Its major concern was that men should be won to the Church rather than to Christ, or at most, to a Christ who lived under the very rigid control of the Church. To be Christian, Catholic, and Churchly, was to participate in the Church's liturgy, celebrate its festivals, and become adjusted to its organizational forms. When, therefore, voices are raised in America regarding "the noise of solemn assemblies," the increasing complexity of the "religious establishment," the dispensation of "cheap grace," the Church's surrender to cultural patterns, the integration of ecclesiastical structures rather than their adjustment to the Christian task, these voices by "angry young men" should be seriously heeded.

There exists also the subtle and increasing peril, that the Churches shall fail to challenge certain phases of the "American way of life," and certain policies of the national Government, at a time when such a challenge should be given in the name of God and the Lordship of Jesus Christ. The more centralized the life of the Church becomes, and the more its organizational structure is dependent upon wealth, the more difficult it becomes for responsible Church leaders, and for national Church councils, to be prophetic. The Christian Churches of America have not taken the stand they should have taken in demanding, in the name of Christ and the Church Universal, that no edict of their Government should prevent American Christians from establishing contact with fellow Christians in countries with which their Government has no official relations. As the situation now stands, Protestantism's largest and most complex structure is fearful to challenge prophetically international policies that put Christ, the Christian Church, and a Christian society to open shame. The American Church in its national dimension is deferential to Christ and makes Him central in its thought and worship. But, like the old Hispanic Church, it becomes, though unwittingly and unwillingly, the servant of the nation and the "American way." We witness a subtle, rhythmic movement from the glory of God to the glory of man.

A SECULAR FAITH THAT REJECTS RELIGION

It is an important part of the Church's prophetic function to set in clear perspective the significance of Marxist Communism in relation to the Christian world mission. In *Creative Society*, a remarkable book written in 1935, John MacMurray (who later became professor of philosophy at Edinburgh University) made this statement: "There would be nothing paradoxical in the discovery that a religion which had lost its faith in God must be overwhelmed by a faith which had rejected religion." [3] He meant to say that Communists, in their approach to life, have what can be designated the "religious equivalent of God." He challenged Christians to face and answer this question: "Do we believe in God, or do we only believe in believing in God?" Which means: Is our ultimate spiritual loyalty religiosity, to which we are emotionally attached, or is it the living God to whom we give total obedience?

It is of first-rate importance that we consider the essentially

[3] John MacMurray, *Creative Society* (New York: Association Press, 1936), p. 28.

religious character of Communism, which is Christianity's chief rival in the world of today and which menaces vast regions in Asia, Africa, and Latin America. Two things can be said regarding Communism's religious spirit. First: We have here a *Christian heresy* which rejects Christianity, just as Nazism was a pagan resurgence which sought to use Christianity for its own purposes. Second: Communism can be described as a *secular faith* which rejects religion, but which as a pseudo-religion has unmistakable religious characteristics. What are these religious features? Ten may be mentioned.

1. The Communist equivalent for God is an inexorable historical process called dialectical materialism, which is considered to be the ultimate driving force in history. Whereas traditional materialism affirmed matter to be ultimate, but static, reality, dialectical materialism conceives matter as the subject of a dynamic creative force which directs the course of events.

2. Communism has its *Holy Scriptures.* Its Old Testament is the writings of Karl Marx, the Communist Moses; its New Testament is the writings of Lenin, the Communist Christ.

3. There is a *Holy People,* comparable to the "People of God." It is the world proletariat. This captive people has begun to be led out of Egypt, the capitalistic system, to the strains of the new song of liberation, "The Communist Internationale":

> Awake ye prisoners of starvation,
> Awake you wretched of the earth;
> For justice thunders condemnation.
> A better world's in birth.

"Holy Mother Russia" is the "first fruits" of salvation and the agent of the revolutionary process, the "grand design." The claim to this honor, it should be observed, is now being disputed by Communist China.

4. The *messiah* of Communism is the Russian, Lenin. He it was who "redeemed his people," after he had returned from banishment, not in the realm of death, but in the Swiss valleys. Lenin's embalmed figure is today enshrined in the Kremlin, there to be gazed upon and adored.

5. Communism's *apostles* are Khrushchev, who is its St. Peter, and the other members of the *Politburo*. The apostolic group has also had its Judas. His name was Stalin, who went in due course "to his own place."

6. The *Church* of Communism is the Communist Party. This is a "gathered Church," a "militant monastic order," as it has been called, which makes absolute demands upon its members.

7. Communism has its *missionaries,* who are found throughout the globe, in the entire *oikoumenē*. Covertly or overtly, according to the local situation, these missionaries are dedicated to the task of world revolution. This task they fulfill by winning the attention of people, whom they then indoctrinate, and in some places, "liberate."

8. The possession of a *theology* is another mark of Communism. There is an official ideology, a rigid system of ideas, to which all Communists are committed, and which they must apply to life with unquestioning devotion. In recent years, there have emerged two schools of Communist "theology," the liberals and the conservatives. The liberals are led by the Russian Khrushchev, who favors a modified Marxism, maintaining that the Communist goal of world revolution can be attained without the necessity of going to war with capitalist nations. The conservatives are led by the Chinese, Mao, who is uncompromisingly committed to orthodox Marxism and to the absolute necessity of violence if the Communist goal is to be achieved. But both schools are equally committed to an *ethic,* whose main absolute is the interest of the revolution, and to an *eschatology,* which envisages world revolution and a classless society.

9. Communists are held together emotionally and inspired to action by a *liturgy.* This liturgy consists of a series of readings, anthems, songs, dances that are designed to produce a sense of liberation and exultation. The accent upon liturgical development is becoming more and more apparent in youth circles and among the forgotten masses of the world.

10. There are "Days of Judgment" in the Communist outlook upon history, quite apart from history's eschatological climax, when the "kingdoms of this world" will come to an end, and the

classless society will begin. These intermittent Judgment Days take the form of purges, designed to maintain party and ideological purity. In Russia, we have witnessed "Days of De-Stalinization," and in China we begin to witness "Days of De-Russianization."

The Christian Church is faced with a major imperative. It is essential that all Christians, and very especially Christians who are concerned about the Kingdom of God in the world, should have an intelligent view of Communism. It is equally indispensable that they make a realistic appraisal of Communism's present status and prospects in the world. An informed and positive appraisal of this dynamic phenomenon is urgently needed. Nothing is more pathetic, or rather, more tragic, than the fact that in so many circles, in both Church and society, the approach to Communism should be exclusively negative and be crusadingly heralded merely as "anti-Communism." Communism, let us be quite clear, does not provide the ultimate answer to the problem of man and society. While it is true, all too true, alas, that religion has often been on the side of vested interests that have oppressed the common people, it is not true that Christianity came into being to buttress a social or political order. We cannot but mourn the fact that in some Communist lands the most sadistic and outrageous cruelty has been shown towards religious groups. In no Communist land, moreover, is there the freedom, religious or cultural, for which Christians should stand. Evidence exists, however, that, while Communism is committed to oppose, and if possible, eradicate religion, Churches will be allowed to carry on their work. They will not be allowed, however, while a Communist regime is in power, to enjoy complete religious freedom. For that reason, let Christians, with a vision of the Kingdom and dedicated to its coming, whatever be the social order in which they live, "cast not away their confidence," but keep ever moving beyond.

Let us be realists, however, in the spirit of Jeremiah. At the present moment, the "Heartland," to return again to Mackinder's prophetic image, has gone Communist. The territory from the Urals to the Yangtse, and from the Arctic to the Himalayas, is under Communist control. The battle is now on for the "World Island." The largest Communist party outside Russia is, strangely enough, in Indonesia, which is located at the southern tip of the "World Island." During a recent visit to Indonesia, I discovered that a large number of Christians, including Christian ministers, who are in no sense Marxists, support the Communist political party. They told me they gave their support to this party because, in their judgment, it is the only party which has the kind of program that the country needs at this crucial juncture in Indonesian history. Their attitude reminded me of simple peasants in Colombia, South America, who, while they know absolutely nothing about Marxists, have come to believe that people called "Communists" are the only folk who understand them and are interested in their problem. Here is the paradox. These peasant folk, some of whom are religiously loyal evangelicals, will allow those who address them to be as critical as they like of the Colombian Church, the Colombian government, and the Colombian social order. But they resent criticism of "Communists." These, they feel, are their only friends!

Certain things are clear and should challenge the Christian Churches of the world. We live in a new "Day of the Lord." The flames beneath the "boiling pot," once fanned by northern breezes from Assyria, are now fanned by eastern breezes from the "Heartland." Christ's Church Universal is summoned to understand intelligently the Marxist Faith and the Gospel of Christ. Marxist Communists display a discipline, an enthusiasm, a determination to change man and the social order, which Christians, in loyalty to Christ and the Gospel, should possess, but which in wide sectors of the Christian world, they woefully lack. Yet Jesus Christ can do more in a revolutionary way for man and society through the Gospel than Marx ever can. But the Church and Christians must take Him seriously, more seriously than they are now doing. For Christ's New Men and Women, for whom the world waits in this hour of judgment, are related to the Eternal, through the satisfaction of the heart's deepest longings, in a way that a Marxist can never be. They can also become more relevant to the world's total situation than the most dedicated followers of Marx or Lenin can ever be. But the Church must have a fresh vision of the Gospel of Christ, of the reality and relevance of the "New Man in Christ," and of the nature and mission of the world community of Christ, if it is to play its part in this "Day of the Lord."

CALL FOR EVANGELICAL CATHOLICITY

We have reached an important point in our discussion. We have considered the Church's worshipping function, and the Church's prophetic function. We have seen that Christians truly worship when they give themselves adoringly and unreservedly to God. We have seen that their outlook is truly prophetic when they see all things, whether pleasant or pestilent, in the Light of God. We are now ready to consider what Christian worship and Christian insight involve for Christian action. For the Church as the "People of God," as the "Body of Christ," can express its true meaning, and fulfill its God-given mission, only in terms of action. The action to which the Church is called involves the exercise of two further functions: the Church's *redemptive function* and the Church's *unitive function*. Before we deal in the next two chapters with these climactic functions of the Christian Church, let us pause to consider, in the spirit that has inspired the present chapter, something to which all the Churches must give unqualified devotion if they are to fulfill their calling. The imperious something is *evangelical Catholicity*. Let me explain.

I have referred in the course of this study to a book entitled *The Spirit of Worship*, by Friedrich Heiler, who is today the Professor of the Philosophy and History of Religion in the University of Marburg, Germany. The Foreword to the English edition of this book, issued in 1926 and dedicated to the Stockholm World-Conference on Life and Work (August 19–30, 1925), was written by G. K. A. Bell, Dean of Canterbury. Dean Bell was later elected Bishop of Chichester. As the first Chairman of the Central Committee of the World Council of Churches, he was one of the most loved and creative figures in the Ecumenical Movement.

> Heiler, said Bell, stands for a type of Catholicity which he would probably refuse to call new—though circumstances may seem to make it such; a Catholicity which hopes more perhaps from the ideals of the Universal Christian Conference on Life and Work than from those of the World Conference on Faith and Order; a Catholicity of Faith and Love. He describes his position as 'neither Protestant nor Roman Catholic, but ecumenically Christian, that is, evangelical Catholic.' His ecumen-

ical Christianity is sustained by the faith that the living Christ moves in all Christian Churches, and that the fullness of truth is not to be found in any particular church (be it even the greatest of all, the Roman), but in the true *Ecclesia Universalis*, which stands behind and above the separate confessions.[4]

Heiler had been ecclesiastically a Roman Catholic until the year 1919. In that year, during a course of lectures which he delivered in Sweden, at the invitation of Nathan Söderblom, Archbishop of Upsala, the great ecumenical pioneer who profoundly influenced the young scholar's life, he received Holy Communion at a Lutheran Service. "By this religious act," says Heiler, "without an open breach and without formal secession from the Roman Catholic Church, I entered the Evangelical Church fellowship." He adopted the position of "evangelical Catholicity." [5]

I am not concerned to discuss at this point the implications for ecclesiology of a Church that would be at once "evangelical" and "Catholic." Neither am I interested for the moment in the development of Heiler's own thinking and Church relationship, as a result of embracing "Evangelical catholicity." I desire only to emphasize this conviction. The future of the Church, and also of the Ecumenical Movement, is contingent upon the status which is given to the Evangel in theological thought and in Christian life, as the Churches dedicate themselves to fulfill the Church's mission and to achieve its unity. This emphasis might be called *dynamic centrality.*

Dynamic centrality represents a concern not for what is Leftist or Rightist, either theologically or ecclesiastically, but for what is *Centric*. But what is Centric in this sense is not what is "middle of the road." It is not a compromise between two extreme positions, to Right and Left. It is devotion to a reality called the Gospel, the center and core of the Christian faith, which is inseparably related to the living Lord Jesus Christ. The Gospel transforms the life of those who take it seriously, and sets in dynamic motion towards new frontiers the Christian Community that becomes possessed by it. What matters today is that those who

[4] *Op. cit.*, pp. xi, xii.
[5] *Op. cit.*, pp. xi–xii.

plume themselves on their strong positions on the right or the
left of the main Highway, should move towards the Figure who
awaits them at the Center, beckoning them to follow Him along
highways and byways towards the Goal. It is in action on the
Road that they will come to know Him better, and one another
better, and the human situation better. It is on the Road they will
be able to organize the fellowship in the way most worthy of their
Leader, and most adapted to do the work to which He has called
them as His Body.

As we now look forward to a discussion of the redemptive and
unitive functions of the Church, and to the question of the
Church's relations that lies beyond, I conclude this chapter by reference to a small volume, *Fifty Years of Faith and Order: An
Interpretation of the Faith and Order Movement*, by John E.
Skoglund and J. Robert Nelson. It was written in prospect of the
Montreal Meeting of the Faith and Order Commission in July,
1963, just as Heiler's book was written in retrospect after the
Stockholm World Conference on Life and Work had finished its
task. The pre-Montreal volume makes reference to an important
statement regarding the Gospel, a statement considered to be the
most memorable deliverance of the First Conference on Faith and
Order, which met at Lausanne in 1927. The same statement was
endorsed the following year in Jerusalem by the first world gathering of the International Missionary Council.

I vividly recall the latter occasion. William Temple had just
drafted the now famous Jerusalem Message. Robert E. Speer, the
vice chairman of the committee, suggested that it incorporate part
of the Lausanne document. This was done. Here, in combination,
is the most glowing and authoritative statement of the Gospel
ever to sound in an ecumenical assembly. Here is the evangelical
soul of whatever aspires to Catholicity, or to be Catholic in activity or organization.

Jerusalem speaks: "Our message is Jesus Christ. He is the revelation of what God is and of what man through Him may become.
. . . By the Resurrection of Christ and the gift of the Holy Spirit,
God offers His own power to men that they may be fellow workers
with Him, and urges them on to a life of adventure and self-
sacrifice in preparation for the coming of His Kingdom in its
fullness."

Jerusalem endorses Lausanne. "The message of the Church to the world is, and must remain, the Gospel of Jesus Christ. . . . Because He Himself is the Gospel, the Gospel is the message of the Church to the world. It is more than a philosophical theory, more than a theological system, more than a program for social betterment. The Gospel is rather the gift of a new world from God to His old world of sin and death; still more, it is the victory over sin and death, the revelation of eternal life in Him who has knit together the whole family in heaven and on earth in the communion of saints, united in the fellowship of service, of prayer, and of praise." [6]

[6] *The Jerusalem Meeting of the International Missionary Council* (New York: International Missionary Council, 1928), I, 402, 403.

The Church's
Redemptive Function

chapter 9

From the Church's response to the presence of God in worship, and its radiation of the light of God in prophetic insight, we pass to its *mediation* of the love of God in evangelical witness. This we call the Church's redemptive function. It is when the Church identifies itself with God as an instrument, a "steward," that is, an administrator, of His redeeming love, that worship and prophecy reach their climactic expression. For it is then and only then that the Church truly glorifies God, unveiling His splendor and fulfilling His purpose for the redemption of the world. It is in the acceptance of its redemptive function as a "fellow worker with God," that the Christian Church makes it unmistakedly clear that it is the "Body of Christ," responsive to Him who is both its Head and its Life.

THE CONCEPT OF REDEMPTION

When we say that it is the Church's redemptive function to *mediate the love of God,* it is important to clarify the concept of redemption. Redemption as word and concept is central in Biblical thought, both in the Old Testament and in the New. "The theme of redemption," says a distinguished Biblical scholar, "is embodied in every part of the liberation and informs the whole course of Israel's history." [1] The concept had its origin, not as an abstract

[1] F. J. Taylor in A *Theological Word Book of the Bible, op. cit.,* pp. 185–87.

philosophical idea, but in a concrete life situation. To "redeem" a person was to buy him from his master or his captor, by means of a ransom, or with something regarded as the legitimate price of his liberation from serfdom. The concept moved from the liberation of a captive person to the liberation of a captive people. Israel was "redeemed," that is, "delivered," by God from her bondage in Egypt, and centuries later from her captivity "by the waters of Babylon." The emphasis came to be laid upon redemption as a *result* and not merely upon the *process* that secured release. But whether the perspective is that of process or result, redemption is always something in which God Himself takes the initiative.

The exercise of divine power becomes manifest, moreover, not only in mass liberation from a sinful foreign power, but in individual liberation from a sinful selfhood. Thus, in the prophets Jeremiah and Ezekiel, the concept of "redemption" passes into that of the "New Covenant," whereby the hearts of the physically "redeemed" become spiritually changed when God writes His law in their inmost being. "I will put my law within them, and I will write it upon their hearts; and I will be their God, and they shall be my people . . . they shall all know me, from the least of them to the greatest, says the Lord; for I will forgive their iniquity and I will remember their sin no more" (Jeremiah 31:33, 34). By the same hand that brought them "out of the land of Egypt" (Jeremiah 31:32), Israel, being forgiven and cleansed, would be redeemed from sinful self-centeredness and all its aberrations. Thus would triumph the God of Abraham, the "Shepherd of Israel," the passionate Lover and spouse of His People.

The most vivid Old Testament image of God's presence as a redeeming, transforming reality in Israel's life, is Ezekiel's vision of the great "redeeming" stream that flowed from beneath the temple altar. Following the coming of God in His splendor through the eastern gate of the temple, in such wise that the "house was filled with His glory," a stream was born. Increasing in volume, the waters of this stream transformed the Judean wilderness into a garden, and "redeemed" the Dead Sea from being a sepulchre of death to being a nursery of bursting life and activity, where busy fishermen plied their craft (Ezekiel 43:1–5; 47:1–12).

In the New Testament, the concept of redemption is inseparably related to the person and work of Jesus Christ. Christ who is set forth as the Galilean son of Mary of Nazareth and of Bethlehem, and also as the Eternal Son of God, given by the Father and being Himself "God manifest in the flesh," whose mission it was to "reconcile the world" to God, was hailed, following His death, Resurrection, and the coming of God and the Holy Spirit at Pentecost, as "our Lord and Savior, Jesus Christ." He came to be in the fullest sense the "Redeemer." Jesus Christ, Himself, what He was and what He did, what He is now and what He continues to do, what He offers to all who give their all to Him, became the theme of the "Gospel of God."

Vast beyond poetic imagination and the ordinary categories of thought, are the implications of "redemption" in its evangelical New Testament setting. Forgiven men are cleansed from the guilt and power of sin; they are delivered from futility and alienation from God, they are set free from servitude to the assumptions and activities of the present world order, they are made a "kingdom and priests unto God" and become members of God's Household. Their dynamism for Christian service is their recollection of the price paid by Christ to secure man's redemption. Redemption in the fullest sense, however, will not be completed until all nations, and all history, come within its embrace, and the "kingdoms of this world have become kingdoms of our God and of His Christ."

No human insight can fully plumb the depths, no intellectual categories can adequately interpret the meaning of the Incarnation, the Life, the Death, the Resurrection, the Ascension, the Descent of the Holy Spirit, and the continuing Presence of Jesus Christ. But certain things are clear. Through faith in Christ and commitment to Him, a new type of human personality was created. Through the association of "New Men in Christ," a new form of community, the Community of Christ, conceived also as the "Body of Christ," came into being. Through the loyal response of the New Community, known as the Christian Church, to the farewell words of Christ to "disciple the nations," the Gospel began to be carried into the *oikoumenē*. Through imperishable belief in the victory of Christ, and expectant waiting for His coming again to inaugurate the Kingdom of God, and make all things new, Christians continued through the ages to witness to their faith in Christ and the Church.

Individual examples of humanity "redeemed" in the early years of Christianity varied in type. Some persons, like the angry young zealot, Saul of Tarsus, for example, were converted to the New Faith in very dramatic circumstances, through personal encounter with the Risen Lord. Others, like young Timothy, had the advantage of a home training in Christianity. Timothy became a Christian undramatically, through the influence of two wonderful women, his grandmother Lois and his mother Eunice (II Timothy 1:15). Eunice's son is typical of a large number of sincerely committed Christians who come into the Kingdom and become members of the Christian Community, with little drama, but in deep reality, through commitment to the same Lord Jesus Christ.

The mandate of the Risen Christ, commonly called the "great commission," which oriented and inspired the apostles and their followers to become world-minded and to be, in the fullest sense, "ecumenical" evangelists, was the dynamic source of the Church's dedication to world mission in the most creative years of its history. Whenever the "great commission" has not been taken seriously by the Church, the Church has ceased to be "in very deed the Church." At such times, the Church, if a free agent, has become more interested in scholastic wrangling or hierarchic ambition, in accommodating itself to the prevailing culture or to the secular power, than in bracing itself for witness to the whole world, beginning with the existing "Jerusalem," and moving onwards through "Judea and Samaria" to the "ends of the earth."

THE CHRISTIAN MISSIONARY MOVEMENT

From the beginning of the Christian era, there have been men and women who devoted their time and energy to the ongoing task of redemption. They proclaimed by word and life that Jesus Christ who had "redeemed" man collectively by what He had done for them on the Cross, could "redeem" men as individual persons, by liberating them from the power of sin, and by becoming Himself the true life of every redeemed person. These men and women accepted a missionary vocation. They became precursors of the greatest spiritual movement in human history, a movement matched only in the past by the missionary movement of Islam, and in the present century, by the missionary movement of that secular faith called Communism.

We now address ourselves to consider the Christian Missionary

Movement as the chief expression in history of God's redemptive action and as the dynamic symbol of the spirit that should possess the Church when it is "in very deed the Church." To do so intelligently it is important that we examine the term "missionary," both as applied to individual Christians and to the Church as a whole.

What is a *missionary?* I would offer this definition. *A missionary is a person who feels called to communicate to others, or share with them, something of supreme worth which he himself has found, and who has been specially sent, or commissioned, to do so, by some group of like-minded people.* A "missionary" is in this sense the dedicated representative of some great idea, some great cause, or some great person, that he, the missionary, considers to be of supreme importance for the thought or life of the people to whom he goes. The missionary's objective can be of a secular as well as of a religious nature. Thus, the members of the famous "cultural missions" that were sent out in groups of five by the Mexican government for the education of the peasants during Mexico's social revolution, were dedicated *"misioneros"* in the secular sense.

A "missionary" is committed to a truth of some kind, to the promotion of which he devotes all his energies. He has in common with a philosopher that he *expounds* the truth in which he believes: but, unlike a philosopher, he actively *promotes* his belief. A missionary shares with a propagandist, the intelligent zeal that makes what is promoted exciting and attractive for others. But he goes beyond the propagandist in striving to secure the acceptance by others of that which he promotes. The "missionary" resembles the "politician" in presenting that for which he himself stands as something that others should endorse, because it is in their best interest to do so. His motive, however, in so doing is the intrinsic worth of what he recommends, and not the gain that would accrue to himself or his sponsors should his recommendation be successful. These distinctions are important, because it is unfortunately true that the concept of "missionary" has frequently been debased or distorted.

What is a *"Christian* missionary?" A Christian missionary is a person who feels called by God to communicate to others by lip and by life, on some frontier of the world, the good news of the

Gospel of Christ. He becomes a "missionary" when he is set apart by the Church, or by an association of fellow Christians, to dedicate his every talent to the task of so presenting Christ to other people that they shall accept Him as Savior and Lord and become members of the Christian Community.

It matters little or nothing, however, what particular designation a Christian missionary may bear, or what the specific work in which he expends his energy may be. For reasons relating to the status and sensitivity of the "younger" Churches, a one-time "missionary" from abroad may now be called a "fraternal worker." Because of the multiple spheres in which the new Christian Communities around the globe need the co-operation of technically trained fellow Christians from other lands to enable them to present Christ, and to make the Christian faith relevant in areas of desperate need, "fraternal workers" may be teachers, doctors, nurses, agriculturalists, engineers, radio experts. In certain instances, a Christian missionary may be so intimately identified with a national culture that he is never thought as being a "foreigner," or even as a "missionary," but only as a loved and revered man or woman. People wish to make their acquaintance because they have become deeply impressed by their dedicated personality. What matters, the only thing that matters, is this. The meaning of the Church, the mission of the Church to the world, and the future of the Christian Missionary Movement in the world are bound up with the measure in which all who represent the Church vocationally, whatever be the designation they may bear, are passionate lovers of Christ and the Gospel. It shall be their overmastering concern that their talents, their work, and their prestige shall serve to draw other people to Christ and to His Church.

Not only, however, must the Christian Church be represented in the world by missionaries whom it sends out and supports, *it must itself be missionary.* In consonance with its nature, in loyalty to its Head, the Church must be so inspired by its worship of God, and so illumined by its insight into God and the world, that it shall be, in every epoch and in every place, the vehicle of God's redeeming love in Jesus Christ. Neither the true worship of God by a true Community of God, nor a true understanding of God by the whole Christian Community, can become a substitute for the missionary service of God. Called by God to participate in His redemptive activity, the Church must, in lowliness and reverence, and in dependence upon the Holy Spirit, dedicate herself to the fulfillment of her redemptive function.

Historically speaking, the Church's exercise of her redemptive function has been most dramatically expressed in what has been known as the "Missionary Movement." After a checkered history through the centuries, during some of which the Community of Christ lived a very static and stagnant existence, quite unworthy of her Lord, a reawakening of missionary zeal towards the close of the Eighteenth Century, carried the Church, as has already been noted, into the uttermost bounds of human habitation. God's redemptive activity through the Church has brought to birth new men and women in Christ in every political area of the globe. It must be acknowledged, and with sorrow, that the motivation which inspired the expansion of Christianity into the non-Christian world was not always of the purest and best. Missionary movements in both the Protestant and the Roman Catholic traditions were in certain instances unduly related to the colonial ambitions of the countries where the "sending Churches" had their seat. While this fact must be recognized in a spirit of penitence, the words of Dr. Kenneth Latourette, the greatest living historian of Christianity, remain gloriously true that the missionary movement of the past centuries has been the most notable outpouring of life, in the main unselfishly, in the service of alien peoples which the world has ever seen. It was a Christ-inspired effort to "redeem" life in its wholeness.

Now that the Christian Missionary Movement is being reappraised, and that the mission of the Christian Church is being studied afresh, it is opportune to examine, in terms of both principle and policy, what it means for the Church to exercise the *redemptive function* to which Christ has called the members of His Body. Only by a thorough exploration of this question can we deal, in true perspective, with the question of the Church's quest for unity and the appropriate exercise of its unitive function.

THE MEDIATION OF THE LOVE OF GOD TO MEN

The Christian Gospel, which enshrines both what God has done for man and what He can do in man, is to be communicated to men everywhere by speech and by life, by words and by deeds. Evangelism is the soul of missionary effort.

During the years of World War I, the Archbishop of the Church of England appointed a Committee of Inquiry on the Evangelistic Work of the Church. That committee made its report in 1918. Years later, in 1943, when World War II was in progress, William Temple, then Archbishop of Canterbury, with the co-operation of his colleague, the Archbishop of York, appointed another committee, whose mandate was "to survey the whole problem of modern evangelism, with special reference to the spiritual needs and prevailing intellectual outlook of the non-worshipping members of the community." This committee, which addressed at its opening session in the Jerusalem Chamber, Westminster Abbey by its initiator, William Temple, published its report in 1945, under the title, "Towards the Conversion of England," and dedicated it to the memory of the beloved Archbishop, who had in the meantime passed away. This famous report adopted as its own the definition of evangelism contained in the report of 1918. The definition in question, which may be regarded as the most classic formulation ever made of what it means to evangelize, is as follows:

> *To evangelize is so to present Christ Jesus in the power of the Holy Spirit, that men shall come to put their trust in God through Him, to accept Him as their Saviour, and serve Him as their King in the fellowship of His Church.*[2]

Before I comment upon this statement, and attempt to show its theological cogency and its implications for the Church's approach to the world and to itself, along the whole ecumenical front, let me present two quotations. These will serve to set in high relief the crucial importance of evangelism in the thought and action of the Christian Church today.

The first quotation cites words spoken by Archbishop Temple at the Jerusalem Chamber gatherings in which he enunciated two principles:

[2] "Towards the Conversion of England" (London: The Press and Publications Board of the Church Assembly, 1945), p. 1.

(1) The message of the Church is the Eternal Gospel. This remains fundamentally the same first to last. The Gospel could not alter, although the setting in which it was given and the method of its presentation, could and did. (2) The first need in evangelism is for a strengthening and a quickening of spiritual life within the Church. "We cannot separate the evangelization of those without from the rekindling of devotion within." [3]

The second quotation is from an address delivered in San Francisco, California, during the spring of 1963 by a Roman Catholic theologian, Father Daniel J. O'Hanlon, S.J. Said this Jesuit theologian:

> Conversion is the ultimate goal of ecumenical work . . . Conversion is every movement by which man turns away from sin and self-centeredness to love God and his brothers and union with them in Christ. As Christians, we know that the central and decisive act of conversion is that by which a man, whether he be Catholic, Orthodox, or Protestant, is converted to God through faith and Baptism to new life in the community which is the Church. The ultimate goal of ecumenism is the conversion of the world to Christ.[4]

In this setting, the Church's function to be "redemptive," to "evangelize," to "convert" takes on the ecumenical dimension which belongs to it. At the same time, the definition of evangelism offered by concerned Anglican Churchmen acquires special significance. To this definition, therefore, we now return.

First, the core of evangelistic effort is to *present Christ Jesus in the power of the Holy Spirit.* A "largely alien world," to use William Temple's phrase, a world that today exists as much within the Church as outside the Church, must be confronted with Christianity's and history's central figure, Jesus Christ, and with the Gospel. This Gospel is the good news from God to man, that centers in Christ. It involves all that Christ was, said, did, is now,

[3] *Ibid.*, Foreword, p. ix.
[4] "Operation Understanding," The National Catholic Action Weekly, May 19, 1963, p. 2A.

and shall be. To have redemptive effect upon those who hear it, the Gospel must be presented by persons who themselves believe passionately in its truth. They allow themselves in humility to be organs of the Holy Spirit. He who made Christ what He was, makes men see what they themselves should be and what through Christ they can become.

Second, the presentation of Christ in the power of the Spirit, disposes men in such a way that they *"shall come to put their trust in God through Him."* The human spirit responds to the love of God as manifested in the person and work of Jesus Christ. Christ, who becomes the object of adoring affection, awakens that trust in God which is Christian faith, and which remains inseparably related to Himself, who continues to be not only the Way, but also the Truth and the Life.

Third, trust in the Eternal God and His sovereign rule in the affairs of men has its abiding and dynamic center in "Jesus Christ, the Son of God, the Savior." [5] Men who *accept Him as their Savior* are delivered from their sinful self-centeredness by Him who gave His life for them, and who now shares His life with them, thereby assuring them of the strength they need for life and of eventual triumph in death.

Fourth, Jesus Christ is also accepted by Christians as their *"King,"* whom they pledge themselves to *"serve."* Renewed by the power of Christ, they will devote their lives to the obedience of Christ. Thus, the saved become servants; and the Savior becomes Lord. The redemption of life is followed by the dedication of life. Jesus Christ the King becomes relevant to every phase of Christian thought and behavior. Obedience, fulfilled in action, is the central category of the Christian religion. Loyalty to the King becomes the central motive in Christian living, whether it be manifested in missionary obedience to the great commission to "disciple the nations," or in revolutionary defiance of a tyrant who claimed absolute Lordship, which inspired the signers of the Barmen Declaration.

Fifth, Christ's Saviorhood-Kingship in the lives of Christians

[5] The English rendering of the Greek words enshrined in the early Christian symbol of the fish *(Ichthys).*

finds its highest spiritual expression, and its chief sphere of action, *"in the fellowship of His Church."* They who belong to Christ belong also to one another, as members of the Community of faith which is Christ's Body. Their names are written one by one in the Lamb's Book of Life and in the Church Roll. Their individual growth in the faith of Christ, and the fulfillment of Christ's mission in the world, both require that Christians shall not act as unrelated units, but as members of the great Fellowship in which Jesus Christ is Savior and Lord.

HOW TO PRESENT JESUS CHRIST

We pass now from the *what* to the *how* of evangelization. We have considered the centrality of Christ in the Christian Gospel, the centrality of the Gospel in the Christian religion, the responsibility of the Christian Church to participate in the redemptive activity of God by evangelistic effort, the fruits and the goal of Christian evangelism. But an important question still remains. Taking it for granted that a faithful presentation of Jesus Christ to men will not produce redemptive fruits except through the "power of the Holy Spirit," what features should mark the process whereby Christ is presented? In a word, what are the principles which should govern the presentation of the Gospel, if Jesus Christ is to be taken seriously by those to whom He is presented? The authors of the definition of evangelism which we have just analyzed, said: "To evangelize is *so* to present Jesus Christ. . . ." It is to this basic and very practical question of the *way* of evangelism, the question of intelligent sensitivity on the part of the "evangelizers" to human nature, and to the concrete situation in which the people find themselves whom they would attract to Christ and the Church, that we now address ourselves.

Certain important principles should govern the presentation of Christ to non-Christians, as well as to nominal Christians. These principles apply wherever man is found. They apply equally, whether Christ is presented by persons who are not known to be Christian, or by persons known to function officially under the auspices of Christian Churches or groups. The same principles are relevant whether the setting be in the East or in the West, in the "Free World" or in the "Communist World," in a rural environment or in centers of culture, in the midst of revolutionary activity or where bourgeois complacency reigns.

THE INCARNATIONAL PRINCIPLE

The *first* principle I would formulate thus: *The evangelical word must become indigenous flesh.* The person who represents Christ, and seeks to communicate the Gospel of Christ, in a community where Christ is not known, or where the people are indifferent or even hostile to everything that is Christian, must identify himself in the closest possible manner with his human environment. This he must do in the most natural and least ostentatious way possible. All mere foreignness in manner, speech, living, and sometimes dress must disappear. He must become one with the people in the fullest sense, observing, of course, the great moral proprieties which, as a Christian, are part of his essential being. But in his behavior and life among the people, he will be humble, sensitive to their needs, concerned about their interests. He will show himself at all times, and in every respect, a friend. He will give concrete expression by word, act, and disposition to the reality of love, of Christian *agape,* mediating thereby the love of God in Christ Jesus.

This principle, which we will call the *incarnational* principle, was given its supreme and unique expression in the incarnation of Jesus Christ Himself. In Christ, God became man for man's redemption; the "Word became flesh and dwelt among us, full of grace and truth" (John 1:14). By being truly man, and being intimately identified with human life, Christ obtained a unique understanding of the nature and dimension of man's problem. He was thereby fitted to be the representative of the human kind in redemptive activity. He who was "perfected through suffering," qualified to become, after His Ascension, a "merciful and faithful High Priest," for men and their abiding Intercessor before God.

The incarnational principle has marked every truly redemptive effort in Christian history. People have responded to Christ and the Church has been established and has grown, in the measure in which Christ's representatives ceased to be mere outsiders in the life of a people, and became, not condescendingly, but joyously and empathically, involved in their common life and concerns. Outstanding examples from among a host of men whose life expressed this principle were St. Paul, Christianity's greatest Apostle; William Carey, the pioneer of the modern missionary movement, for whom everything truly Indian became a passion; Bartolomé de las Casas, the pioneer Spanish missionary in Mexico and Guatemala, whose incarnational approach to the Indians was rejected by his own Church and is being revived today; William Morris, an Anglican clergyman, founder of the "Philanthropic Schools and Institutes of Argentina," who, when he died, was hailed by the Buenos Aires press as *"el santo argentino,"* the Argentine saint.

A unique contemporary expression of the incarnational principle in the service of Christ and the Gospel is the approach which is made both to governments and to primitive people by the Wycliffe translators; another is the road-building activities devotedly carried on at odd moments by simple Pentecostalists in the wilds of Mexico, which drew the attention and admiration of a government traditionally hostile to religion. Still another example is the increasing practice of dedicated young men and women who, in order to be able to present Christ and Christianity to people in such a way as to deal intelligently and sympathetically with their particular problems, become their fellow students in foreign universities, or their fellow workers in industrial establishments at home.

What has just been said concerns the expression of the incarnational principle in the lives of individual persons. The same principle, however, has marked, and always must mark, the approach to the human situation of the Christian Church as a whole. The love of God, which became manifest in the Incarnation of Christ, and the love of Christ, which became manifest in His passionate concern for the temporal welfare of people, provide the Church with both inspiration and a pattern for its own approach to men. He who "spoke with authority," who said, "Come unto me—Believe upon me—Follow me," lived a life which merited the affirmation of Peter to the Roman officer Cornelius. "He went about doing good" (Acts 10:38). This "doing good," which marked the life of Jesus and in which He incarnated that spirit of "caring" which He bequeathed to His followers as a precious legacy, has been reproduced down the ages by the Christian Church in fulfillment of its mission. Only in periods when the concrete figure

of the Galilean failed to inspire Christians, and the implications of
the Incarnation for Christian living were forgotten, did the
Church fail to recognize that "caring matters most." Historically
speaking, however, philanthropy in the full meaning of the term,
is the creation not of the cultures of Greece, Rome, or the Orient,
but of Christianity.

It was natural and inevitable, therefore, that the historical
movement of the Body of Christ into the world should be marked
by the provision of media for human welfare, dedicated to relieve
suffering and to equip people for living. And this was done,
whether or not the people who benefited from Christian philanthropy at its best accepted, or did not accept, Jesus Christ as
Saviour and Lord and became members of the Christian Community. While it is true that the Christian Church had occasion,
in some epochs and in certain countries, to found hospitals,
orphanages, schools, and colleges, primarily as a needed contribution to the welfare of its own members, let this also be remembered. Many a time the Church set the pace for secular
civilization, and to a superlative degree in the United States, by
the establishment of philanthropic and educational institutions
designed to "redeem" people from sickness, poverty, and ignorance. But on the frontiers of the world, in the vast areas of Asia
and Africa, where the non-Christian religions have predominated,
the Christian Missionary Movement, in the true spirit of Christ,
has been concerned with the physical and temporal needs of
the inhabitants, and not merely with the propagation of the
Gospel and the development of the Church. Whatever be the
social or the political future of Asian and African countries, they
can never forget the debt they owe to the educational and philanthropic efforts of Christian missionaries and of Christian missions from overseas.

At this point, certain reflections, which have a bearing upon
the incarnational principle and its expression, are in order.

1. The efflorescence of welfare institutions that accompanied
the establishment of Christian missions in many lands had their
origin in the missionary's sensitivity to human need, in the spirit
of Christ, and not to considerations of religious strategy. Still less
were those institutions designed to influence the nationals in
favor of the civilization or country to which the missionaries be-

longed. It is true, nevertheless, that much of the support received for such institutions came from individuals and organizations whose exclusive interest lay in the contribution which the institutions they supported might make to the development of new nations, in the interests of western civilization. When, therefore, the break came, as in the case of China, between a "mission land" and the countries in which the "missions" had their seat, the latter were charged with having been the conscious tools of western imperialism.

2. The practice, in certain instances, of missionary establishments, to locate their personnel and offices in separate areas called "compounds" violated the incarnational principle at a very crucial point. Consequent upon the growth of nationalism and racism, this practice resulted in an unhappy breach between national Christians and Christians from abroad, thereby dividing the Christian Community.

3. There have been cases when Christian missions, in the relations of their missionaries with the people among whom they worked, substituted other principles for the principle of love-inspired incarnation. Sometimes the principle of incarnation was no more than an attitude of condescending patronization. Christ's representatives from abroad never ceased to feel, and never failed to convey, a certain superiority. Outside the occasions when they were related professionally, or let us say, vocationally, to citizens or even fellow workers, of the adopted country, they spent their leisure hours in their own company or in that of citizens of western lands. This represented a revival of pre-Christian Judaism, with its practice of cultural segregation. It spelled the betrayal of the nature and mission of the New Humanity and gave rise to a violent reaction on the part of the nationals, when the political situation changed.

A contemporary instance of substituting another principle for the principle of incarnation is a very delicate one, because of its sacred associations. I have in mind the substitution of reverence for life for incarnation in life. This substitution is linked to the revered name of Albert Schweitzer.[6] It becomes clear, however, that the venerable missionary doctor, philosopher, and musician,

[6] Schweitzer first became famous as the author of *The Quest of the Historical Jesus.*

who went to Africa in early manhood because he felt he owed it to Jesus Christ to consecrate his life to the most forgotten people in the world, and who embraced as his motto "reverence for life," will in the years to come belong more to Europe and America than to Africa, where most of his life has been spent. The reason is this. Albert Schweitzer has been a great Christian in Africa, but he has never belonged to Africa, nor has he been concerned about the transformation of Africa. He has made a tremendous contribution to our understanding of western civilization, but he has made no contribution to the reorientation of African life. The reason is that he never became "incarnate" in the African people, nor has he been devoted to the redemption of their life. Schweitzer's dedicated career will remain a symbol of passionate concern that primitive people should be given a chance to live in biological normalcy. But he has not shown concern that they experience redemptive change in their spiritual selfhood or in the sociological conditions of their life. To this day, no representative of the new revolutionary Africa is a medical colleague of the eminent founder of the Hospital of Lambarene.

4. There is clear evidence that whenever a Christian mission from abroad devoted itself exclusively to evangelistic activity in a narrow, technical sense, without its component members identifying themselves closely with a community and its welfare, the work became sterile. In not a few instances it came to an end entirely; or else the mission continued to exist as a pure façade, to satisfy the conscience and witness to the "zeal without knowledge" of its founders, or of its supporters in some foreign land.

5. It is equally true, on the other hand, that when missionaries have succeeded in establishing indigenous Churches, the members of which develop a missionary passion to bring their fellow countrymen to accept Jesus Christ as Savior and Lord, the Christian Community grows. Foreignness disappears. There takes place a movement of the Holy Spirit in the lives of "newly born" men and women. The new Christians take pride in belonging in the fullest sense to their country and become leaven in their environment.

This precisely is what began to happen in Chile fifty years ago.

In this country, Pentecostal Christians who were originally inspired by a single foreign missionary who took the Holy Spirit seriously, combine today a rich reborn humanity, spiritual enthusiasm, and complete dedication to Christ and their country. The growth of Pentecostal Churches in Chile and in all Latin America has been literally phenomenal. The whole Chilean nation has been profoundly affected. The government has recognized the sociological importance of a movement that in the profoundest and also in the most practical sense, has embodied the incarnational principle. Christ became "born" in people, who in turn became "incarnate" in the most concrete sense in the life of their fellow Chileans. These people, witnessing to what God can do when the Gospel of Christ and the reality of the Holy Spirit are exalted, are a living witness to what that eminent Anglican, Roland Allen, called the *spontaneous expansion of the Church.*[7]

THE RIGHT TO BE HEARD

While the incarnational principle, embodied in the life and attitude of those who would lead others to accept the Christian faith, is an indispensable precondition for successful effort, it is not in itself sufficient. The moment comes when persons who have won the esteem of a community because of their identification with it must also win the *right to be heard* by the members of that community on a matter which is affirmed to be of transcendent importance. It is not enough for Christians, wherever they live and whatever their work, to be simply likable and Christ-like people. There comes a time when they must become *vocal* concerning their faith. In loyalty to Christ, and for the sake of people, they must move toward the hour when others are ready to listen to their witness concerning Christ. The Church and its institutions, whether by the Ganges, the Nile, or the Hudson, fulfills its redemptive function when it inspires and equips both its officers and its members to present the *Kerygma,* the Christian message of salvation.

[7] The mention of Roland Allen leads me to say that a study of his works and the works of Donald McGavran, Alexander McLeish, and David Paton, are of first-rate importance for a study of the way in which the Christian Church may become truly incarnational and fulfill its redemptive function in the world.

It is surely not an unwarranted presupposition that, if the Church is to be "in very deep the Church," if it is to match the secular faith of Communism, if it is to be truly relevant to the deepest needs of men in this revolutionary time, Christians should be eager to communicate their faith and should win the right to be heard regarding it. This right is won when non-Christians, or merely nominal Christians, are eager to know what Christians have to *say* because they have learned to respect them for what they *are*. Nothing, on the other hand, is more tragic for the Church or for Christians than when "outsiders," concerned but disillusioned people, are heard to remark or imply, "I cannot hear what you say, what you are sounds too loudly in my ear."

History, from New Testament times to the present, is gloriously full of episodes in which the Christian Church, Christian institutions, Christian individuals, and groups, won the right to be heard and, upon that basis, said things that had redemptive significance. It is unnecessary to refer to the manner and the occasions when Jesus Himself, and His apostles Peter and Paul, won this right and how they used it. Their spirit has pervaded the Christian ages and has appeared at times in most unexpected places. Here are some illustrations, taken from different times and cultures of Christians who won a right to be heard on behalf of their Lord.

I begin with the land of my ancestors. Presbyterianism in Scotland, especially in the northern region of the country, has sometimes been accused of religious legalism and "social" Puritanism in their most extreme and objectionable forms. But at a time when Sabbatarianism was one of the chief clerical absolutes, this incident occurred. A young minister found on arriving at his new parish of Loch Carron that his parishioners, instead of going to Church on Sunday morning, were accustomed to assemble by the loch-side to watch feats of athletic prowess. The new parson mingled with the throng. He challenged Big Rory, the local Goliath, to a wrestling match. To the stupefaction of all, young Parson David won the bout. Shaking hands cordially with the vanquished, he said to him, "Rory, I'm the new minister, won't you help me to get the people to the Church?" They acted together. The simple country folk, who had never found religion to be very exciting, readily followed their two heroes. The Church was filled with folk eager to hear what the wrestling champion had to say. He preached a sermon. Big Rory was converted by that sermon. Other conversions followed, and a new day dawned in the Parish of Loch Carron.

It was an old custom in the Scottish Highlands that, when a person was converted, he should break with every social practice associated with "worldliness." A young man, John Macdonald, who was famous as a bagpiper, became spiritually a "new man." He immediately laid aside, for what he thought would be forever, the instrument with whose strains he had often thrilled gay dancers. Years later, however, in the city of Dundee, the erstwhile master of the bagpipes, now a famous evangelical preacher, could not endure the poor performances of a piper who marched back and forth in a public square to enliven the passersby and earn their bounty. Taking his old beloved instrument from the man, the preacher marched up and down, thrilling the Scottish hearts of the crowd who came together at the sound—and also to see the unusual sight. The bagpiper parson had won his *right to be heard*. He thereupon took advantage of the occasion to speak to his thrilled audience in a quite informal manner about Christ and the Gospel. If only Christians show themselves to be "real" men and women, responsive to challenges in a myriad of situations that may arise, there is no limit to the opportunities that will come to them to bear witness, in a very natural and effective way, to the "unsearchable riches of Christ."

Let me further illustrate the "right to be heard" principle. Here are two instances from Asia. In 1949, I was informed by the Prime Minister of Thailand that the name of the American, Francis Sayre, is enshrined forever in the annals of his country. I asked him why, and he gave me the story. Here it is. Young Sayre resigned a teaching position at Harvard University to become a consultant to the Thai government. The Christian conscience of the young diplomat was outraged when he came face to face with the "extraterritoriality" tradition which deprived Thailand of jurisdiction over foreign interests within the nation. He did not rest until he succeeded in getting foreign governments, including his own, to revoke the objectionable statute. Thailand became "free." After this political problem had been solved, Francis Sayre, trusted and loved by the Thai government and people, was spending an evening in the home of the Prime Minister. The young daughter of the latter appeared to be at the point of death, and her life was despaired of. The guest, who had won on another ground his "right to be heard," suggested prayer. The Buddhist host consented, whereupon the loved American diplomat prayed earnestly to God for the girl's life.

Many years later, after Sayre, the dedicated Episcopal layman, had served as Assistant Secretary of State and was finally retired from public office, he happened to attend a reception in Washington, D. C. In the course of the evening, as Mr. Sayre himself told me sometime later, the wife of a diplomat from the Orient came up to him and said, "You are Mr. Sayre, I believe. They tell me I owe my life to you." It was the girl who years before had been at death's door! God had answered the prayer of His servant, after he had won the right to engage in prayer in a Buddhist home.

One of the leading and most trusted naval officers in the Islamic land of Indonesia is a Christian layman, Commander John Lie. A number of years ago, Lie, while a young lieutenant, passed through a profound experience of Christian conversion, which he vividly described to me some years ago during a visit to his home in Jakarta. I learned from others that Commander Lie had established such a reputation in government circles for technical skill and personal integrity that he was frequently entrusted with very important assignments, such, for example, as the raising to the surface of vessels that, with valuable cargoes on board, had been sunk during wartime. A few years ago, our commander was asked by President Sukarno to ready his ship to take him and a group of diplomats, including representatives of Communist countries, on a special voyage. As it happened, the Christian captain had, with the full consent of his officers, introduced on the ship the practice of reading each morning a passage from the Bible, and of offering prayer just as they and he sat down together to breakfast. He informed President Sukarno of this custom, but offered to forego it should the Chief of State consider it inappropriate while he and the ambassadors were guests aboard. But no objection was voiced. So family prayers were quietly conducted on shipboard next morning by a man who had won the right to give devotional expression to his Christian faith.

We come now to the western world. One of the most disturbing problems in the religious life of the United States is the fact that the vast majority of teen-agers remain aloof from the churches and come under no direct Christian influence. A young Presbyterian minister, Jim Rayburn, became alarmed about the situation. He was confident that teen-agers would respond to Christ with enthusiasm, if only His relevancy to their life were interpreted to them by young men and women whom they came to admire for their friendliness and good sportsmanship. Backed by a group of young Christians who were members of the Churches and students in the universities he was able to make a new "redemptive" approach to the teen-age problem. Schoolboys and schoolgirls, in gymnasiums, sports fields, social gatherings, excursions, wherever teen-agers came together, began to meet friendly young people, just a little older than themselves, whom they came to admire for some particular accomplishment. The young Christian crusaders would spend weeks and even months establishing rapport with gangs of youths, winning their esteem for the stunts they could do, the songs they could sing, the tales they could tell, the feats they could perform, the advice they could give, the help they supplied.

The time would come at last, when, as a result of growing admiration on the part of the teen-agers, relations became more personal. Individuals or groups would get together to unburden their souls, and ask the young man or woman who had won "a right to be heard," what their view was on some of the things that concerned them. The opportunity thus came in an atmosphere of concern and trust to "present Jesus Christ in the power of the Holy Spirit," and it was done. Extraordinary things began to happen. The "Young Life Campaign" was under way. I have been close to this movement, with which pastors and Churches in many parts have begun to co-operate, and from which they have learned things that they now apply in congregational life. I have listened to the personal testimony of outstanding boys and girls of seventeen or eighteen years of age, some of whom occupied leading positions in the large high schools they attended. They had been gripped by Christ through *Young Life* and were led to commit their lives to His service. A striking book on this movement has recently been written by a distinguished Christian scholar.[8]

Two things are clear. First, a policy of adjustment to the realities of youth acquires Christian meaning only when it is inspired by

[8] Emile Cailliet, *Young Life* (New York: Harper & Row, Publishers, 1963).

a Christian vision for the redemption of youth. Second, a deep
spiritual yearning underlies the exhibitionism and boisterous activity of modern youth. Youth is awaiting what the Churches in
general are not providing. The ordinary Church is not offering
youth what youth feels it needs, simply because religion has become passionless. The entertainment of youth and, at most, the
education of youth have become substitutes for the conversion of
youth and for the presentation to youth of something really great
and exciting to live for.

What of the higher cultural realm where the secular Cult of the
Uncommitted is regnant, and whose devotees, in increasing numbers, proclaim that religion makes no appeal, or even sense, to
them? None are more responsive than are university men and
women to a Christian interpretation of life, when it is presented
by one who has won his right to be heard on other than religious
grounds. When such a person makes his case for Christ and the
Gospel, not as part of a religious service, or during a conference
on religion, but as a conclusion reached after a vigorous and
luminous analysis of a human problem of recognized importance,
he will be listened to. Not at the beginning, but at the end of a
basic presentation, should an academic audience be challenged to
face the reality and relevancy of Christ in relation to the problem
of man and his world.

This is a matter on which the writer feels strongly, and in connection with which he has had personal experience. Because of
what he feels to be the relevancy of this experience to academic
communities in other parts of the world, he ventures, though with
diffidence, to become autobiographical.

It can be said, without exaggeration, that the cultural atmosphere in Latin American universities has been the most thoroughly
secularized in the world. The breach between religion and culture
has been traditional and absolute for generations. At the same time,
academic freedom has been maintained as a most sacred right.
Provided a teacher or a lecturer has given clear evidence that he
understands his subject and has done justice to conflicting viewpoints, he is considered to be entitled to present his own conclusion, whatever that conclusion may be, and however much it may
run counter to traditional views or prejudices prevailing among
his audience.

It has been the author's privilege, in the course of the years, to lecture in some twenty-five universities, or centers of higher learning, in Latin American countries. Some of those lectures were given at times of religious crisis, or where religion was anathema, or at least, was considered unworthy of academic attention. But invariably, whatever the topic, thought would move, in a natural, logical manner, to the figure of Jesus Christ and His relevancy to the question under discussion. The theme might be "The Vocation of Man," "The Meaning of Existence," "Intellectuals and the New Era," "Metaphysics and Life," "This Revolutionary Springtime," "The Concept of Freedom in Contemporary Culture," or it might be a discussion of Kierkegaard, Nietzsche, Dostoevsky, Unamuno, or "The Spanish Mystics." But there was always one refrain and it was He, He who was the Center of the lecturer's life passion. And the audience responded, and some saw Christ, God and Christianity, and life in a new perspective.

How could this happen? It could happen because the lecturer was not regarded by his audience as a mere foreigner, but as "indigenous flesh," as a lover of the "Hispanic," as one who had been part of their own academic life. They received him and listened to him in the great tradition of Hispanic personalism. The man from abroad had founded a school in Lima, Peru, in which Spanish was the official language; he had been a member of the editorial staff of Peru's leading cultural journal, *El Mercurio Peruano;* he had held the Chair of Metaphysics in the old University of San Marcos; in the days when he was a graduate student in Spain, he had come to know Miguel de Unamuno, who created within him a passion for the Hispanic. This is not written for self-glorification. Far from it. I can make my own the words of Raymond Lull, "I have one passion in life and it is He," and also the words of William Carey, which he wished inscribed, and which are inscribed, on his tombstone, "A wretched, poor, and helpless worm, on Thy strong arm I fall."

I have said what I have said because I am profoundly convinced that a new and less conventional approach needs to be made by Christians and the Christian Church to the presentation of Christ and the Gospel in the universities of the world. It is here that laymen, especially men and women who are recognized scholars, who are unashamedly Christian, and who have the gifts of utterance and human geniality, should be used by the Church in the intelligent fulfillment of its redemptive function. Let there be occasions in which the Christian message is not announced as itself the theme, but when it will become the luminous and moving conclusion to a theme recognized by the promiscuous audience to be important. Such presentations need not necessarily be made under official religious sponsorship.

But whatever be the sphere or the circumstances in which the message of Christ is presented, whoever the people may be who present it, and whether the message be communicated by vocal utterance or the printed page, two things are needful: First, the person who has won a right to be heard by others must present his case *with passionate conviction*. This does not mean brashness or sentimentality. But it does mean that the hearer shall get the unmistakable impression that for the one who addresses him it is a really exciting thing to be a Christian.

Second, the message must be conveyed with *crystalline clarity*. This is equally true, whether the audience be in a Church sanctuary, a club room, a public hall, a movie theater, a sports arena, at a street corner, or in a university auditorium. The language, as language, must be such that those who are addressed can understand it. The truth of Christ must be presented in language understood by the auditors, and in terms that they find meaningful and appealing. What a shock came to a man who was speaking about God as Father to a group of boys and girls in a slum area of an industrial city in England! He discovered that for them the word "father" was a name accursed and damned! For most of them did not know who their fathers were, except that they had abandoned them and their mothers. This is a parable. Words have different meanings in different environments. When the words of witness come over radio and television, it is still more imperative that they be in the language of ordinary people, with theological clichés and pious jargon at a minimum.

It might be said that nothing has been suggested regarding a collective approach to evangelism on the part of the Churches. The reason is that I have had chiefly in mind the non-Christian, or the purely secular frontier, where people are unwilling to attend Christian services and reject Christian assumptions. On the other hand, evangelistic efforts carried on within the context of the Church and which are unmistakenly Christian in character should be given an increasingly important status. In this connection the Church should never cease to thank God for the campaigns associated with the names of George Whitefield, John Wesley, and Dwight L. Moody. In our own time, the principles enunciated in this chapter regarding a truly redemptive approach to the human situation have been worthily expressed by certain Christian enterprises which have recently been carried on in many lands. I have particularly in mind the "Billy Graham Crusade," "World Vision," and "Evangelism in Depth."

The writer, moreover, can never cease to thank God for the great evangelistic effort of 1936. Sponsored by the Federal Council of Churches, it was organized by Jesse Bader and led by E. Stanley Jones. All the Protestant Churches of America co-operated. The participants in that campaign crossed the country together. In every city visited, members of the group spoke in churches, schools, hospitals, factories, and prisons, quite apart from participating in great public gatherings. It was a case in which the American Church, in the context of the national situation at that time, sought to be "incarnational" and to "win a right to be heard"—and to a remarkable degree succeeded. It was a glorious example of unity in action.

As a concluding word on this subject, let it be said how deeply the Christian Churches throughout the world stand in debt to the great Bible Societies. These have been pioneers in studying the language of the world's peoples, and in translating the Word of God into their vernacular. The Book of Redemption, thanks to the consecrated efforts of master linguists and phoneticians, for whom Jesus Christ is Savior and Lord, and among whom the name of Eugene Nida is becoming a symbol, heads the vanguard of the world's "great books" in the movement toward the ecumenical frontier.

The Church's
Unitive Function

chapter 10

We come to the fourth and final phase of what I have ventured to call the Church's functional quadrilateral. The Christian Church, if it is to be "in very deed the Church," must dedicate itself, in its diverse empirical expressions, to the achievement of unity that belongs to its nature as the Church of Christ. This chapter will be devoted to a consideration of what has come to be called "Ecumenism," by which is meant the Church's efforts to bring about unity and understanding in all things pertaining to the life and thought of the Churches.

It is unfortunate that, in the mind of many people, Christians and non-Christians alike, the Church's *unitive function* is regarded as exhausting the connotation of "ecumenical." While the view in question runs counter to the basic thesis of this book, the pursuit of unity on the part of each Christian congregation, denomination, tradition, and the Church Universal must be regarded as a major responsibility of Christ's Church. Without that oneness which the Lord of the Church desired His followers to have, the Church cannot be truly the Church, nor can it succeed in fulfilling its mission to the world. We address ourselves, therefore, to the question of Christian unity.

GUIDEPOSTS TO UNITY

It is important to begin by inquiring what unity means in a Christian context, when it truly reflects the mind of Christ and breathes His Spirit. At the heart of every genuine manifestation of Christian unity there must be the reality of *love*. Toward the close of His life, Jesus spoke these words to His disciples: "A new commandment I give to you, that you love one another; even as I have loved you, that you also love one another. By this all men will know that you are my disciples if *you have love for one another*" (John 13:34–35). This "Eleventh Commandment," which goes beyond the precepts contained in the ancient decalogue "to love God with all one's heart and one's neighbor as oneself," is the commandment which Christians have tragically broken through the ages. How often, and in how many places around the globe, have professing followers of Jesus Christ loved God and people outside the family of faith but have been guilty of not loving, and even of hating, men and women called "Christians," who happened to belong to a Christian fellowship which the violators of the Eleventh Commandment could not accept.

There can be no substitute for that love of Christ and of one another which inspires and makes possible the "Communion of Saints." This love goes far beyond a passionless love, which is essentially intellectual, and a sentimental love, which is no more than emotion—a being "in love with loving." It enshrines "holy affections" to God and to one another. It is equally distant from the coldness of protocol and the hilarity of mere togetherness. It leads to reconciliation with one another and to the rededication of life to God. It is a meeting transfigured and crowned by the celebration together of the Lord's Supper, as happened in the Upper Room, the same evening that the Lord added His "New Commandment" to the traditional Ten. I have spoken in symbols, but the reality is plain. No unity is worthy of being called Christian, or of being pursued as a Churchly goal, where love is not present as the soul of togetherness. For where love is lacking, the pursuit of Christian unity, and every project of Church union, will be no more than monuments to human expediency.

The second guidepost bears the word *obedience,* and beneath it the explanatory saying, "If you love me, you will keep my commandments" (John 14:15). The Christian fellowship whose members are knit together in the love of one another and for whom Jesus Christ is Lord, are responsive to His word of command. Obedience, let it be said again, is the climactic category of the Christian religion. True Christian Community involves dynamic action. Oneness in Christ, love for the brethren, do not receive full expression when tensions disappear or when a true family spirit is created, but when the community responds to a command which is discerned to be God-given. Peace in the Christian sense is not the peace of the cemetery, however replete a graveyard may be with masterpieces of nature and of art that soothe the spirit. Nor is it the peace that came to the Palestinian hillside with returning spring. The peace which Christ bequeathed to His disciples when He said, "My peace I leave with you," is a dynamic peace, whose symbol is the river. Though the waters of the river go cascading over rocky boulders, or swirl through "caverns measureless to man," the river is at peace, because its bed is made. So, too, with the People of God, the Community of Christ, the fellowship of love. Its members are at peace in the deepest Christian sense when together they respond to the command of Christ, allowing themselves to become part of God's great scheme of things, emissaries of His grand design.

Unity, therefore, is never so real or so Christian as when it is fulfilled in mission. For it is in mission and only in mission that individual members of the community achieve true stature, when each discovers his place within the whole and becomes equipped to play his part worthily. When this happens, the work of the Church's leaders is not in vain, for then Church members as "God's people" do not learn merely to "enjoy religion" or to have a "wonderful time" together but are "equipped for work in His service" (Ephesians 4:11, 12).

The third guidepost is *God-likeness*. "Copy God," it says (Ephesians 5:1). Churchly unity at every level, and in all its manifestations, will express the reality of Christian Community when its inspiration and prototype is the Holy Trinity. The Trinitarian concept is no mere theological dogma. It enshrines a profound spiritual truth which provides the People of God with a dynamic pattern for their corporate life. The three Persons of the Godhead—Father, Son, and Holy Spirit—are related to one another in terms of their respective roles in the fulfillment of the grand design. The Christian Trinity conveys to us the ineffable truth that the Father sent the Son into the world, that the Son came to be the world's Savior, that the Holy Spirit descended upon the Church from the Father and from the Son to equip the Church to be God's "minister of reconciliation." The Christian Community takes the doctrine of the Trinity seriously when it perceives more than a luminous idea, more also than a liturgical motif, and when, with understanding and joy, it accepts the Trinity as the missionary pattern and inspiration for its own life.

On the fourth guidepost appears the word *man-likeness*, and underneath it, the injunction, "Understand Man." The appropriate pattern for Christian unity or Churchly union must take into account the human situation in which Christians are called upon to join in united witness to God. The designers of Christian unity must never forget that Christian men and women differ in different parts of the world. Europeans, Asians, Australians, Africans, Latin Americans, and North Americans who belong to the Church Universal vary in temperament and race. Their cultural backgrounds and political situations differ. They confront different problems and different environments. For that reason, the Holy Catholic Church, in its empirical manifestations around the globe, and even within the territory of a single large country, will inevitably bear the imprint of man-likeness. Redeemed man, transformed by the grace of Christ and indwelt by the Holy Spirit, will not and should not cease to be man. The apostles of Christian unity and the architects of Church union must never forget the complexity of the anthropological problem, and the legitimacy of varying structures within the unity of the one Church, the *Una Sancta*. This is not a concession to Fallen Man; it is not pessimism about Historical Man; it is the recognition of Eternal Man.

THE ECCLESIASTICAL SPECTRUM

Let us now look at the Church situation as it exists in the world today. It is no part of our purpose to offer an exhaustive, or even a cursory, treatment of the varying ecclesiastical organizations which are known as the "Churches." The attempt to do so would carry us beyond the objective of this study. Innumerable tomes exist, in which the theological position, the historical development, and the contemporary stance of the "Churches" are set forth. Important studies that deal in an authoritative and basic manner with these important topics are in progress, some of them under the auspices of the World Council of Churches. Our present purpose will be achieved if we succeed in discerning and crystallizing the core feature of the several Church types regarded as representative in the current ecclesiastical spectrum.

In contemporary Christianity there are, as there have been for more than four centuries, three main Christian traditions: Roman Catholicism, Eastern Orthodoxy, and Protestantism.

ROMAN CATHOLICISM

The Roman Catholic Church, which claims to be the oldest Christian tradition, coming in unbroken hierarchical succession from the Twelve Apostles, has the largest constituency of members. It affirms that "Jesus Christ founded His Organization," which it identifies as the Church of Rome. Inspired by the spirit of Roman law and order, this Church stresses the *institutional* aspect of the Christian Church. It functions under the leadership of a supreme hierarchy of cardinals. Their head, when elected by his fellow cardinals, is designated the Pope, who is considered to be the successor of St. Peter. The Supreme Hierarch is regarded as the infallible vehicle of the Holy Spirit in the official pronouncements (papal encyclicals) which he makes, and in his direction of Church affairs. In this view, the essence of the Christian Church is order, institutional reality. The clergy constitute the Church, and belong to it in a way that the laity do not. The status given to the clergy in the Roman Communion has led historically to the phenomenon of *Clericalism,* meaning the intervention of the clergy in the affairs of the state and society. The Church is equated with the Kingdom of God. Thus, loyalty to the Church as an institution has constituted the central and crucial loyalty.

EASTERN ORTHODOXY

Eastern Orthodoxy, which allegedly broke with Roman Catholicism over the famous *"Filioque"* controversy, maintaining that the Holy Spirit comes exclusively "from the Father," and not "from the Father *and the Son*," is associated with the eastern area of the Old Roman Empire. It is made up of fourteen Patriarchates or self-governing Churches, of which the largest is the Russian Orthodox Church. These Churches, which reflect the influence of Greek philosophy, as the Roman Church reflects the influence of old Roman law, are mystical and communal in spirit, in contrast to the legalism and institutionalism of Roman Catholicism. Stress is laid upon the unity of all believers with Christ, the Head of the Church. The Community of Christ, *Sobornost,* takes the place of the Organization of Christ. Yet the Church as community is both "Orthodox" in its ideas, and infallible in its practice. Eastern Orthodoxy claims in fact to be the true Church, the authentic heir of the apostolic tradition and the ancient Church. In relationship to the state, the Orthodox Churches have been "Erastian"; they have tended to recognize the supremacy of the state, while the Roman Catholic Church has sought to dominate the state. Traditionally, Eastern Orthodoxy has been lacking in missionary spirit and has been weak in social concern. However, as stated in a preceding chapter, it has led the Christian van in liturgical brilliance.

PROTESTANTISM

The name "Protestant" is attached to all Church bodies that owe their birth to, or share in the spirit of, the Protestant Reformation of the Sixteenth Century. Most unfortunately, Protestantism, because of the term, has been associated in some minds with negation, dissent, or rejection. It is therefore important to remember that in its pristine, or root meaning, to "protest" is to "aver" to "solemnly avow," to "state as a witness." Protestantism is that Christian tradition which owes its ecclesiastical form, its confessional position, its spiritual attitude to the attempt made in the Sixteenth Century to give a more adequate expression to Christianity than that which was current at the time. The great Protestant reformers rediscovered the Bible as the supreme source of truth and an abiding fountain of life. They stressed the doctrine of Justification by Faith, the Priesthood of all Believers, and, in varying degrees, the Sovereign Lordship of Jesus Christ over the Church, the State, and Society.

Protestant Churches can be divided into two main types. There are what may be designated *the Churches of Classical Protestantism,* and also *the Churches of Radical Protestantism.*

CLASSICAL PROTESTANTISM

The Churches of *Classical Protestantism* are the Lutheran, the Reformed, and the Anglican Churches. Apart from what each of these Communions has in common, through sharing in the waters of New Testament Christianity that welled forth at the time of the Reformation, each has a distinctive trait which defines it as a Church and marks it off from sister Churches.

Anglican, or Protestant Episcopal Churches, as they are called in the United States, stand for what may be called a *mediating* view of the Church. The Church is regarded as an extension of the Incarnation, the medium through which Christ becomes related to man. Because of what it has in common with the pre-Reformation Christian tradition in ecclesiastical claim, episcopal government, and liturgical form, and with sister Protestant Churches in its evangelical emphasis, the Anglican Communion has regarded itself as being called to mediate between Churches which stress their being "Catholic" and those which stress their being "evangelical." Anglicans have shown an extraordinary capacity for inclusiveness. They give full status within their ranks to High Churchmen called Anglo-Catholics, to Evangelicals, who give centrality to the Gospel, and to Modernists, who challenge some of the basic tenets of the Christian religion. It is an acknowledged fact that Anglican clergymen and Anglican laymen have given pioneering leadership in the Ecumenical Movement. Symbols of that leadership are two revered figures whose names we have had occasion to mention in earlier chapters, William Temple and J. H. Oldham. To which may be added the name of the father of "Faith and Order," Bishop Brent, of the Protestant Episcopal Church in the U. S. A.

The *Lutheran* Communion, which has the largest membership of any of the Churches of the Reformation, represents what might be designated the *sanctuary* view of the Church. Churchly reality has centered in the sacred edifice which is the home of the Word and the sacraments, the place where the Word is preached and the sacraments are administered. To be truly Christian in the Lutheran tradition has centered in the loyal attendance of members upon sanctuary services. Lutherans have not in general been encouraged to carry their faith into the affairs of state, to challenge government policies, or to orient public relations. Lutheranism has been marked by detachment from the secular order. Doctrine has occupied a place of supreme importance, but liturgical forms and organizational structure have never been regarded as absolutes. Following World War II, Lutherans have moved into the *oikoumenē* as never before. They have organized the Lutheran World Federation and have taken an increasingly active part in the Ecumenical Movement. The present chairman of the Central Committee of the World Council of Churches is a distinguished American Lutheran, Dr. Franklin Clark Fry, who is also President of the Lutheran World Federation.

The *Reformed* tradition in Protestantism is represented by Churches which are variously called "Reformed" or "Presbyterian." Central in this tradition are the names of the Frenchman, John Calvin, and the Swiss, Ulrich Zwingli. In the English-speaking world, where Presbyterian Churches predominate in numbers and influence over Reformed Churches, the great historic names are those of John Knox and John Witherspoon. The view of the Church that has dominated thought and life in the Reformed tradition as a whole may be designated the *instrumental* view. The Church has been regarded, to use Calvin's phrase, as the "instrument of God's Glory," the organ through which God has carried on His eternal purpose in Christ for the world. It can never be an end in itself. The Church, therefore, must not pass its life in detachment from the world, but be active within it; for the world is "the theater of God's glory" where God carries on His work. "Truth is in order to goodness," said John Witherspoon, who was the central figure in American Presbyterianism, when the United States became an independent nation. Christian goodness, Witherspoon declared, must be expressed in the secular order as well as in the religious order, in the direction of public affairs as well as in the direction of Church affairs. Churches in the Reformed tradition have, with some minor exceptions, been consistently "ecumenical" in outlook, in the spirit of Calvin, who abhorred schism and longed for the restoration of unity in the Church. The World Alliance of Reformed Churches, organized in 1876, was the first attempt in the Protestant world to draw together the Churches belonging to a single Confession. It is not insignificant, moreover, that the first General Secretary of the World Council of Churches is a distinguished Reformed Churchman from Holland, Dr. W. A. Visser 't Hooft, and also that the first General Secretary of the National Council of Churches in the U. S. A. was an eminent Presbyterian, Dr. Samuel McCrea Cavert.

THE CHURCHES OF RADICAL PROTESTANTISM

The Protestant Churches to which the term "radical" is applied, represent Churches whose founders severed their connection with existing Protestant Churches because of a "radical" disagreement with them on matters of Christian doctrine, Church discipline, or Church organization. Emphasis was laid upon something which was regarded as so important that loyalty to it warranted, and even demanded, a break with the Mother Church and the organization of a new Church body. Thus came into being Baptists, who as Anabaptists antedated the Reformation, Congregationalists, Methodists, Disciples of Christ, the Society of Friends (called also Quakers), and Pentecostals. For all these Churches, or Christian groups, to be loyally Christian, to be "in very deed the Church," had nothing whatever to do with the continuation of a mere ecclesiastical tradition. What mattered, both in the individual and in the corporate life of Christians, was loyalty to some truth regarded as basically Christian, according to the Scriptures. Their devotion to this truth made them willing to suffer persecution and to constitute a separate Christian Community through which to carry on their witness.

Thus, *Baptists*, for example, emphasized the importance of individual conversion on the part of those baptized in infancy, and stressed the importance of Believers' Baptism as essential for true Christian witness. It was a Baptist, John Bunyan, who, while confined to prison for his faith, wrote *Pilgrim's Progress*, the greatest, as well as the most popular, religious classic outside the Bible. In the United States, Baptists belonging to several Baptist denominations constitute the most numerous Protestant Community in the country. Today, Baptist Christians are, in general, ecumenically minded and play an important part in the World Council of Churches and in the National Councils of Churches. At the same

time, the great Southern Baptist Convention, the largest Protestant
Church in the United States, is not a member of the World Council of Churches. Protestant Christians who adhere to the Baptist
principles are found today at the ecumenical poles. At one extreme are the *Plymouth Brethren,* a Baptist sect, many of whose
members, the "Close Brethren," refuse to have religious associations with any other Christian group. They consider themselves
to be the one true Church of Christ, which must be kept pure and
undefiled. At the other pole is the denomination called *The Disciples of Christ,* which is Baptist in principle, and enthusiastically
committed to inter-Church relations.

Congregationalists have been the traditional symbol of the
"gathered Church," that is, a Church Community made up of
committed Christians, a community of which the ultimate unit is
the local congregation. Congregationalists constituted the majority
of the Pilgrims who were the founding fathers of the United
States. They played a decisive role in the early history, cultural
and political, of the American nation. The great universities of
Harvard and Yale were founded by Congregationalists. The chairman of the Department of Faith and Order of the World Council
of Churches, which held its third world gathering in Montreal,
Canada, during July 1963, is a distinguished churchman and
scholar, Dr. Douglas Horton, who was, until recently, Dean of
the School of Divinity of Harvard University. An historic fact,
also to be remembered, is that the Unitarian Churches, which are
not related to the Ecumenical Movement, because they cannot
"accept Jesus Christ as God and Savior," were in their origin, an
offshoot of Congregationalism.

Methodism, which had its birth in the thought and witness of
the famous Anglican brothers, John and Charles Wesley, represents today one of the great spiritual forces in the Protestant
family of Churches, and in the Ecumenical Movement as a whole.
Originating in the emphasis laid by the Wesleys on the *witness
and sanctifying work of the Holy Spirit* in the life of the Christian
believer, Methodism, through its "camp meetings" and "circuit
riders," won the American frontier more successfully than the
Episcopalians and Presbyterians in the early years of the Republic. Methodist fervor and geniality captivated the hearts of lonely

frontiersmen who were left unmoved by theological dogmatism and cold religious formalism. In more recent times, American Methodists, who constitute the overwhelming majority of Methodists throughout the world, have reacted against religious subjectivity and have transferred their zeal and chief emphasis from the life of the soul to the life of society. Many Methodists have given outstanding leadership in the achievement of social reform and the betterment of human relations. Symbols of the two poles of Methodism, which are by no means mutually exclusive, are E. Stanley Jones and his Ashrams, and G. Bromley Oxnam and his historic encounter for human rights with the Un-American Activities Committee. But both men have been outstanding ecumenists. Jones has been a vigorous advocate of the Federal Union of Churches, while Oxnam was one of the Presidents of the World Council of Churches. Today *The Methodist Church* in the United States has a membership of over ten million.

The *Society of Friends,* which has eschewed the use of the term "Church," is associated with the name of the Englishman, George Fox, the first Quaker. The Society places emphasis upon the "Inner Light." Quaker gatherings are associated with the Worship of Silence, and with spontaneous, unprogrammed, utterance inspired by the Spirit. Members of the Society of Friends have given leadership in scholarly pursuits, especially in the study of mysticism and the Inner Life. They have taken the lead in movements for social justice and world peace, and for the general betterment of human relations. They have emphasized the centrality of personal commitment and true community in everything that presumes to be Christian. Scholarship and sainthood will continue to be associated with the names of Rufus Jones, Douglas Steere, and Elton Trueblood.

Pentecostal Protestants constitute a worldwide, though highly diversified fellowship, consisting of many groups bearing different names of which the best known is "The Assemblies of God." One of the most significant happenings at the Third Assembly of the World Council of Churches in New Delhi, India, was the incorporation into the Council of two Pentecostal Churches from Chile.

The Pentecostal Movement, whose beginnings go back to the early years of the present century, is becoming a growing force in contemporary Christianity, especially in the lands of the "younger" Churches. There are areas, especially Latin America, where Pentecostal Christians are increasing in numbers more rapidly than the membership of the so-called historical Churches, whether Roman Catholic or Protestant. They constitute, moreover, the largest single group of Protestant Christians in that great region where there are today some ten million Protestants.

Pentecostalism represents the rediscovery of the Holy Spirit as a reality in the life of the Church and in the lives of Christians. Despite all the aberrations that may be attached to it in certain places, neo-Pentecostalism is a rebirth of primitive, First-Century Christianity. Protestants who glory in belonging to Classical or Radical Christianity will look down their noses at Pentecostal Christianity only at their peril. For this is a phenomenon of God's springtime. Ecstatic utterance, "speaking with tongues" (glossolalia), has begun to sound in the lives of sober and well-balanced people in university circles, in ministerial groups belonging to the historical Churches, as well as among downtrodden masses in Asia, Africa, and Latin America. It is a symbol of the fact that the manifestations of the Spirit are not limited to the formulation of sound doctrine, to the development of liturgical worship, or to the creation of Church order. Moreover, the working of the Spirit begins now, as it began in the origins in the Christian faith, in the lives of individual people. The beginnings may be crude, just as the beginnings of man's biological birth are crude. But here, according to every contemporary evidence, is the beginning of new life. And let me repeat what I have often said: Uncouth life is better than aesthetic death.

The advent of Pentecostalism in contemporary Christianity and the entrance of two small Pentecostal Churches into the ecumenical fellowship are symbolic facts. What lies at the heart of the Pentecostal movement of today must be given due attention by all Christians who are concerned about Christian unity, and who would help the Churches to fulfill their *unitive function*. One of the significant moments in my personal life in recent years was when I first became acquainted with the world Pentecostal leader, David du Plessis; one of the most significant moments in his life was when I subsequently introduced him to the Ecumenical Movement.

MANIFESTATIONS OF CHRISTIAN UNITY

Christians may differ on questions relating to the nature of the Church, but they are in general agreement that the Christian Church, however unity may be interpreted, is *one* in Christ. It is consequently under obligation to manifest its unity in Him. When the question arises as to the concrete mandate which calls the Church to manifest its essential oneness, the words of Christ Himself in the great prayer recorded in the Fourth Gospel are of classical importance. These words are: "I do not pray for these only [His apostles], but also for those who believe in me through their word, that they may all be one; even as Thou, Father, art in me, and I in Thee, that they also may be in Us, so that the world may believe that Thou has sent me. The glory which Thou hast given me I have given to them, that they may be one, even as We are one" (John 17:22).

Our Lord, in contemplating the great ecumenical family of faith that was to come into being as a result of apostolic witness, prays that the unity among Christians be patterned upon the unity that exists between Him and His Father, and, also, that the outward manifestation of this unity in history be conducive to convincing the world of the God-given mission of the Son. Here is unity not only in being, but in action. Ontology is clearly involved, but still more, *soteriology*. The Son is dynamically related to the Father, and the Father to the Son, within the context of God's overarching purpose of reconciliation in Christ. Oneness, unity among Christians must, therefore, express the dynamism that characterizes relations within the Godhead. Such unity must be validated by the response of society to the mission of the Church. God-like unity is, therefore, unity in mission. True Christian unity is the *fruit* of mission and should never cease to be the *source* of mission.

In this perspective let us consider a variety of representative projects in which Christian Churches have succeeded in achieving not only a spirit of unity, but the reality of Church union.

The present century has witnessed an increasing number of organic unions among the members of the Protestant family of Churches. The centrifugal movement that had marked Protestant history since the Reformation became centripetal. Concrete objectives were pursued, whether to blot out old differences that no longer had significance, or to face new frontiers that demanded a united approach.

The years of my childhood and youth in Scotland were marked by both schism and reunion. The year 1893 was darkened by schism; the year 1900 gleamed with the radiance of reunion. That year there came into being the United Free Church of Scotland. In this Church were joined together the Free Church of Scotland, which in 1843 had severed its connection with the Established Church in loyalty to the principle of the Church's freedom from state control, and the United Presbyterian Church, which had consistently opposed any connection whatever between Church and State. A quarter of a century later, in 1929, the United Free Church was reunited with the Established Church of Scotland. The reunion was based upon the understanding that the State, while giving special recognition to the historic Church of the Scottish Reformation, would not exercise the slightest authority over it and would grant also the most complete religious freedom to all Churches and to all people in Scotland. Scottish Presbyterianism is still unhappily divided, but some "unhappy divisions" that marred the reality and effectiveness of Christian witness through Presbyterians in Scotland have been removed.

Church unions, or reunions, of this type, *between Churches belonging to the same Confessional family*, have been numerous in recent years in different parts of the world. In the western world, several important reunions of this kind may be mentioned. The British Methodist Union was constituted in 1932. Soon thereafter American Methodism brought to an end the tragic rift (a result of the Civil War) between Methodists living in the northern and southern states. The Methodist Church, as it now exists, has succeeded in transcending a division caused by a political and military clash. It is most unfortunate, however, that neither Presbyterians nor Baptists in the U. S. A. have succeeded in restoring the ecclesiastical unity that became shattered by warfare in the mid-Nineteenth Century. The reason for this unhappy failure is that in both Church families, new factors of a sociological character have contributed to prevent reunion. On the other hand, two historic Presbyterian denominations in the United States have succeeded in recent years in transcending traditional differences of a purely religious character that had kept them apart. In 1958, they became the United Presbyterian Church in the U. S. A., constituting the largest single denomination in World Presbyterianism.

These are illustrations of family consolidations that have been taking place within Protestant Communions throughout the world. It must be admitted, at the same time, that denominational family relations have still a long way to go before they achieve the oneness that is called for by their common heritage of faith and by the current needs of the society which they should serve in unison.

Other instances there are in which the *confrontation of a common problem* has led to the organic union of Churches of different denominational backgrounds. A striking example of this type of Church union is *The United Church of Canada*. The awareness that, unless their Churches united, they might lose the country's western frontier, as well as fail to grapple adequately with the problems of Canadian society, led to the union of Methodist, Congregational, and Presbyterian Churches. A considerable number of Presbyterian congregations, however, abstained, for diverse reasons, from entering the union; they constitute today *The Presbyterian Church in Canada*. The uniqueness of the United Church of Canada, among the Churches of the world, lies in the fact that it represents the first successful attempt to unite several different ecclesiastical traditions in a single unified Church structure. It is no less significant, as has been already indicated, that this Church union was primarily the creation of a common concern to be "in very deed the Church," amid the challenges of a changing society. It was inspired by the necessity of missionary witness, and not by the logic of ecclesiological discussion. It was a Church born on the Road and not in the cloister.

The most outstanding example, however, of a Church body being formed by the union of Churches of diverse denominational backgrounds is the Church of South India. The urgent need for fragmented sectors of the "Household of God," all of them foreign to traditional Christianity in India and all confronted with resurgent Indian faiths, to constitute a single united Church, led to the creation of the great new denomination just named. Episcopalians, Methodists, Congregationalists, Presbyterians, and Reformed all combined to form the Church of South India. Missions and national Churches were fused. Missionaries and Indian pastors became the servants of one Church. The liturgy of the new Church reflects the influence of the Indian spirit when renewed by the Gospel of Christ and controlled by the Holy Spirit. Its creedal basis enshrines the great verities of the Faith. It contains emphases and formulations inspired by the doctrinal statements of the uniting Churches.

The new Church showed wisdom in leaving certain questions of doctrine and policy open for subsequent consideration, after its members had spent time together on their pilgrim-crusading journey. The outstandingly important thing was to bear witness to oneness in Christ, and to summon the Church and its members to dedicate their all to the Christian cause in India. A bishop of the Church of South India may be Indian or foreign, provided the latter, as was remarked to me in Bangalore, has "an Indian heart!" Another outstanding feature of this Church is that, for the first time in history, a union was constituted between Episcopal and non-Episcopal Communions. It now remains to be seen whether the Church of South India will be accorded full ecclesiastical status by the next Lambeth Conference, and whether bishops of the Church, who have not been ordained by Anglican hands, will be regarded as having an authentic place in the Apostolic Succession. It should be remarked that the projected union of Churches in North India, after the model of the Church of South India, is at present being delayed by difficulties with the Anglican Communion on the question of ordination.

REPRESENTATIVE APPROACHES TO CHRISTIAN UNITY

Having considered certain representative types of Church union, we will now give our attention to some representative approaches to Christian unity.

THE DRAMATIC APPROACH TO UNITY

We begin with what I venture to call the *dramatic approach.* This approach centers in personalities who, by a striking gesture at a moment when a cherished proposal can be assured of wide publicity, succeed in winning sympathetic attention for their idea. This approach was the one utilized by two distinguished clergymen, one a United Presbyterian, the other an Episcopalian, when, in a dramatic setting, they called upon their two denominations to invite The Methodist Church and the United Church of Christ in the U. S. A. to enter into discussions with a view to Church union between the four Churches. The United Church of Christ had been constituted several years before by a union of the Congregational Church and the Evangelical and Reformed Church.

This proposal made an unprecedented impact upon the public mind in the United States, because of the combination of dramatic circumstances that accompanied its nationwide and worldwide announcement. The elements of high drama may be described thus: Dr. Eugene Carson Blake, the stated clerk, that is, the chief permanent officer, of the General Assembly of the United Presbyterian Church in the U. S. A., made the proposal referred to in a carefully prepared sermon that he delivered in 1960 at the Episcopal Cathedral of San Francisco. He did so in the presence of the Bishop of California, Dr. James A. Pike, who, having been made aware of the proposal to be made, gave it his full endorsement immediately following the sermon's delivery. The setting for such a pronouncement was thus very dramatic.

No less dramatic were the attendant circumstances. The National Council of Churches of Christ in the U. S. A., of which Dr. Blake was a former president and a continuing member, was holding its triennial meeting in San Francisco during the same week, but its members were unaware of what was coming. The officers and general constituency of the four Churches involved received their first notification of the Church union proposal in the secular press. The impression received by most readers, was that, for the first time in American Church history, a serious proposal was being made for Church union. It was deduced that the Churches immediately concerned, not having themselves officially sponsored such a proposal, were now being told, as they should be told, what to do.

The Churches were clearly on the spot. For Churchmen to be unresponsive to the "Blake-Pike Proposal," about which everyone was talking, could only give the impression that they were indifferent or reactionary. So there came into being "The Consultation on Church Union." The four Churches that were mentioned in the original proposal have now become six. Representatives of the Methodist Church, the Protestant Episcopal Church, the United Presbyterian Church, U. S. A., now sit down with colleagues from the United Church of Christ, the Evangelical United Brethren Church and the Christian Church (Disciples of Christ). In no part of the world, and at no time in Protestant history, have so many Churches, so diversified in their background, met together officially as a group to consider becoming a single ecclesiastical unit. This is significant and encouraging. There is no doubt, moreover, that the *Consultation on Church Union* owes its existence and its particular character to the original *drama* that brought it into being.

But now a serious question arises. How can the *Dramatic* become the *Epic*? How can an event that had its origin in Drama become an integral and creative part of ongoing history? How can personalities be transformed into abiding principles that determine policy and shape destiny? Let me set the dramatic proposal of two eminent and admired churchmen into the perspective in which its status may be duly appraised.

First, it was an unhappy circumstance that Methodist leaders were not apprised in advance of the projected proposal regarding a union in which their church would constitute by far the largest group. Their ignorance was all the more unfortunate in view of the fact that a distinguished Methodist bishop, now retired, though intensely active, Dr. Ivan Lee Holt, had given many years of his life to the promotion of a scheme of Church union. Dr. Holt had been chairman of what was known as the Greenwich Group. It consisted of the representatives of eight Protestant Churches in America, including Episcopalians and Presbyterians, who had actually drafted a scheme of union.[1] Human nature being what it is, and the proprieties of ecclesiastical relationship being what they are, it was not to be unexpected that Methodist Churchmen should feel wounded and resentful when they learned suddenly through

[1] This scheme, under the title *A Plan for a United Church in the United States*, was presented to the Churches for study in 1953.

the public press of the dramatic proposal that had been addressed to their Church. Subsequent happenings would seem to indicate that a serious psychological and ecclesiastical error had been made in the method adopted to create what is now known as the *Consultation on Church Union.*

Second, for a number of years, beginning in 1938, official representatives of the Presbyterian Church, U. S. A. and the Protestant Episcopal Church had been negotiating the organic union of their two Communions. A document entitled "Proposals Looking Toward Organic Union" was drafted for submission to the governing bodies of both Churches. The document in question was in three parts: (1) Things Believed in Common. (2) Things that Might Be Undertaken in Common. (3) The Proposed Concordat. "The Proposed Concordat" began as follows: "The immediate purpose of this agreement is to provide means whereby each Church may, wherever it seems locally desirable, assume pastoral charge of the members of the other Church, and offer them the privilege of The Holy Communion, thus establishing one congregation."

But high hopes were blasted. The Episcopal Triennial Convention, which convened shortly after the "Proposals Looking Toward Organic Union" were approved by the joint committee of the two Churches, unexpectedly rejected the "Proposals," due to the preponderant influence of "High Churchmen." These rejected the suggestion that Presbyterians and Episcopalians should be free to celebrate the Lord's Supper in one another's Churches, and that each Church should recognize the validity of ministerial ordination as practiced by the other. This set back the movement toward union between these two bodies. As a member of the Joint Committee I vividly recall the shock sustained by my fellow members and myself when the Episcopal action became known.

The work which had been carried on by the Greenwich Conference since 1949 was thus seriously shaken. Presbyterians now began to concentrate their attention, so far as Church union was concerned, upon a plan of union between Churches belonging to the Presbyterian and Reformed family. This led eventually to the union consummated in 1958 between the Presbyterian Church, U. S. A. and the United Presbyterian Church in America. There came into being the United Presbyterian Church, U. S. A. The Presbyterian Church, U. S., popularly known as the Southern

Presbyterian Church, had been a party to the union negotiations. Unfortunately, however, for reasons largely sociological, which, in potent Church circles, were rationalized theologically, that beloved denomination did not enter into the union of 1958. Yet, the longing for Presbyterian reunion continues to be deep and eager among the descendants of men and women whose Church fellowship was broken by the Civil War.

Third, it was a tragic misfortune that the dramatic proposal of San Francisco took no cognizance whatever of the epic problem of American Presbyterianism. It ignored the guidepost of "manlikeness," as well as the "incarnational principle." Human nature, even redeemed human nature, being what it is, and Presbyterians, Southern as well as Northern, being what they are, that is, committed together to the Ecumenical Movement and engaged together in co-operative activity in all the countries where their missionaries are at work, the exclusion of the South Presbyterian Church from any gesture looking towards Church union could not fail to be a devastating blow to the sensitivity of fellow Churchmen, and to the harmony of ecclesiastical relations. These are sores which drama can create but which it cannot cure. The only way in which situations of this kind can be avoided in the Ecumenical Movement and in Church relations in general, is that the exercise of the dramatic, and, where other Churches are concerned, the role of Church officers, shall be confined within boundaries whose frontiers are constitutionally determined.

Fourth, the Consultation on Church Union has now become related, so far as Presbyterians are concerned, to the Church's Permanent Committee on Inter-Church Relations. The success of this able and dedicated group will be intimately related to the amount of realistic, creative study which its members find possible to devote to the role of the Church and the fulfillment of its mission in contemporary America and the world. For unity that is worthily Christian and truly churchly is the fruit of a vision of what it means for the Church to be "in very deed the Church," an instrument which God can use to carry out His purpose in the Eternal Christ for the redemption of man and the coming of His own Kingdom. This is important because of the tragic paradox that, in certain circumstances, the pursuit of unity can be mere escape from reality and from concern about the Church's mission. Church unions can be formed, which, because of an exclusive concern to transcend or heal historical differences between the bodies concerned, may prove discontinuous with the Eternal and become irrelevant to the contemporary.

Let it be recognized at the same time that the *dramatic* has a very real and legitimate role to play in the pursuit of Christian unity. Classically dramatic and historically creative was the call of Pope John XXIII to non-Roman Churches to send representatives, in the capacity of observers, to the Second Vatican Council. In addressing this call to "separated brethren," the Pope did what he, and he alone, had a right to do, because of his ecclesiastical status in his own Communion. But the Hierarch with the greatest personal authority in Christian history was careful to take members of his Church's Curia into his confidence. In this way, his appeal, when heralded abroad and hailed as an unprecedented event in history, went forth with full ecclesiastical approbation and with all the perfume of proprieties fulfilled.

While no one can foretell the future of Roman Catholic-Protestant relations, history will assuredly record that the dramatic gesture of the late, saintly and ecumenically spirited Pontiff, will mark the beginning of a new Christian epic. It is cause for rejoicing that the dialogue between Protestants and Roman Catholics, which has been taking place for the past decade in many parts of the world, should have received such dramatic approval. Let us also give thanks to God, the Holy Spirit, that Pope Paul VI has quietly sanctioned the reconvening, under the same conditions, of the Second Vatican Council. In the hands of the Spirit is the question whether, at the close of the Council, there will be left, as part of its legacy to the Church Universal, a visible means whereby, with the necessary sanctions, Christians of the three great traditions may meet to talk and pray together. Let Christians await the unfolding of the epic of unity, as under the sole Lordship of Christ, they face together Yesterday, Today, and Tomorrow.[2]

[2] See Hans Küng, *The Council Reform and Reunion* (New York: Sheed & Ward, 1962) and *The Council in Action* (Reflections on the Second Vatican Council).

THE CONCILIAR APPROACH TO UNITY

A true pioneer on the road to unity has been *conciliar unity,* which is unity expressed in the formation and work of Christian councils, local, national, regional, and ecumenical.

Of particular significance has been the work of the councils, some thirty-five in number, which together composed the *International Missionary Council.* These councils, which continue to exist, though perchance with different names and under different ecumenical auspices, came into being because of a desire on the part of Christian organizations to confer together and, where possible, co-operate together, in the fulfillment of the Church's mission. Integrated in these councils were the representatives of national Churches, missionary societies of all types, Bible societies, and in some places the representatives of Y.M.C.A.'s and Y.W.C.A.'s. The International Missionary Council, which that great Christian statesman, John R. Mott organized in 1921 to be the center of consultation on missionary matters (but not for the control of missions or the determination of their policy) played a truly creative role for forty years in the co-ordination of missionary activity, in the development of Christian literature, and in the formulation of a theology of mission. The council, in the course of its history, held epoch-making conferences in Jerusalem in 1928, Madras (India) in 1938, in Whitby (Canada) in 1947, Willingen (Germany) in 1952, and Accra (Ghana) in 1957. It became finally integrated into the World Council of Churches at New Delhi, India during December 1961. Today the historic I.M.C. is The Division of World Mission and Evangelism of the World Council of Churches.

Representatives of national councils of Churches make up the National Council of Churches of Christ in the United States of America. This body is integrated by thirty-six of the major Protestant and Orthodox Churches in the U. S. A. It represents a constituency of some thirty-six million Church members, and is, organizationally speaking, that is, in terms of the complexity of its work and the number of its officers, the largest co-operative enterprise in contemporary Christianity. It is the successor to what was called the Federal Council of the Churches of Christ in America, which in 1951 became integrated with seven other co-operative Church enterprises to form The National Council of Churches.

The best known, and also the most ecumenical of the conciliar approaches to unity, is the World Council of Churches. Founded in 1948 in the City of Amsterdam, Holland, through the integration of the two bodies, the Conference on Life and Work and the Conference on Faith and Order, and in "association" with the International Missionary Council, the W.C.C. embraces some two hundred Protestant and Orthodox Churches. With headquarters in Geneva, the World Council of Churches, through its several divisions and departments, and the Churches' Commission on International Affairs, which functions under its auspices, exercises a profound influence upon the leadership of its component bodies in all that relates to the quest for Christian unity. Each world gathering held under its auspices—the Amsterdam Assembly in 1948, the Evanston Assembly in 1954, and the New Delhi Assembly in 1961—was a landmark in the manifestation of ecumenical fellowship. They expressed the determination of the component members to stay together and to work together, under the supreme leadership of Jesus Christ, who is "God and Savior," the Hope of the World, and the Light of the World. Repudiating the idea that it is a super-Church or aspires to be one, forbidden by its constitution from being an agency to promote organic union among its member Churches, and functioning as a literal microcosm of Churchly reality outside the Roman Communion, the World Council of Churches has become at once the symbol and the dynamic center of efforts directed towards the visible expression of the Church's oneness in Christ. There is not the slightest doubt that the Council has become the leading contemporary symbol of Christian unity.

One of the major factors in bringing about a changed attitude towards the Ecumenical Movement on the part of the conservative Roman Curia, apart from the attitude of Christian love revealed by John XXIII and others like him, has been the recognition of the World Council of Churches as a "great new fact." The Church of Rome, aware of the serious situation in which it finds itself in many parts of the world, could ignore the Ecumenical Movement only at its peril. Whether the Church's leadership will acknowledge it or not, a new ecclesiological problem has been created for the Roman Catholic Church. In the meantime, the Churches that compose the W.C.C. are confronted with an analogous question. Should conciliar unity be regarded as the highest visible expression of Christian unity which it is proper, or possible, for our diversified Church family to expect in history? This is not a new question, but, because of circumstances, it is becoming an increasingly real question, and one which is in urgent need of an answer. In ultimate terms, when does a Church belong to the true Church? What constitutes true Christian unity? When and how do different Churches become truly united? What is the ecumenical goal for the Churches of the world? These questions have been already raised in varying contexts in the course of this book, and certain criteria have been laid down. There will be occasion to return, in due course, to this basic matter. In the meantime, let us consider some other ways in which Christian unity is being pursued in our time.

THE CONFESSIONAL APPROACH TO UNITY

One of the phenomena of the Ecumenical Movement is that, simultaneously with the development of the World Council of Churches, there is being established an ever closer and more dynamic bond of relationship between the Churches in different parts of the world that have a common Confessional origin. Reference has been made in another connection to this development, which began with the creation of the World Alliance of Reformed Churches in 1875, and which paradoxically has grown in strength and significance since the organization of the World Council of Churches. The dominant figure in the council, outside its secretariat, is the chairman of the Central Committee, Dr. Franklin Clark Fry. Dr. Fry was until 1963 the president of the Lutheran World Federation, which is the largest and most powerful of the World Confessional bodies. The present writer was president of the World Presbyterian Alliance during part of the time that he occupied the chairmanship of the International Missionary Council.

What is happening? How do we interpret the Confessional resurgence that marks our time? As one who has been involved in this movement and who is deeply concerned regarding its contribution to ecumenical unity, let me crystallize some reflections that I have made from time to time in diverse circles of the Church Universal. The truth is this. The reborn sense of the Church, together with the new aspiration towards Christian unity, has awakened in the several Confessional groups a fresh interest in their own religious heritage. Each Confession begins to explore its historic roots in quest of the "tradition" that gave it birth. It wishes to be clear regarding its own essential character and witness. It desires to have a clear conception of the contribution which it may be called upon to make to the Church Universal. The realization grows that a Christian cannot belong to the Church in general, any more than he can belong to the human race in general or have a mere general relationship to his own country. A person becomes truly and richly human only through life in a family circle, in a community, in a nation. So, too, a Christian is introduced into the fullness of Christ through a specific Church tradition. But this tradition he need not treat idolatrously as the sole empirical expression of the one true Church. He should regard it, rather, as a providential instrument through which he was introduced to the Christian faith and nourished in the Christian life.

The new Confessionalism is thus different from the old. There is no disposition on the part of Anglicans, Baptists, Congregationalists, Lutherans, Methodists, or Presbyterians to absolutize their respective confessional structures or loyalties. No single Protestant Confession believes that it represents the one and only Church of Christ, the *Una Sancta*. Each does believe, however, that it enshrines in its heritage something unique that is also authentically Christian. It is precisely this "something" that each Confession should make its own specific contribution to the ecumenical treasure house of Christian faith and life, to the one Church of Christ, for the fulfillment of its world mission. Even the leadership of the Roman Catholic Church begins to recognize that it has much to learn from the Churches of the Reformation.

During the present decade, a leading publishing house in the United States, having become intuitively aware of the Confessional resurgence and desire of clergy and laity alike to know more

about their own and other Church traditions, has been issuing the
"Way of Life" series.[3] Each volume has been written by a leading
exponent of his own tradition. The series began in 1957 with *The
Episcopal Way of Life.* In 1962 appeared *The Catholic Way of
Life.* In the United Kingdom equally significant volumes have
been published.[4]

Whither bound? The Confessional Movement could conceivably
develop in such a way as to reduce the World Council of Churches
to a venerated ecclesiastical façade. It could prevent unions taking
place between the "younger" Churches in the traditional mission
fields of the world, and, for that matter, between "older" Churches
in new situations. On the other hand, the Confessional Movement,
if wisely directed, can and should enrich the Ecumenical Movement. Our hope and prayer is this. Under the guidance of the
Holy Spirit, let all the Christian Confessions re-examine themselves in the light of Holy Scripture, in the light of Christian
history, in the light of all the Christian Confessions and traditions,
and in the light of the challenge to Christianity and the Church
in the world of our time. By doing so, each Confession may discern what it has in its heritage that is authentically Christian and
legitimately unique. Sloughing off those elements in its thought
and life which, however sacred, may be no more than accretions
produced by ecclesiastical conceit, or perchance by human blind-
ness and prejudice, let each Church, Confession, and Tradition
bring the pure Christian gold into the storehouse of the one Faith,
for the mission of the one Church, and for the glory of the one
Lord.

In the ranks of the "younger" Churches, great concern has become manifest with regard to the menace of Confessionalism to
the unity and freedom of the Church in non-Christian lands. Preceding the meeting of the Third General Assembly of the W.C.C.
in New Delhi, 1961, representatives of the Asian Churches gathered together in Bangalore. They expressed themselves thus, on
the Confessional issue:

> The desire of a Church to serve its nation and people is
> legitimate and necessary. World Confessional ties may be

---

[3] Prentice-Hall, Inc., Englewood Cliffs, N. J.
[4] The *Star* books.

vitally useful to enable a Church to serve without allowing the demands of a nation to dominate its life—*but*—however good the intention, it seems that the expression of World Confessionalism, in increasingly complex institutional structures, results in the perpetuation and reinforcement of patterns of paternalism and continued exercise of control.

This concern of the Asian Churches began to become a concern of the present writer during a sojourn in Asian lands in 1949. He subsequently raised the delicate Confessional issue with officers of the World Council of Churches—with Reformed Churchmen at two world gatherings of the Alliance of Reformed and Presbyterian Churches, and also at a private gathering of fellow presidents of World Confessional bodies. He is happy and proud to be able to report that, so far as the World Presbyterian Alliance is concerned, nothing will be left undone to set the interests of the Church Universal in every place above Confessional craving for world status. An action taken at Basle, Switzerland, in 1951, by the executive committee of the Alliance, has become foundational, insofar as concerns the outlook and attitude of the worldwide family of Reformed Churches. In this document we read:

> It is the highest glory of the Reformed tradition to maintain the vision and viewpoint of the Church Universal, seeking continually its welfare and unity, in accordance with the mind of Jesus Christ, the Head of the Church, and through the power of the Holy Spirit who indwells the Church . . . Presbyterians want to bring as their contribution to the Ecumenical Movement a Presbyterianism which has been scrutinized by the eyes of Christ and purified by the Holy Spirit. . . . It is the true glory of this tradition to seek and promote Christian solidarity and also Church union when the local or national situation demands it. . . . If the great world denominations, the Reformed Churches among them, pursue denominational pre-eminence, they will betray Jesus Christ.[5]

THE REGIONAL APPROACH TO UNITY

We have just considered an approach to Christian unity that is inspired by the existence among Christians in different parts of

[5] "The World Presbyterian Alliance in the Present Ecumenical Situation," *The Reformed and Presbyterian World*, September, 1951.

the world of traditional beliefs, practices, and forms of Church organization which they hold in common. We move now to consider a bond of unity which is not ecclesiological but *sociological*. It consists in the awareness on the part of people in a given area that they belong together in the living present. Any attempt to create a Christian structure to which "regionally" minded people are invited to belong, and which is designed to promote the unity and mission of the Church in that "region," must take cognizance of the basic realities that combine to make the area in question what it is, and the people who inhabit it what they are, or feel themselves to be.

A *region* in a country or a continent differs basically from a *section*. The latter is determined exclusively by physical features. It lies to the north or to the south, to the east or to the west of a given point; it is mountainous or forest country; it is made up of valleys or occupies a wide plateau. A region, on the other hand, while it has a physical basis so far as the location and size, the character and the contours of the ground, are concerned, is a unity. Regional unity is created by the fact that the people who dwell within the physical boundaries of the region are united by a common history, common interests, common problems, common aspirations, and, perchance, by a common outlook. The people may be disunited in many ways, but they recognize that they belong together and must work out co-operatively a common destiny. It might be observed that, while a mountain range is a creator of regions, as in the case of the Rockies and the Himalayas, and thus becomes a natural and inevitable boundary between regions, this is not normally true of a river. A river is usually the life of a region and not a dividing boundary. When a river divides or is accepted as dividing, a monstrosity is created in the natural life of mankind. All this has a bearing upon the approach which the Church should make to the problem of Christian unity and to the fulfillment of Christian mission within a natural region. Let me offer two illustrations of regional reality that challenge a united approach on the part of Christian Churches. One of these regions is Metropolitan New York, the other is East Asia.

Metropolitan New York is a complex urban and suburban region that occupies parts of three American states, New York, Connecticut, and New Jersey. Within an area highly diversified racially, culturally, and industrially, through which flows the Hudson River, there exists a very definite regionalism so far as life and its great issues are concerned. The northern boundary of this region extends to the town of Poughkeepsie, seventy miles up the Hudson; its southern boundary is the City of Trenton, the capital of New Jersey, on the bank of the Delaware River. This populous and highly complex area constitutes, in sociological terms, a single region, the complex phases of whose life are all interwoven. For a long period, because of a law which forbids the City of New York from crossing the Hudson, the shipping situation in the world's leading seaport was hopelessly confused. To meet this situation, there was created the Port of New York Authority in which was vested the power to deal with all problems relating to shipping on both the New York and the New Jersey sides of the river. Commercial intelligence overcame the problem created by political boundaries and sensitivities.

But while commercial intelligence succeeded in solving a secular problem in this region, Christian intelligence, as represented by the great Churches within its bounds, has not begun to confront the regional situation from the viewpoint of the unity and mission of the Christian Church. Take Presbyterianism, for example, as represented by the beloved Church to which I personally belong. This single region is under the ecclesiastical jurisdiction of three different Presbyterian synods, the Synod of New York, the Synod of New Jersey, and the Synod of New England. Each synod consists of a number of autonomous presbyteries that function within the bounds of the region in question but make no provision whatever to face regional reality as a whole from the viewpoint of the United Presbyterian Church.

There is a clear call to American denominations, individually and collectively, to take our sociologists seriously. Let them begin to make a common approach to Christian unity not exclusively from the viewpoint of the doctrine, the liturgy, and the structure of each, but from the viewpoint of the human situation within which their Church services are held and their institutions function. A decade ago, the General Assembly of the United Presbyterian Church, U. S. A., following favorable action by more than two-thirds of the Church's presbyteries, decided to confront the regional issue. It was agreed to consider the organization of synods, not within traditional political boundaries that ignore natural phenomena and human reality, but along boundaries within which people really belong together. But some influential leaders did not favor the idea, and creative action awaits a new generation which will take the assembly's action out of the archives.

Within the context of the Ecumenical Movement, and in association with the World Council of Churches, there has been organized the East Asia Christian Conference. The secretary of this group, which is representative of East Asian Churches and of missionary societies in East Asia, is Dr. D. T. Niles of Ceylon. Niles is an Asian Christian who has given eminent leadership in the Ecumenical Movement and is a strong advocate of the regional principle in the development of the Church Universal. Related to this council are Churches in Pakistan, India, Ceylon, Burma, Thailand, Malaysia, the Philippines, Indonesia, and Australia. Between all these countries there are common bonds, and they face common problems. The Churches within their bounds happily enjoy Christian leadership that is intelligent, dynamic, and Christ-centered. In their efforts to promote the cause of Christian unity, the Church leaders in East Asia have envisioned the necessity of taking into account the concrete human situation which marks their region. These men and women are convinced that national Churches and national Christian Councils are not in themselves sufficient to develop adequate and progressive Church policy within the nations they serve unless they take into account the region of which their several nations are a part. They are equally opposed, on the other hand, to having their policies determined by any organization, whether it be the World Council of Churches, or by the World Confessional bodies.

It may be of interest to observe that the regional idea in Asia received its first concrete expression in the conference which met at Bangkok in November, 1949. It was the first time that a Christian conference had met in Asia under direct Asian leadership, and at which Westerners were present only as invited guests. The conference chairman, Dr. Rajah Manikam, a distinguished Lutheran from South India, now Bishop of Tranquebar, was asked to become pastor-at-large for East Asian countries. In the course of his journeys, Manikam established a close bond between the churches of the vast region which he traversed.

There is little doubt, however, that the luminous regional idea, which was envisioned at Bangkok and was subsequently developed by the pastoral journeys of Manikam, would have succumbed before the forces of ecumenical centralization but for one providential circumstance. That circumstance was the vision and zeal of the late Charles T. Leber. Charles Leber was a dedicated ecumenist, who at the same time, was committed to the principle of granting to the "younger" Churches complete autonomy in the management of their own affairs and the shaping of the Christian mission in their own countries. Committed to the idea of regional autonomy within ecumenical harmony, Leber, with the co-operation of some like-minded spirits, and with the full support of his own mission board, the Board of Foreign Missions of the Presbyterian Church in the U. S. A., created the Asia Council on Ecumenical Mission of which an outstanding Filipino pastor Enrique C. Sobrepeña was elected chairman. That Council was viewed with concern by some ecumenical leaders. But with the support and statesmanship of Leber's distinguished successor, Dr. John Coventry Smith, and others like him, and following meetings in Thailand and Indonesia, the regional idea triumphed, and a new chapter was written in the pursuit of Christian unity. A major contemporary task of all the Christian Churches of the world is to discover and understand regional reality, and, in the light and strength of the Holy Spirit, to establish and develop within the bounds of each region the most appropriate organ of Christian unity.

THE COOPERATIVE APPROACH TO UNITY

This particular phase of the Christian pursuit of unity has been undoubtedly the most dynamic and creative. It is an ecumenical platitude, but it is gloriously true, that the Christian movement towards unity was born on the mission fields of the world. It was there that Christians, in the tradition of Bishop Brent of the Philippines, the founder of the Faith and Order Movement, became acquainted with one another across denominational boundaries. There, too, they learned to co-operate with one another in the cause of Christ and His Church. Inasmuch as obedience to Christ, in response to the love of Christ, is the central category of the Christian religion, let it never be forgotten that it is in action together on the Road that Christ's followers come to know one another and become united in love with one another. Where love and obedience are lacking among its members, no Church can be "in very deed the Church." But where Christians meet one another in love, across dividing barriers and chasms, and together obey Christ as members of the One Holy Catholic Church, there is no limit to the ecclesiastical miracles that can be accomplished.

Let God be thanked, therefore, for the Bible societies, the tract societies, the evangelistic campaigns which Christians of all denominations have sponsored and in which they have worked together, and now for the new and outstanding work of the Theological Education Fund Committee. Let Christ be praised for the number of institutions inspired by His spirit—orphanages, hospitals, schools, agricultural institutes—and for the literature, radio, and television enterprises, in which Christians, Christian missions, and Christian Churches have co-operated and continue to co-operate. Let Christians everywhere pray without ceasing that the Holy Spirit may lead all Christ's followers into those paths of co-operative service which will dispose their hearts and prepare their minds for common membership in whatever form of Church fellowship, local, national, regional, ecumenical, that He Himself may design as their Church.

The Holy Spirit has not yet revealed the ultimate historical structure for the One Church which is Christ's Body. While it is important, therefore, that Christian thought be devoted to questions relating to the true ministry, the true liturgy, the true sacraments, it is still more important that Christians of all Churches, in passionate devotion to Christ and engaged in common talks, should be united in love with one another—on the Road. For it is on the Road, and only on the Road, that the ultimate empirical pattern for the Church Universal will be revealed by the Spirit.

ISSUES THAT CONCERN UNITY

We conclude this chapter with some reflections on three major issues that deeply affect the question of Christian unity.

INSTITUTIONALISM

The first of these questions is *institutionalism*. It is the viewpoint of this book that the Christian Church is primarily Community. For that reason, the Church can be true to its nature in God's design only when it continues to maintain its communal reality, while it structures its life in such a way as to fulfill its mission. The necessary emergence of organization in the Christian Community is accompanied by the inevitable temptation of institutionalism. Church organization, whatever its form, whether it be simple or complex, can, in a great variety of ways, become an end in itself, the instrument of a church power bloc, and not the organ of the Holy Spirit. This can happen equally in the life of a Protestant sect and in the life of the Roman Communion. It can happen also in Ecumenical Councils.

The problem of institutionalism is at present receiving unprecedented attention in ecumenical circles. And a profoundly difficult problem it is proving to be, for both ecclesiastics and theologians. Sociologists and politicians, moreover, have been concentrating their gaze increasingly upon the Church in society. Certain things are clear. First: The Community of Christ must have some institutional form, in order to be itself and to do its work. But let it beware of becoming a mere religious establishment, controlled by a hierarchy or by a lay bureaucracy, and used as an organ of power. Second: Let the Church, in the expression of its life and in the fulfillment of its mission make use of all the insights and devices that the secular order can provide for the promotion of the Church's work. But let the Church and the Churches beware, in their life and relationship, of the dictatorship of "Organization Man," who uses the "noise of solemn assemblies" for objectives that run counter to the mind of Christ and the witness of His Church. Third: Let measures be taken in the Churches to secure that participation in ecumenical gatherings and discussions shall not be limited to persons hierarchically or bureaucratically chosen.

A great deal of attention is being focused at the present time upon the two major ecumenical institutions, the World Council of Churches, and the National Council of the Churches of Christ in America. Books have recently appeared, written by younger men, some of whom once held secretarial positions in the Ecumenical Movement. These books are very critical of trends in "high places," whereby policies are shaped by hierarchs and bureaucracies that perpetuate clichés, committees, and personal-

ities. Current policies, it is maintained, will not stand enlightened
scrutiny, in the perspective of what is best for the unity and
mission of the Church and of the Ecumenical Movement as a
whole. What is happening is this. The Ecumenical Movement, as
represented by the great institutions that are its symbols, and that
are the centers of discussion on all matters relating to the unity
and mission of the Church Universal, enters upon a crucial period
in its history. This is happening, moreover, at the very time that
a new attitude toward non-Roman Christians and Churches has
begun to manifest itself in Roman Catholicism.

THE ROMAN CATHOLIC CONCEPT OF UNITY

Reference has been made on a number of occasions to the
Roman Catholic concept of the Church. Whereas the official attitude of the Roman Church to other Christians and Christian
Churches has undergone a dramatic change in recent years, so
far as contacts and relations are concerned, there is no evidence
that this Communion is prepared to lower its stand on the traditional contention that it alone, as an institutional entity, is the one
and only true Church of Jesus Christ. The ecclesiastical organization, as at present constituted, is the Body of Christ. That is the
contention, a contention that is conscientiously and unequivocally
held. The new graciousness of spirit, the encouragement given to
members of the clergy to enter into dialogue with other Christians,
and to attend meetings under the auspices of other Churches, the
recognition that certain traditional policies have been unwise and
should be changed, the invitation to non-Roman Churches to
send observers to the Second Vatican Council, the rediscovery and
reinterpretation of the word "ecumenical"—all this is evidence
of a very profound and sincere change on the Roman front. On the
other hand, there is no indication that the Roman Catholic Church
would be prepared to alter its absolutist position on the Infallibil-
ity of the Pope in all matters pertaining to Christian doctrine, or
on the exaltation of the Virgin Mary to a status which, in view of
the assumption of Mary and the Fatima Cult, can with all objectivity, be described as that of Executive Director of Deity. In a
very real sense, this historic Church, having taken seriously the
unwarranted assumption regarding its institutional relationship
to Deity has, to all intents and purposes, become God's patron. No

amount of graciousness or evasiveness can disguise this fact. But Jesus Christ is Lord. Let dialogue and friendly relations, in the spirit of Christ, and under the guidance of the Holy Spirit, continue between Protestants and Roman Catholics. And let both together seek to rediscover the great evangelical tradition of the "New Man in Christ," which Romans lost officially many centuries ago and to which Protestant ecumenists have tended to accord a very secondary place.

There is one thing, however, above all others, which Protestants in their several Churches and in the pursuit of Christian unity, have to learn from the Roman Catholic Church. It relates to the number and status of the religious orders, which are a phenomenon of Roman Catholicism. While no religious organization in history has been so monolithic and so highly centralized in all matters relating to doctrine, worship, and discipline as has the Church of Rome, this Church has more than six hundred religious orders, whose number continues to increase. While each of these orders is bound by the faith of the Church, and all together acknowledge the authority of the Pope and are expected to observe the proprieties of diocesan relationship, they are free, nevertheless, to carry on their own work and to initiate projects with virtual autonomy.

These autonomous religious orders have been the dynamic agents of the Church's growth and missionary activity. They have been a witness to the immense variety of ways in which the Roman Catholic Church relates itself to neglected phases of human need. They awaken interest in new aspects of belief, to which the Church gives sanction. Between some of these orders great rivalries exist, with little fraternal relationship between them. This is particularly true of such powerful fraternities as the Jesuits, the Dominicans, the Franciscans, and the Benedictines. Speaking in terms of Christian love and community, the members of these orders are much more separated from one another by institutional boundaries than are the clergy of the representative Churches of Protestantism. It is a case in which theological dogma, or institutional structure and practice, make difficult the manifestation of Christian love, despite common allegiance to the essential faith of the Mother Church, the revered "*Mater Et Magistra.*" The acuteness of this tension between some of the great Roman Catholic orders in this Ecumenical Era, at a time when the Papacy encourages friendly relations with Protestants as "separated brethren," might be illustrated in many ways.

On the other hand, the variety, the autonomy, the vision, and the dynamic action of the great orders of the Roman Catholic Church raise an inescapable question for Protestant Churches. It is equally germane to ecumenical organizations in which authority becomes increasingly centralized, with power politics running rampant. The question is this: How can Protestant Ecumenism, whether it operates in a world council, a national council, a national denomination, or a national Church union, provide the equivalent of the great orders of the Roman Catholic Church, with their freedom to take initiatives and their autonomy in the execution of their tasks? Do we witness in the Protestant quest for unity the birth of a dream which would identify the ecumenical goal with a union, or with unions, in which power to carry on the fourfold function of the Christian Church would be concentrated in the hands of a central curia?

AN ECUMENICAL THEOLOGY

It is clear that the need for an ecumenical theology was never greater than in this crucial hour of inter-Church relations. By an "ecumenical theology," I do not mean a conspectus of the theological viewpoints that are representative of all Christian Churches. Nor do I mean a ghostly minimum statement, a so-called lowest common denominator formula, from which affirmations of faith that failed to win universal approval would be eliminated. As I ponder afresh the question of ecumenical theology, I feel that the best contribution I can make to the ongoing discussion on this subject is to set the problem in the perspective in which it began to appear in me in the years before the organization of the World Council of Churches in 1948. While World War II was entering its most crucial state, a group of friends founded a theological journal called *Theology Today*.[6] In an editorial, "The Times Call for Theology," written for that journal in April, 1945, I wrote what continues to be my strong conviction—which I believe to be relevant to the present ecumenical situation. Let me reiterate thoughts

[6] Founded April, 1944.

that I expressed at that time and was accustomed to share with members of the course on Ecumenics at Princeton. What I said then and endorse today runs thus:

> Now that the Church is co-extensive with the inhabited globe, the hour has arrived to survey afresh the whole course of Church history. Let each Church in the three great traditions, Roman, Eastern, and Protestant, be studied for the witness it has borne to Christ in the course of its life, whether in the nurture of the saints, in the elucidation or defense of truth, or in its contribution to the effective reign of God among men. Let each be surveyed to discover whatever stains of sin, or marks of shame and error, its history may reveal. Such a study will show that no Church in history can claim a monopoly of insight or sainthood, of evangelical zeal, or transforming power. Those things which God has taught the Church through the glory and shame of the Churches will provide data for an ecumenical theology. A theology of revelation, which cherishes without idolatry the historic Creeds and Confessions, which studies the life history of the Churches in search of insight regarding Christ and the Church, which embraces within its sweep God's dealing with the new Churches in Asia, Africa, Oceania, and Latin America, can lay the foundation of that theology which is needed by an Ecumenical Church in an ecumenical world.
>
> Let the Churches of the Reformation acknowledge their many sins and shortcomings, admitting freely that the Church can sin and has sinned. In penitence and humility, in faith and in hope, let them prepare themselves for the tasks that await them in the coming time. And about one thing let them be clear. The theological statement to which the Church Universal must look forward in the years ahead must be no doctrinal syncretism or theological dilution. It must have at its heart no pale, lowest denominator formula. Never must the Church sponsor a blanched, eviscerated, spineless statement of Confessional theology. It must give birth in this revolutionary transition time, to a full-blooded, loyally Biblical, unashamedly ecumenical, and strongly vertebrate system of Christian belief.

This I feel more strongly today than when these words were written eighteen years ago.

Let me give my endorsement to another statement made in that same period. In a chapter on Protestantism written for *The Great Religions of the Modern World*[7] I stress the "demand for an ecumenical theology." The new situation created by the Second Vatical Council gives to the words in question a still greater relevance than when they were first uttered in a mood of ecumenical longing. The statement is as follows:

"The new orthodoxy that takes shape in the Protestant mind, the new catholicity that inspires its ecclesiastical outlook, the Christian concern for the human situation in its global aspects that marks the Protestant Churches of today, combine to create a longing for an authoritative Ecumenical Council. This was what the Reformers of the Sixteenth Century desired above anything else, 'the next free General Council of Holy Christendom,' and of which they were defrauded in their time by the action of the Council of Trent in 1546. An invitation to such a council will undoubtedly be issued in due course 'to all whom it may concern.' One of the chief tasks of the new Ecumenical Council will be the formulation of an ecumenical theology."

Little did I dream that in 1962 new vistas in this direction would be opening.

With this, we bring to a close our discussion of the functional quadrilateral of the Church Universal and pass to the final phase of the Science of Ecumenics.

[7] Edward J. Jurji, ed. (Princeton, N.J.: Princeton University Press, 1946).

The Church
and the World

PART IV

The Relations
of the Church Universal

chapter 11

So vast is the range of this phase of Ecumenics, and so important
are the issues involved, that adequate treatment of the Church's
relations would necessitate a separate volume. Inasmuch, however, as the ideal procedure if followed would carry us beyond
the contemplated dimension of this book, I will do my utmost to
set this aspect of the main theme in due perspective, dealing
briefly and synthetically with its essential facets in a single, concluding chapter.

Included within the province of discourse are the relation of the
Christian Church to the non-Christian religions and also its rela-
tion to society, to culture, and to the state. We begin with the
Church in relation to the non-Christian Religions.

THE CHURCH AND THE NON-CHRISTIAN RELIGIONS

The resurgence of the non-Christian religions is one of the spiritual phenomena of our time. There was a period following the
close of World War I when the prevalent opinion in the western
world was that the great ethnic faiths of Asia and Africa—Islam,
Hinduism, Buddhism—were decidedly decadent. They were regarded as ceasing progressively to be a dynamic force in the life
and culture of the peoples with which they had been historically

associated. In some academic centers, the subject of Comparative Religion was given a lowered status. During the years referred to, a famous theological seminary in the United States dropped its Chair of Comparative Religion altogether after the incumbent had reached the age of retirement.

But changes have occurred. *The historic religions have begun to take on new vitality.* In Asia and Africa their resurgence has become related to an upsurge of nationalism. This trend is particularly marked in the spirit and policy of the United Arab Republic. While India is constitutionally neutral, so far as concerns any official relationship between the Indian government and Hinduism, the traditional faith of the country, the influence of the old religion is very real in political circles. Recent decades have witnessed, moreover, the emergence of diverse expressions of Reformed Hinduism. These show a decidedly missionary spirit.

In the course of a visit to India in 1961, I visited in Delhi one of the centers of the Ramakrishna Mission. This mission, as was told me by one of the leaders of the movement, has one hundred and twenty mission centers in India and six in the United States. A missionary spirit of this kind is something entirely new in Hinduism. On the main wall of the lecture hall in the Delhi mission there is a striking portrait of Vivekanada, a famous missionary mystic of the Ramakrishna Mission. He is represented standing on India's southern tip with his gaze directed northward. Underneath the portrait are written these words that interpret his missionary concern: "Arise, awake and stop not till the goal is reached."

It was impressive to see in Rangoon, Burma the enormous hall where thousands of Buddhists had held a world gathering after the lapse of several hundred years. Buddhist services are now held in Washington, D. C. In Japan, there is clear evidence of the revived influence of Shintoism among a great people in quest of new life and light.

How does the situation stand as regards relations between Christians and non-Christians? It is axiomatic, or at least should be, that Christians, both individually and collectively, and as citizens of countries called "Christian," should never be a party to the exercise of any kind of discrimination towards the members of other faiths. Non-Christians should not only enjoy the most complete religious freedom for the exercise of their faith but should also, at all times and in every circumstance, be the objects of human consideration and Christian affection. Christians should make every effort, in the most disinterested manner, to promote the interests of their non-Christian fellow men and, wherever necessary, seek to better their lot. With sensitivity and devotion, they should obey the law of Christ "to love their neighbor as themselves."

On the question of the appropriate Christian approach to non-Christians in the interests of religious truth and of human salvation, positions vary. There are Christians who take the view that God has been equally at work in all religions. Christians should, therefore, take the lead in discovering in other religions those truths which are God-given, and which, for that reason, should be combined with specifically Christian truth in order to constitute a religion expressive of man's spiritual achievement, and so adequate for all mankind. This viewpoint was classically expressed in the famous book, *Re-Thinking Missions: A Layman's Inquiry after One Hundred Years.* Written by the distinguished Harvard professor of philosophy, W. E. Hocking, who was chairman of a group of Americans who devoted several years to a field study of Christian missions and their policy, *Re-Thinking Missions* takes what is commonly called the syncretistic approach to the religious problem. Thus we read, "All fences and private properties in truth are futile: the final truth, whatever it may be, is the New Testament of every existing faith." Then referring to the non-Christian religions, Professor Hocking goes on to say, "The Christian will look forward not to the destruction of these religions, but to their continued coexistence with Christianity, each stimulating the other in growth toward the ultimate goal, unity in the completed religious truth." [1]

The classical reply to the Hocking syncretistic viewpoint of man's religious future, and to the supreme objective of Christian mission as formulated in *Re-Thinking Missions,* was given by Hendrik Kraemer in the outstanding volume he prepared as basic study material for the Madras Missionary Conference of 1938, to which reference was made earlier in this book. The former mis-

[1] (New York: Harper & Row, Publishers, 1932), p. 44.

sionary and world-famous authority on Comparative Religion took the viewpoint that, whereas the other great religions are no more than the product of man's religious genius, the Christian religion is in the most absolute sense the product of God's self-disclosure of Himself in Jesus Christ. For that reason, the Christian missionary task, says Kraemer, consists in this: "to persuade the non-Christian world to surrender to Christ as the sole Lord of Life." But this task, he goes on, "must be accomplished in the present complicated world with all the means that human intelligence, ingenuity, and devotion put at our disposal, because it is our plain duty to make the hearing and expression of God's revelation and message as palpable as possible." [2] In a word, Christians must win a right to be heard and to make their meaning clear and attractive. That being so, "Theology, history, psychology, anthropology must be exploited to achieve one aim and one aim only: to be a better instrument in conveying the conviction that God is speaking in Jesus Christ, His decisive Word to individuals, nations, peoples, cultures, and races, without any distinction." [3]

Since the founding of the World Council of Churches in 1948, official ecumenical sponsorship has been given to the intensive study of the great religions by a group of scholars. Among the hills above Hong Kong, for example, there is a center where outstanding authorities on religion devote themselves exclusively to an objective examination of the non-Christian faiths in their relation to Christianity. Representatives of those faiths are invited to visit the center and make their contribution to the elucidation of religious truth from the viewpoint of the religion they profess. Not in a spirit of compromise, but in the interests of intelligent understanding, interfaith dialogue has become a reality. The quest is afoot to know other religions, not in terms of the aberrations and extravagances by which all historic faiths have been plagued, but through a study of them at their best and as interpreted by their most competent exponents.

In the study of the great religions the approach that inspires the research currently conducted in Christian ecumenical circles

[2] *The Christian Message in a Non-Christian World* (New York: Harper & Row, Publishers, 1938), p. 444.
[3] *Ibid.,* p. 445.

is marked by two theological presuppositions. On the one hand, there is affirmed the ultimacy of God's revelation of Himself in Jesus Christ. The words of the Jerusalem declaration of 1928, "Our Message is Jesus Christ," is re-echoed today among the Churches that compose the World Council in the slogan, "The Finality of Christ in an Age of Universal History." A high Christology marks the Church's approach to the study of Comparative Religion. With equal seriousness, the Pauline declaration is affirmed, "Jesus Christ is Lord," and the Johannine transcription of Christ's own words, "I am the Way, the Truth and the Life," is unashamedly heralded abroad.

On the other hand, there is no disposition to affirm the view that was implicit in Kraemer's famous volume, reflecting the theological position of Karl Barth in the thirties, that the Eternal Creator and Lord of the Universe has not conveyed glimpses of truth regarding Himself, man, and the meaning of life in the non-Christian religions. For God, who in the most absolute sense disclosed Himself and His grand design in Jesus Christ His Son, as recorded in Holy Scripture, did not deny to mankind His Common Grace. He made it possible for men to attain some insights derived from human reason and the human heart in a world which, though alienated from Him, was controlled by Him, and by Christ was reconciled to Him. But only in Christ can the human insights and longings that have marked man's quest for God through the ages reach true fulfillment and achieve redemptive significance.

Of special interest and importance is the recent trend of relations between Christians and Jews. More and more, and in all sorts of occasions and contexts, reference is made to the Hebreo-Christian tradition. For several decades, Jews and Christians, especially in the United States, have co-operated closely together in projects relating to human welfare and the quest for truth. Symbolical of this co-operative relationship is the National Conference of Christians and Jews. The traditional feeling of mutual antagonism and alienation has come to an end. Jews have come to a deeper appreciation of the figure of Jesus Christ, and many are proud of the fact that He was a member of the Hebrew race.

Thoughtful Jews are eager to have the Christian viewpoint interpreted to them. It was my privilege a number of years ago to give the official address at the inaguration of several new professors in the leading theological seminary of American Judaism. I recall the profound impression made upon me at the close of the ceremony, when the president of the institution expressed his appreciation of the fact that, while observing all proprieties that should mark utterance at a function sponsored by another faith, I had spoken unashamedly as a Christian. "We want Christians to speak as Christians," he said, "when they occupy this platform." He was not interested in mere religious platitudes, but in the expression of a viewpoint. This man, who was no other than President Louis Finklestein of the Jewish Theological Seminary, New York, became the Founder of the Conference on Science, Philosophy, and Religion, of which I was privileged to be a charter member. I can recall the pleasure with which the eminent Jewish theologian was listened to subsequently by the faculty and students of Princeton Theological Seminary.

Many other organizations might be mentioned in which Christians and Jews confer or co-operate. The important thing, however, is that a spirit of friendliness and common concern exists between members of the two historic faiths. It should be recognized, at the same time, that religiously, Jews are deeply divided among themselves. American Judaism is composed of three main groups: Orthodox, Conservative, and Reformed. Very many Jews, moreover, have no religious faith or affiliation of any kind. It should be noted also that politically, especially on the Palestinian issue, the world of Judaism is tragically rent asunder. A very large number of Jews are bitterly opposed to the idea that Jews should have a national political territory. They resent the Zionist thesis that to be a true Jew, you must become a citizen of Israel. They consider that Jews belong, and should belong, to their countries of residence, and not to one country in particular.

Controversy continues to arise among Christians as to the propriety of organized mission work among Jews. On that score, it is clear that, whatever be the particular approach made to Jews in the name of Christ and in the spirit of Paul, Jews, as human beings, need the Gospel. They need the Gospel as do all other members of the humankind, in order that they, too, may become part of God's New Humanity.

THE CHURCH AND SOCIETY

We now move on to consider the relation of the Church to the secular order, traditionally spoken of as "the world," which consists of three distinct phases—society, culture, and the state.

While the Church Universal can never be true to its nature or fulfill its destiny without being a missionary community that takes seriously the constitutive functions already dealt with, it dare never forget that it is itself an integral part of human reality. It has a mission to the world; but it has also an obligation, individually and collectively, locally and ecumenically, to take seriously its responsibility within the family of mankind. In their roles, therefore, as God's men and women, pilgrims and crusaders, colonists of heaven, who accept the Lordship and finality of Jesus Christ and rejoice in the grace that made them members of the New Humanity, Christians must play their part in relation to the Old Humanity. Persons who have been called by God to be His servants in the fulfillment of His purpose in Christ for the world, are equally called by Him to attain an intelligent understanding of the world and its problems, and to achieve a sympathetic involvement in the world's life. This means that Christians and the Christian Church, while living by a light and a power not derived from the world, and for a Kingdom that transcends the world, must never spend their lives in detachment from the affairs of the world. They must rather—to use the words of Dietrich Bonhoeffer, a Twentieth-Century saint and martyr—cultivate a "holy worldliness." For this world is God's world for which Jesus Christ gave His life, a sphere where the Holy Spirit is at work, where all men are God's guests, a community for whose happiness and welfare He is concerned, and whom He desires, through their own personal decision, to become members of His family.

The Christian Church, which is today, in a geographical sense, *ecumenical* for the first time in history, a new diaspora in the midst of all nations, is becoming increasingly sensitive to the realities of the human situation around the globe. This is as it should be. Without ever forgetting its missionary role, the Church must develop more and more an intelligent, realistic, understanding of the world in which its lot is cast. It must appraise the forms of its involvement in the life of mankind, whether these forms of involvement be imposed upon the Church, as happens in totalitarian societies, or are freely chosen by the Church, as in democratic societies. Evidence of the Church's concern in this regard is the increasing number of significant names which begin to sound. Publications, committees, and departments bear the titles: "Religion and Society," "Christianity and Society," "Religion and Race," "The Church and Society," "Church and State," "Rapid Social Change." In 1965 the World Council of Churches will sponsor a world gathering to deal with these issues. This projected meeting will be the successor of the historic conference on "Church, Community, and State," which met at Oxford in 1937.

CHRISTIAN PERCEPTIVENESS

The human family is growing numerically in a most fantastic manner. We witness a veritable population explosion of literally appalling proportions, a phenomenon which statesmen and Churchmen must both face and which raises all sorts of new questions. Problems of birth control and of eschatology are forced upon every serious-minded person, whatever his religion, race, or nation. Humanity is on the march in an unprecedented manner, but also in a very ominous setting.

Boundlessness, in its most diversified form, has become the hallmark of human life today. A multiplicity of new nations in Asia and Africa, some of major, some of miniature, size, have been born, and have already acquired social and political significance. There is boundlessness, too, in the growth of a nationalistic, and even racialistic, passion among nations, new and old. In leading centers of civilization, boundless wealth and luxurious living glitter in the shadow of unspeakable poverty and appalling delinquency. Centers of these tragic contrasts are great American cities like New York and Washington. No less symbolical of the environmental coexistence of wealth and poverty, are Lima, the capital of Peru, and New Delhi, the capital of India. In the outskirts of Lima a vast slum called the "Barriadas," which is populated by half a million people who have recently arrived in search of a living from Andean plateaus and valleys to the lovely and famous "City of the Kings," is an example of the revolutionary portent that casts its shadow over Latin America today. As, with boundless celerity the rich become richer and the poor become poorer over vast areas of the globe, the poem of Edwin Markham, "The Man with the Hoe," becomes ominously relevant. Inspired by the stooping figure of the peasant in the famous canvas of the French painter Millet, the American poet breaks out:

> Through this dread shape the suffering ages look;
> Time's tragedy is in that aching stoop;
>
> O masters, lords and rulers in all lands,
> How will the future reckon with this Man?
> How answer his brute question in that hour
> When whirlwinds of rebellion shake the world
> How will it be with kingdoms and with kings—
> With those who shaped him to the thing he is—
> When this dumb Terror shall reply to God,
> After the silence of the centuries? [4]

The same boundlessness takes on a psychological but no less ominous dimension in the inordinate passion for pleasure and power that marks contemporary man. This is happening in lands once noted, due to Christian influence, for the sobriety of their citizens. In the United States at present three problems, all related to physical appetite and indulgence, have begun to cause supreme concern, both in Governmental circles and in the general public. These problems are created by excessive smoking, alcoholism, and promiscuous sexual relations.

A Government-appointed commission of eminent scientists has stated in its report that there is clear evidence that cigarette smoking is one of the chief causes of cancer, a disease which has become a staggering national problem. There is equally indisputable evidence that excessive indulgence in alcohol is responsible for the degeneration of human personality through the proliferation of "alcoholics." Alcoholic beverages are also the source of a very large proportion of the crimes and traffic accidents that plague American society. It is no less true that the exaltation of sex, in its most revolting forms and undisciplined expressions, as the great absolute for human enjoyment, together with the promotion

[4] The World's Great Religious Poetry (New York: The Macmillan Company, 1938), p. 376.

of this ideal in literature, art, and the glamor of Hollywood stars, is creating a debased image of manhood and womanhood.

Agape has been dethroned and is replaced by *eros,* who has become the supreme divinity in the new Sodom. Unrestrained appetite, at its very lowest levels and in its most loathsome form is being glorified. The Biblical meaning of sin and of a fallen world thus takes on fresh meaning and is given a new dimension. The current revolt against everything that spelled order and harmony in the Christian and Platonic traditions, and which Shakespeare called "degree," is being given dramatic significance. Most timely and prophetic are these words of the great dramatist:

> Take but degree away, untune that string;
> And hark! what discord follows!
>
> Then everything includes itself in power.
> Power into will, will into appetite,
> And appetite, a universal wolf,
>
> Must make perforce a universal prey,
> and last eat up himself.*

What are Christians and Christian Churches saying and doing about this sodomic boundlessness? What should they say and do by way of relating themselves to this social issue?

In addition to this boundlessness which characterizes contemporary society, many phases of which are due to "appetite," there is also to be noted the sociological fact of *polarity.* By social polarity I mean the contrasting, often conflicting situations, that are a direct consequence of technology, and in some important instances, of ideology.

In recent times both the city and the countryside have been taking on a new look, and have entered into a new kind of relationship. On the one hand, a steady movement continues towards the city and its environs. This is due to industrial developments in urban areas and to the quest of work by dwellers in the back country. Rapid social change of this type has been taking place equally in older countries of the West and in the new lands of Asia, Africa, and Latin America. A representative, if somewhat

* Shakespeare, *Troilus and Cressida* (Act I, Scene 3).

extreme, case of this phenomenon, is the growing depopulation of the Scottish Highlands, where the writer was born. A recent survey has shown that in this region, where lived, nearly twenty centuries ago, the kilted barbarians who defeated the Romans at the Battle of Mons Graupius, and whose sons and daughters have played a significant role in Church and society in Scotland and in the world, there are today ninety thousand fewer inhabitants than there were a hundred years ago. The trek city-ward, whether the city be in the rural dweller's old homeland, or in a new, creates obvious problems for the Christian Church.

Another phenomenon in the same realm is the increasing polarization between the city and its suburbia, and between the form of life and human relations by which each is characterized. And then there are the inner city and the outer city, the city by day and the city by night, the luxurious hotels and apartment houses and the human ghettoes not far away. As I think of fantastic contrasts of this kind, my thoughts turn to Rio de Janeiro, Glasgow, Calcutta, and to many an American metropolis.

Technology's achievement in making the machine, in the form of automation, a substitute for human hands and feet, contributes to the tragic growth of unemployment in many highly industrialized countries, especially the United States. Automation in the great farming areas and the replacement of small farmers by great corporations reduce the number of men and women who can engage in agricultural activities. The nearly two million migrant farm laborers who are obliged to move as families from one part of the United States to another, and who have been, and continue to be, the objects of shameful exploitation, cast a shadow over society in a great and beloved nation. In all this what is the role of Christians and the Church?

There is, in contemporary society, another form of polarization, caused not by technology but by ideology. The terrible conflict between white and colored people which has marked social relations in the United States and South Africa in recent years, and which continues unabated, is another issue which confronts the Christian Church. Negroes were introduced into the United States as slaves from Africa by men who justified their action on grounds of Christian theology. They maintained that God the Creator had willed that the Negro race, which they claimed was by nature inferior, should serve the white race. Its servitude, they alleged, was the just and inevitable consequence of the perpetual judgment upon its racial ancestor (Genesis 8:24–25). Following the bloody Civil War between the northern and southern states, Negro slavery came to an end a century ago during the presidency of Abraham Lincoln. But the struggle of the colored people for social equality has not yet been fully won, notwithstanding the verdict of the Supreme Court of the United States, which in 1953 held that racial separation violates the national Constitution, and despite the growing support of white citizens. As these lines are being written, the conflict continues to rage with fury, while the civil rights bill, designed to give legislative force to judicial decision, is being debated in Congress. Once again the question rises, where do Christians stand, what should Churches do? Let us hope and pray that the new church organizations relating religion and race may succeed not only in guaranteeing judicial rights, but in creating human respect and Christian love.

Still more serious is the racial situation in South Africa. In recent years there has emerged among the descendants of the white colonists from Holland, who in the Nineteenth Century gained possession of territory inhabited by Negro tribes, in what is now called the Union of South Africa and where Negroes today constitute the vast majority of the population, a doctrine called Apartheid. At a time when the colonial era has come to a close and the "Black Continent" as a whole has achieved political freedom, at a time when the new independent Negro republics begin to have world significance, at a time when the Christian conscience has become increasingly sensitive on the racial issue, a white nation, with a great religious heritage and for allegedly Christian reasons, carries out a policy of racial segregation which, in some respects, is unique in human annals. The Churches in South Africa and the world are confronted by a major question in the sphere of social relations.

But the most acute and widespread expression of the polarization of society by ideology is found in the Communist world. In Russia, China, Poland, Hungary, Czechoslovakia, Bulgaria, Rumania, and Cuba, non-Communists, and especially Christians, do not enjoy the status in the life of the nation to which their capacity would entitle them. They cannot occupy the public positions that are the native right of fellow citizens of equal or less ability who profess a Marxist ideology. They spend their lives under very severe handicaps, even though there be no such thing as active persecution for ideological reasons or religious connections in the countries to which they belong. It should be recognized, at the same time, that conditions vary from one Communist country to another and that there is an increasing trend towards liberalization. What should be the attitude of Christians and Christian Churches towards Communist societies, whether their lot is cast within or outside such societies?

INVOLVEMENT

Perceptive awareness by Christians of the human situation in which they live should lead them to confront their particular situation in a positive manner. It should be a manner consonant with their responsibility as members of the Community of Christ who are called by God to represent humanity at its truest and best, both in private and in public. This calls for the expression of warmth and friendliness on the part of Christians toward all people with whom they mingle. These may be persons belonging to a lower social stratum, members of another race, or foreigners living in a strange environment far from their native land. All projects designed to provide hospitality for those who need it, to make possible friendly encounter with those who are lonely, to give equality of status to men and women whose skin is black or brown, or yellow, to promote friendship towards citizens of countries hostile to one's own, or to representatives of faiths of philosophies opposed to Christianity—all such projects should receive the support of Christians and Christian Churches. Symbols of such projects are Christian student centers where no discrimination, religious or racial, is practiced, Christian homes for wayfarers, such as those conducted by the Salvation Army, and the Church Center for the United Nations recently established in New York City. Everything that Christians can do to *humanize* relations between people and between peoples, with a view to their welfare, in order to produce understanding between them and peace on earth, is part of that "holy worldliness," which God requires of all members of the New Humanity.

It is also the responsibility of all Christians, so far as their age and health permit, and opportunity is provided them, to engage in work that is in the interests of truth or in some phase of human welfare or progress. Christians should be associated with "good works" in the New Testament sense, and with the highest values. They should not be identified with the purely glamorous, or the empty pursuit of mere social recognition. They should be workers in the fullest sense, workers like God the Creator, like Christ the Carpenter, like Paul the tentmaker, all of whom are represented in Scripture as working in the natural order, not limiting their endeavors to the spiritual sphere. Christians should excel all fellow citizens in exemplifying what it means to be truly alive, to live with a dedicated sense of vocation, to pursue a goal that is more than mere self-interest or egotistical display.

To be a real human being in this "earthly" sense, whatever be one's secular environment, has more than ordinary relevance in this revolutionary period of history. At a time when the foundations of complacent western society are being shaken, when more than a billion people live in Marxist communities in which there is no place for the "idle rich," or for the social hangers-on to ancestral privilege and prestige, Christians in affluent societies must rediscover forgotten truths regarding personal life and work —such truths as are found enshrined in the writings of the Hebrew prophets, in the Gospels, and in the letters of Saint Paul. Very especially must Christians in the West take a fresh look at that maxim which Karl Marx discovered in a Pauline letter and made pivotal in his own philosophy of life, "If a man will not work, he shall not eat" (II Thessalonians 3:11 tl. B. Phillips). Any society in which parasites abound who eat but never work, and where a multitude of unemployed desire to work but there is no work for them to do, can be assured that the Judge of all is not far from the door.

What has just been said regarding life and work is applicable primarily to Christians in democratic societies where citizens in general are free to choose their own paths as to what vocations they shall follow and what kinds of persons they shall be. But what about Christians whose life is spent, and whose work must be done in a Communist, a Fascist, or an Apartheid society? For in none of these does the individual citizen have full freedom of choice. So the question arises: What is the meaning of Christian involvement in societies where the great freedoms do not exist, and where those values that have come to be associated with "Christian civilization" and "democratic society" are not regnant?

In the course of the past decade, the writer has had the privilege of visiting the Churches in three Communist countries, Hungary, Czechoslovakia, and Cuba. He also visited Indonesia where a national Communist party exerts powerful influence upon the thought and attitude of many citizens of that country, among whom are found a considerable number of Christian students and Church leaders, who are not themselves Marxists. Let me give expression to some reflections which took shape in my mind following those visits.

1. I found it to be the mature judgment of many devoted evangelical Christians in the countries mentioned that the Communist regimes under which they lived had grappled as no previous governments had ever done with three traditional problems; namely, the enserfdom of the rural masses by the great feudal barons, the unequal distribution of wealth, and traditional corruption in government circles. In Czechoslovakia even the liberal government of great men like Masaryk and Benes had failed to take issue with the age-long feudalism in the agricultural province of Moravia. There was a feeling in Protestant circles that a great liberation had taken place from age-long oppression. Freedom was now given the basic connotation of release from man-made conditions which had made it impossible for workmen and peasants, and many other people, to live truly human lives, lives free from want and oppressive burdens. Those evangelical Christians accepted the view that certain freedoms have to be taken from the rich and from the heirs of ancestral power, if freedom is to have any real meaning for the common man. In their judgment, freedom is unacceptable if it simply means that a man is free to do anything he likes, in accordance with traditional practice, even though his freedom of action should result in the unemployment and dehumanization of others. This is the view of freedom that has become regnant, and is being given vocal, and even vociferous expression in Cuba, a country whose government proclaims it to be "The First Free Land of America." [5] And let it not be forgotten

[5] *La Primera Tierra Libre de América.*

by all who belong to the Free World that this is the view of freedom which is producing volcanic rumblings among the disinherited masses in other Latin American countries.

2. In the three Communist countries I have mentioned, Christians and Christian Churches have been confronted with the problem of their attitude towards the new order. They are forced to decide the degree and the form of their involvement in a society organized on a Marxist pattern. Not a few Christians, including Christian ministers, in Czechoslovakia, Hungary, and Cuba have left their native country for some other, because they found the new order uncongenial. They, therefore, sought a different environment for their life and witness.

On the other hand, the great majority of their fellow Christians stood fast. While those who remained may differ among themselves in their views of Communism and vary in their attitude toward the government in power, they accept their situation as God-given. They strive, as loyal citizens and dedicated Christians, to show the relevance of Christ and the Gospel to the total life of their people. While Christians in these countries are not free either individually or collectively, to make public pronouncements on political issues, they enjoy perfect freedom to carry on their religious work. Protestant Christians in Communist lands enjoy far more freedom and are given much greater status, than can be affirmed of Protestants in Spain.

Because Cuba has drawn the attention of the world in recent years, and because the Cuban situation in all its phases is followed with the most intense interest by the other Latin American lands of America, let me refer in a special manner to the Church situation today in the historic "Pearl of the Antilles," now more generally known as "Tragic Island." Because of their relevancy to the issue under consideration, let me repeat words which I wrote regarding a visit paid to the Cuban Churches toward the close of 1963. With deep feeling and conviction I said: Never in journeys through Europe, Asia, Africa, or the Americas had I envisioned more clearly what it means for a Christian to be a Christian, or for the Church to be "in very deed the Church," than I did during those days in Cuba. Cuban Protestants are convinced that the moment was never more opportune to confront fellow Cubans with the revolutionary significance of Jesus Christ, the Gospel, and the Church. These devoted men and women stand ready to accept the present situation as one in which the Sovereign Lord of history has cast their lot, and where their witness must be given. They brace themselves to be militant followers of the Crucified and Risen Christ, the Head of the Church, who was Himself history's greatest revolutionary, the common people's most devoted friend, the potent Savior whom the contemporary Church and the world of today must rediscover. They are cheered by the fact that since the present crisis began, Protestant congregations in Cuba have had a notable increase in membership and have accepted greater responsibility for the Church's work.[6]

3. There is evidence that dialogue between Christians and Marxists has not only become possible in some Communist countries but is growing in frequency and significance. This dialogue, moreover, has government sanction and begins to assume great cultural significance. It heralds the dawn of a new freedom and augurs the advent of Christian ideas into the national culture. As the dialogue advances it will become clear that concern for the common people, the revolutionary quality of "caring," was not born with Karl Marx in the library of the British Museum, but with Jesus Christ in the fields of Galilee.

Very significant progress in dialogue between Christians and Communists has recently been taking place in Czechoslovakia. This development bears testimony to the decisive influence within his native country and in other Communist lands of Europe, of that great evangelical Churchman, Joseph L. Hromadka, who has long been the symbol of dynamic cultural encounter between the disciples of Marx and of Christ.

THE CHURCH AND CULTURE

Let us now pass to the Church's confrontation with culture. Thus far we have considered the relationship of Christians and the Church to situations relating to the personal or social welfare of people; we turn now to situations in which mind and spirit are primarily involved.

What is meant by culture, whether the term be related to a per-

---

[6] See *The Christian Century*, February 12, 1964, pp. 200–203.

son, a people or an epoch? Said that loved and lamented American theologian H. Richard Niebuhr, "Culture is the artificial, secondary, environment which man superimposes on the natural. It comprises language, habits, ideas, beliefs, customs, social organization, inherited artifacts, technical processes, and values." [7] Niebuhr emphasized the fact that "culture" is always "social," expresses "human achievement," and is concerned about the "conservation of values."

When the Christian Church contemplates the world of today in the perspective of "culture," it gazes upon a very confused and confusing situation. It is a situation, in fact, that becomes more and more complicated both in the Communist World where diversity and conflicts are growing, and within the Free World, where "freedom" becomes more and more mysterious, anarchic, and unreal. Words spoken to a researcher when he was investigating the situation in a prominent country in Southeast Asia are becoming increasingly applicable to contemporary culture. The researcher was addressed thus: "If you are not thoroughly confused, you are not fully informed!"

The reasons for this worldwide confusion in the realm of culture, of which the situation in the particular country mentioned is but a symbol, are due in no small degree to what is called the "Cold War." The Christian Church finds itself today in a moment of history when it can no longer take at its face value anything that is said officially by any country involved in this cultural struggle. The reason is that in the "Cold War," a new culture, with a new set of values, has emerged. Truth means nothing anymore. If a lie will serve the interests of the country or the group concerned, why not canonize falsehood? Let the liar, if successful, become a candidate for sainthood in the new cultural order. In this vicious and titantic conflict we are confronted not only with the de-Christianization of culture and the dehumanization of man, but also with the desecularization of the secular. We witness, in effect, a virulent attack upon the ideal of the new secularism, which in wide sectors of society has been becoming a substitute for religion, and even presumes, in some instances, to be itself a religion.

[7] H. Richard Niebuhr, *Christ and Culture* (New York: Harper & Row, Publishers, 1956), p. 32.

SECULARISM

The first major occasion on which the Christian Church was challenged to consider the spiritual significance of the "secular" was at the Jerusalem meeting of the International Missionary Council in 1928. Among the preliminary papers prepared for this gathering was one by that eminent Quaker philosopher and saint, Rufus M. Jones. Entitled "Secular Civilization and the Christian Task," the paper began with these words: "No student of the deeper problems of life can very well fail to see that the greatest rival of Christianity in the world of today is not Mohammedanism, or Buddhism or Hinduism, or Confucianism, but a worldwide secular way of life and interpretation of the nature of things." Dr. Jones explained what he meant by "secular"—a term little used in Church or cultural circles in those days—by a footnote which reads thus: "I am using secular here to mean a way of life and an interpretation of life that include only the natural order of things and that do not find God, or a realm of spiritual reality, essential for life or thought." [8]

In a section of his paper which he entitled, "Values of Life in Non-Christian Circles," Rufus Jones had this to say, "There are spiritual values of a high order, interpenetrating the secular ranks. Men and women live for high and noble ends of life outside the Church as well as inside it." [9] Some pages later he pleads for a "synthesis of truth." "What ought to have happened long ago," he says, "and what must happen now as soon as possible, is that the leaders of the Church and the leaders of the Christian forces generally should joyously welcome all freshly discerned truths as from God, and should reinterpret Christianity in the light of all the truths that can be demonstrated as truth. That is what Clement of Alexandria insisted upon when Christianity was still young. 'Truth by whomsoever spoken,' he declared, 'is from God.' " [10] A little later the Quaker philosopher, after referring to the attitude of St. Augustine on the issue and also to positions taken by Thomas Aquinas and Dean Inge, remarks: "The most important single spiritual task before the religious world of today is the discovery of a similar use of the present-day intellectual conquests of

[8] Jerusalem Meeting, I.M.C., 1928, I, 230.
[9] Ibid., p. 241.
[10] Ibid., p. 245.

thought for the enrichment and expansion of our Christian faith." [11]

In the council's own statement, the famous "Jerusalem Message," in which are enshrined the historic words, "Our Message is Jesus Christ. He is the revelation of what God is and of what man through Him may become," there is found an echo of "secular" civilization and the Christian task. "We confess our neglect," the message runs, "to bring the ordering of men's lives into conformity with the spirit of Christ. The Church has not firmly and effectively set its face against race hatred, race envy, race contempt, or against social envy and contempt and class bitterness, or against racial, national, and social pride, or against the lust for wealth and exploitation of the poor or weak." [12] After expressing appreciation of the views on social issues which were affirmed by the Universal Conference on Life and Work held in Stockholm in 1925, the statement thus calls the Church to action in the cultural and social sphere: "We call on all Christian people to be ready for pioneering thought and action in the name of Christ. Too often the Church has adopted new truth, or new goals for enterprise, only when the danger attached to them is over. There is a risk of rashness: but there is also possible an excessive caution by which, because His Church hangs back, the glory of new truth or enterprise which rightly belongs to Christ is in men's thoughts denied to Him." [13]

I have included these citations for two reasons: First, because they are taken from documents that were prepared for, or issued by, a conference convened under the auspices of a "missionary council" concerned with confronting the whole world with Christ and the Gospel. Second, because these sentiments, uttered nearly forty years ago, have prophetic significance. They are, moreover, particularly relevant at a time when the Christian Church, belatedly, it is true, but in a concerned spirit and practical manner, is devoting itself ecumenically to significant manifestations of thought and life in the secular order.

In the intervening years between Jerusalem, 1928 and Columbus, 1964, when there was held in the state capital of Ohio, the

[11] *Ibid.*, p. 246.
[12] *Ibid.*
[13] *Ibid.*, p. 409.

first National Study Conference on Church and State, many pronouncements have been made by Roman Catholic and Protestant Church bodies on questions arising out of secular developments that challenge Christians and the Church Universal. Outstanding in this regard are such papal encyclicals as *"Mater Et Magistra"* and *"Pacem In Terris,"* together with a diversity of messages and statements issued by the World Council of Churches, Regional and National Councils of Churches, World Confessional bodies, and individual denominations.

The awareness has been steadily growing both in the West and in the East that a cultural era, variegated in character, is coming to an end for all peoples. Shadows are falling, and streaks of a fresh dawn that is being ushered in by signs at once bright and ominous appear upon the horizon of our time. In a new setting that old Hellenic dictum, "The owl of Minerva takes its flight when the shades of night have fallen," takes on contemporary meaning and calls for reflection on what has been happening.

Several things are clear in the new cultural situation. A spirit of introspection is being born. Great Britain, for example, which in the grand days of empire was marked by pure objectivity in her thinking and by a very overt and practical attitude in her policies, has recently been stricken by a new type of concern. That concern was symbolized a decade ago by a placard in one of the buildings erected in connection with the centennial celebration in London of the First International Exhibition. The inscription read, "English is understood everywhere; the Englishman is understood nowhere."

After World War II, Scotland went all out to attract tourists to "Caledonia stern and wild," which in her greatest days had belonged to, and lived for, the world. A book entitled *The Face of Scotland* appeared. Its object was to describe the country's scenery and history. Sometime later another book, *The Heart of Scotland*, was published. This volume was introspective and self-critical. It contained a very frank critique of some of the sanctities of the Scottish character and tradition!

Unlike the countries of Latin America, all of which have been in quest for a century and a half of a more satisfying "way of life," the United States has not generally indulged in self-criticism. It has tended rather to glorify and make normative for all nations the "American way of life." But that era is drawing to a close. The international rejection of the "American way," and growing impotency to impose it upon others, has begun to produce a new self-appraisal on the part of concerned American citizens.

The most recent evidence of this concern in American Church circles, appeared at the Columbus Study Conference on Church and State, to which I have already referred. One of the sections had as its assignment "Christian Faith and the Worship of 'Our Way of Life.' " The members went on record with this affirmation: "In recent times there have developed in what is commonly called the American way of life, certain aberrations which are very disturbing in character. These aberrations should be diagnosed and challenged by the Church in the light of the Christian faith and the true interests of American society." The aberrations in question were described as "anarchic freedom," the "apotheosis of power," and the "idolatry of national self-interest."

A book recently published by a distinguished Mexican writer Octavio Paz is entitled *The Labyrinth of Solitude*.[14] It is an expression of the increasing sense of loneliness that marks thoughtful and concerned people, not only in Mexico, but in other lands where Western culture has been a predominant force.

Neo-Secularism

In the meantime there begins to appear what is designated neo-secularism. It represents, among other things, a disposition to introduce into traditional secularism a religious quality. We witness the emergence of a religionized culture, a secularism with a religious motivation, the virtual advent of a secular God. Traditional religion shows symptoms of becoming acculturated religion. It is becoming so completely absorbed by contemporary culture that it tends to be little more than the soul, the sanction, and the sanctifying force of a given cultural form. When this happens, religion, and, in some instances, the Church, no longer challenges culture in the name of a higher truth; instead it accommodates itself to culture as being the real truth. Something is emerging that closely resembles what happened in the secular sphere when Auguste Comte, the father of positivism, moved beyond pure naturalism

[14] *El Laberinto de la Soledad*, Fondo de Cultura Económica, Mexico-Buenos Aires.

and created the "religion of humanity." Men, human capacities and human concerns, took the place of Deity. In the Republic of Brazil, positivism actually became an established religion, with its temple and its rites. It supplied that country, moreover, with its national emblem, "Order and Progress."

In the Protestant world of today, very especially among the historic Churches of the West, there is a disturbing trend towards substituting obeisance to secular pluralism for subjection to Christian absolutes. God's self-disclosure in Jesus Christ, commitment to Christ as Savior and Lord, the new life in Christ, the Christian mandate to confront the world with the Gospel, are regarded as belonging to the past and to a culture that is outmoded and irrelevant. The idea obtains that any harassing problem of a psychic nature can be dealt with by the psychiatrist, "whose God is the analytical." The multiple facts, facets, and persons that make up our complex culture are represented as parts of a world that God has reconciled to Himself. Christians and the Church are asked to accept the cultural order as it is and to accommodate themselves to its art, its mores, and its philosophy. Let them, it is advocated, take the lead in becoming genial participants in the existing order, manifesting appreciation of its diversity and being sympathetically condolent of its vagaries.

The view is being propounded that, inasmuch as the world has already been reconciled to God, commitment to God as a ground for acceptance by Him and of reconciliation to Him has no meaning. God is nice and accommodating. "Cheap grace" thus becomes regnant. Ultimates of Christian life and behavior are eschewed. There is no such thing as New Humanity. What matters is to take seriously humanity as it is. As regards values which a previous culture presumed to be absolutes, the great task for the Christian scholar today becomes essentially analytical in character. Christian Truth is no longer something that grips you like a belt or that you unfold like a banner. It is best symbolized by the bird of the old German philosopher, Lessing. The real thinker pursues the winged creature over hill and meadow, calling it by different names, studying its names by semantic processes, watching its movements with hermeneutical precision. Whether the illusive creature is ever caught does not matter. What does matter is the exciting experience of quest on the trail of a capricious songster, whose chirping beguiles the ear. The really important thing is not to possess Truth, or to be possessed by it; intellectual greatness consists in the ability to prove that it is impossible to catch up with Truth. Intellectual integrity means to go skipping in Truth's train.

When this attitude toward Truth prevails, the Biblical scholar and the Christian theologian become absolute relativists, for whom the relative is the only absolute. There is then reproduced in Christian thought what has become the mark of contemporary philosophy in many western lands, and which is the ominous harbinger of cultural sterility: the Cult of the Uncommitted. The hour will then have arrived when western culture can no longer stand up against the massive structure of Marxist-Leninism and the disciplined approach to life of its adherents. The future of a Christianity that aspires to be luminous and dynamic will then pass from the custody of a secularized Protestantism, to that of a new and radical evangelicalism. This new evangelicalism, which is luminously related to the Eternal and dynamically relevant to the Temporal, begins to make its presence felt in diverse sectors of contemporary Protestantism and in many circles of traditional Roman Catholicism. No problem of thought dare be ignored, no issue of life dare be sidestepped. But in all questions relating to ultimate truth let Christians never forget there is a Light and a Way.

Despite a bleak cultural situation, both in Christian Churches and on university campuses, there is taking place a rediscovery of the timeless reality and the contemporary significance of Jesus Christ. Even Marxists have a veneration and affection for Christ, as can be shown from their works. No secularist can ignore Him. Persons gripped and transformed by Him, whatever their culture or cult, adore Him and await a call to action. All is not gloom. Amid the prevailing secularism we can greet tomorrow with a cheer. God reigns.

THE CHURCH AND THE STATE

There remains to be considered the Church's relation to the state. To this final topic we now address our thought.

The relationship between religion and secular government, or, as it is more commonly expressed in countries within the Christian tradition, the relationship between Church and state, is a most crucial issue.

Government as such represents a creation of God, or, as might be expressed in theological terms, of God's Common Grace. God designed government to serve the best interests of people, to guarantee order, to execute justice, and to maintain humanity among men.

The supreme criterion by which a particular government must be judged is whether those in authority manifest concern, and are successful in their concern, to make it possible for all citizens, whatever their background or status, to live a truly human existence, in the enjoyment of elemental rights and with the assurance of unprejudiced justice.

The true meaning of the natural order, in the life of mankind, is fulfilled when rulers recognize the reality of God's absolute sovereignty over nations and civilizations. Such recognition does not involve, of course, that it be formally written into a country's constitution.

In so far as official government attitude towards religion is concerned, there are three different types of national state in the world of today.

THE RELIGION-COMMITTED STATE

A religion-committed state may be described thus: *A state that is committed by its constitution, or by tradition, to recognize the importance of religion, or of a particular religion, in its national life.*

First and foremost, as illustrative of this type, stands out the United States of America. This nation, which is constitutionally uncommitted to any religion, is related traditionally, and to a certain degree in practice, to the Christian religion. On the one hand, there exists in the United States, an absolute constitutional separation between Church and state, together with the most absolute religious freedom. On the other hand, there is in the American nation what might be called a traditional God-consciousness, by which I mean, a sympathetic attitude towards religion as such.

That the United States is what may be designated a *God-conscious* or *God-affirming* nation may be illustrated in a variety of ways. In the Declaration of Independence, human rights are regarded as inalienable and God-given. Inscribed in American currency are the words, "In God we trust." The oath of allegiance to the flag involves the repetition of the words, "One nation *under God*, indivisible, with freedom and justice for all." Thus the United States cannot be regarded, in any sense of the term, as a purely secular state. Moreover, so far as religion as such is concerned, it is in no sense neutral. A new president is inaugurated into office by the offering up of prayer to God. The daily sessions of both Houses of Congress are begun by prayer, which is offered by specially appointed chaplains. The armed forces of the Nation have their chaplains, Protestant, Roman Catholic, and Jewish, whose salaries are paid by the Government. Property that belongs to religious organizations is exempted from taxation. The problem is how this traditional sense of Deity can be expressed in public education without violating the First Amendment to the American Constitution, which "prohibits the establishment of religion."

There are two other modern states to which may also be applied, though to a lesser degree than is true of the American nation, the designation "God-conscious." They are the republics of Indonesia and the Philippines. The Indonesian Republic is constitutionally established upon belief in five elemental realities. First and foremost comes "Belief in God." The other four are: "Humanity," "Nationalism," the "Sovereignty of the people," and "Social justice." In the preamble to the constitution of the Philippine Republic we read, "The Filipino people, imploring the aid of Divine Providence, in order to establish a government that shall embody their ideals. . . ."

Among the governments that, in some way or another, recognize the importance of religion in the national life, should be noted the very unique case of the Republic of Lebanon. The government of this small nation might be designated a *Confessionally constituted government*. For political reasons the Lebanese constitution requires that all members of the government shall be related to some religion, or to some religious body. Their number and the position they may occupy are dependent upon the strength of the religious body to which they belong. No person unrelated to some religious group is eligible for election to congress, but when elected, a congressman is perfectly free to express whatever view-point he desires.

There is in this same general category a type of *religion-related government* which is so culturally, and not merely symbolically. Examples of this type of government are the United Arab Republic, Pakistan, and Burma. While in the constitution of the U. A. R. and Pakistan, Islam does not figure officially as the state religion, it is such to all intents and purposes, because of the racial tradition in both countries. Buddhism, after having been declared the state religion of Burma, ceased to be regarded as such by a revolutionary movement. For all practical purposes, however, it continues to enjoy particular status as the country's traditional faith. At the same time complete religious freedom, and even government appointments, are given to members of other religious traditions. In the case of Thailand and Ceylon, however, Buddhism is the state religion in both countries. That being so, adherents of other religions find themselves at a disadvantage, so far as government positions are concerned.

THE CHURCH-RELATED STATE

We come now to governments that are officially related to some branch of the Christian Church.

First and foremost within this category stands out *the clerical state*. The clerical state may be defined as: *a state so dominated by a particular form of the Christian religion that, both officially and practically, religion and nationality become equated.*

The most completely clerical state in the world of today is Spain, as it exists under the present Franco regime. Only Spaniards who belong to the Roman Catholic Church are regarded as truly belonging to the Spanish nation. No member of a non-Christian religion, or of a Christian communion other than the Roman, enjoys full political status. Such a person can hold no public office, nor can he be a doctor, a lawyer, or an officer in the armed services. This position expresses the doctrine of *Hispanidad,* an extreme form of the equation of nationality and religion, a doctrine to which reference has already been made. It was revived under the aegis of the present regime and was consecrated by a concordat between Spain and the Vatican in 1947. This doctrine is being buttressed by a secret organization called *Opus Dei* which, to all intents and purposes, constitutes a new religious order.

In Spain today, Protestant churches can bear no sign to indicate their identity. Worship is limited to buildings officially licensed. A religious service conducted in a private home exposes those who attend to fines and imprisonment. Protestants cannot be buried in the public cemeteries. A Spanish Protestant who was baptized as a Roman Catholic in childhood finds it extremely difficult to get married.

The second type of church-related state may be defined as *the state where one church is established, but where all churches and all religions are recognized and enjoy freedom.*

Representative examples of this type of church-state relationship are Sweden and England. In Sweden the state appoints the bishops of the Lutheran Church and controls ecclesiastical policy. Recently, in opposition to the wishes of the episcopate, the Swedish government sanctioned the ordination of women. Only very recently did non-Lutheran Churches in Sweden come to enjoy complete religious freedom.

The situation in England is somewhat similar. The British government, after consultation with churchmen and others, appoints the bishops of the Anglican Communion, which is the established Church of the nation. Several decades ago, when the Church of England desired to change its historic Prayer Book, it was unable to do so because of opposition in the British Parliament. On the other hand, in all matters that do not involve basic ecclesiastical structure, the Church of England enjoys the fullest freedom. In England all religions, and all non-Anglican denominations, are allowed to function with the most complete liberty.

Church-state relations in Scotland are of a quite unique character. The British Government recognizes the traditional Presbyterian Church in Scotland as the Church of Scotland. Because of this distinction, the Established Church enjoys special status in its relationship to the Crown. But, unlike the Church of England, the Church of Scotland is in no respect under the jurisdiction of the Crown or of Parliament, in any matter relating to its basic constitution or its particular policies. Symbolic of this is the fact that in 1960, on the occasion of the Four Hundredth Anniversary of the Scottish Reformation, Queen Elizabeth, when she appeared before the General Assembly, was the first to make a bow. By doing so, she recognized that she was in the presence of the representatives of the King of Kings to whom all earthly authority is subject. After the Queen had bowed, the Churchmen bowed. It need scarcely be added that in Scotland, as in England and throughout the British Commonwealth, all other churches and all religions enjoy perfect freedom.

Belonging to the type of Church-related state are also a number of Latin American republics, such as Peru, Colombia, and Argentina. With the single exception of Colombia, which still lags behind, there is complete freedom for non-Roman Catholics in all Latin American countries, both to worship and to propagate their faith.

THE SECULAR STATE

There is, finally, the secular state. By the secular state I mean *a state that gives no status, whether in its constitution or its governmental procedures, to any religion or church, but in which the official attitude towards religion and religious bodies may vary in practice.*

So-called secular states are of quite different types. There is, first, *the secular state which becomes itself a Church, creating thereby the practical equivalent of religion.* The outstanding example of this type of secular state is the Soviet Union. Let me synthetize in this context what was said more extensively in an earlier chapter.

Inherent in the constitution and attitude of the Soviet Union is the Marxist thesis that religion is "the opiate of the people," having been created by a ruling aristocracy in order to facilitate their continuing subjugation of the people. Yet here is the paradox. Russia today has its Holy Book, with both its Old Testament and its New Testament, namely, the writings of Marx and Lenin. Karl Marx stands in Moses' place as the lawgiver; while Lenin is the messiah who inaugurated the New Order. Russia is the "elect nation," and the world proletariat are the "People of God" who replace the Church as the worldwide Community of Christ. The *Politburo* constitutes the new apostolate, with Khrushchev as St. Peter, and Stalin as Judas, who has duly met his deserts and gone to "his own place." God's Eternal Purpose, which the Jewish philosopher, Marx, transformed into the dynamic force of dialectical materialism, will insure the great eschatological hope. This hope is the victory of the proletariat, and the reign of universal peace. And this goal will be achieved by the Community Party, which is the secular equivalent of the "gathered Church," a missionary body through which world revolution will be brought about and the New Order will come into being.

Here we have a mystic secularism in which devotion to the cause of the proletariat, through the medium of a political party, produces self-discipline and crusading missionary passion and becomes thereby the equivalent of religion.

It has become evident in the recent history of the Soviet Union that the official attitude towards religion is being modified. There is a growing appreciation of the fact that religion is native to the human spirit and cannot, and perhaps should not, be eliminated. In Russia today within certain limits, religious freedom obtains for worship and witness. A growing trend can be noted towards the recognition of the Church and of Churchmen as being in no way opposed to the best interests of the state or of the people, but as representing elements of positive worth. In this respect, as in others, the Soviet Union has passed beyond strict Marxism, which continues to be adhered to, however, by the Peoples' Republic of China.

In Communist Czechoslovakia, and to a lesser extent in Hungary, there is a type of secular state which *patronizes religion and uses it for its own purposes.* Could anything be more paradoxical than this? The present Czech government actually subsidizes the Church, whose theological seminaries and clergy receive state support. Within seminary classrooms there is complete freedom of thought, even to the extent of criticizing Marxism. But such criticism cannot be made in public.

Let me give a symbolical illustration of the attitude of the Czech government towards religion in the country's tradition. The figure of John Hus, the Czech national hero, who was a pre-Reformation Protestant and suffered martyrdom at the hands of the medieval Church, continues to be acclaimed by the New Order. The old John Hus Chapel has been restored and converted into a great national museum. In this ancient shrine I was privileged to preach some years ago, with the sanction of the authorities, on the occasion of a meeting in Prague of the Executive Committee of the World Presbyterian Alliance. It was the first sermon preached from the Hus pulpit in more than three hundred years. During that visit the members of our committee were shown an extraordinary film on the life of John Hus. Hus was presented as a proletarian leader who was persecuted by the religious hierarchy of the Middle Ages and was burned to death at the stake. When the embers were being lit, and the martyr was being offered his life in return for a complete recantation of his heretical position, the words put into the condemned man's mouth were these: "I cannot forsake my people." But what the great hero and friend of the masses did actually say, according to the irrefutable historical record, was this: "I cannot forsake my Christ." Here is a striking example of how a liberal and progressive Communist state can patronize religion and interpret a country's religious history and legendary Christian personalities in the interests of a secularist dream.

There is a third type of secular state. It is the secular state, which, *while being completely neutral in its attitude to religion, grants absolute religious freedom.* Two outstanding examples of this type of state are France and India.

Since the French government disestablished the Roman Catholic Church in the Nineteenth Century, in consequence of a violent anticlerical movement, France has officially maintained a neutralist attitude on all matters pertaining to religious thought, religious life, religious structures, and religious propaganda. The result has been the development of a very virile, intelligent, and ecumenical type of Christianity in Roman Catholic, Protestant, and Eastern Orthodox circles. All three Christian traditions are confronted in contemporary France by a highly secularized environment and a persistently antireligious intellectualism.

In the constitution of the new India, something which is quite unique among modern states must be noted. The Indian constitution, while committed to religious neutrality, provides that all who live in India shall have complete freedom to "profess, practice, and propagate" their faith. Most contemporary states grant the right of religious propaganda, but India alone has explicitly written this right into the national constitution. It is to be hoped that this right will not be affected in the years ahead by the development of a new Hindu nationalism.

A fourth type of secular state is *that which is benevolently neutral towards religion.* While Roman Catholicism is the religion of most Belgians, all religious groups in Belgium are not only tolerated, enjoying complete religious freedom, but are also the recipients of government aid. On the ground that they contribute to the welfare of the Belgian people, all recognized religious bodies in the country receive state subsidies. The amount of the subsidy, as well as the number of chaplains which each body can have in the armed forces, is proportionate to the size of its membership.

Uruguay, that small and very democratic country of South America, offers a fifth and quite unique type of secular state. Here is a state which, *while it grants complete religious freedom to all faiths, is, officially speaking, cynically disdainful of religion as such.* In the early years of the Twentieth Century, the Uruguayan calendar was changed by a radical government in such a way that all religious associations traditionally linked to special days and seasons, were eliminated. In Uruguay today Christmas Day is officially designated "Family Day," [15] while Easter Week is called "Touring Week." [16] When the leading newspaper, *El Día* has occasion to print the Spanish equivalent for God, Deity appears as *"dios,"* instead of *"Dios."* The Almighty is not given the distinction of a capital letter to His name!

But there is still another type of secular state. It is *the state which grants freedom to individuals and groups to profess, practice, and propagate their religious faith, but imposes severe restrictions upon all religious institutions and members of the Clergy.* This is the situation that obtains in Mexico.

Mexico is today the most stable country in Latin America. It is also the country which had the first social revolution in the modern world. Because, however, of a violent reaction in Mexico against the power of the traditional Roman Catholic Church, which had been for centuries the chief property owner in the

[15] *El Día de la Familia.*
[16] *La Semana de Turismo.*

country, the revolutionary government imposed the severest strictures upon all organized religion. Today no religious organization can own property. Members of the clergy do not have the right to vote in local, state, or national elections. Priests and bishops, monks and nuns, as well as Protestant ministers, are required by law to wear civilian garb in public. Religious bodies, moreover, cannot conduct educational institutions except for the training of men and women for vocational service.

While the foregoing conspectus cannot be regarded as fully covering the growing complexity in the relationship between government and religion in the more than one hundred independent nations in the world of our time, the panoramic view here presented will, I trust, set in perspective one of the greatest of contemporary issues.

REFLECTIONS ON THE CHURCH-STATE ISSUE

From considering the diverse types of relationship which actually exist between Church and state, and between religion and government in the world of today, let us now consider briefly and synthetically, as we bring this study to a close, the type of relationship which *should* exist between Church and state in a so-called "free society." I am not thinking, at this point, of the constitutional, or judicial, relationship between Church and state. For our present purpose this relationship must be taken as a fact. Taking this fact as our starting point, let us consider the moral responsibility of the Church as the Community of Christ towards state policy.

Echoing the Pauline viewpoint, let it be affirmed that all government as such is "ordained by God." Speaking as a theological son of John Calvin, I would add, in the words of the Genevan master, that the state is "God's vicegerent." It dare not presume to be, either an end in itself, or that for which everything exists (becoming thereby a substitute for Deity and assuming absolute authority). In a word the state is not, and dare not essay to become, "God walking upon earth," as the philosopher Hegel declared the German state to be, and that which the tyrant Hitler strove to make it.

It is the responsibility of the Church to co-operate with the state in every way possible, even when its structure and policy can in no way be regarded as ideal from a Christian viewpoint. The Church, however, must be prepared to disobey the state when the latter demands of Christians and of the Church adherence to ideas or forms of action which violate conscience and are incompatible with loyalty to Jesus Christ and the Church's Lord. The Church must also stand ready to call upon the state, and the institutions of government, to conduct policies, both within the nation, and in relation to other nations, that conduce to justice, understanding, and peace. Herein lies the abiding ethical responsibility of Christians and Christian Churches in a democratic society towards the state to which they give their loyal allegiance.

A new science is emerging, to which has been given the name "Metapolitics." It is expressive of an effort to move beyond politics, in search of the values and principles that determine, or should determine, political action or policy. Looking at the human situation metapolitically, what do we find? We find that the major forces which determine governmental policy are the quest of security, the acquisition of economic power, the passion for national sovereignty, violent anti-Communism, and the craving for international stability and peace.

Developments that should bring great satisfaction to Christians everywhere are the achievement of a Test-Ban Treaty, which banishes for the present the spectre of thermonuclear warfare, and the effort to secure disarmament in the interests of universal peace. The Churches have reason to rejoice in the reality and aims of the United Nations and should never cease to lend their support to this world body.

There are two phenomena, however, which should give increasing concern to the Church Universal, from local congregations to Ecumenical Councils. I refer to the "Cold War," and to the spectre of hate which, under the name of "anti-Communism," haunts some lands, especially the United States of America, one of the traditional homes of vital Christianity. All Churches are called upon to combat by every means at their disposal the methods and practices of the "Cold War," and to indict the baneful anti-Christian premise upon which it is founded, namely, that whatever helps to win the current propaganda struggle, is right whether it be a specious lie, a subtle theft, or a scandalous deed. There is no clearer evidence that civilization is in the post-Christian era than the demonic reality of the "Cold War." The Christian Church is under obligation to God and man to make its voice heard and its influence felt. It is summoned to seek the grace of Christ and the power of the Holy Spirit to multiply the number of encounters between actual enemies, to seek new bases of understanding, to provide platforms for corporate action, and, not least, to unmask professional liars.

As regards anti-Communism, a crucial issue has been confronting the Churches, very especially the American Churches, for a number of years. That issue is the official attitude of their country towards China and Cuba, and their own lack of a definite stand upon a question which involves both relations between Church and state, and the future of Asia and the Americas.

As one who has been involved in this issue, may I be allowed to clarify the standpoint I have taken, because I believe it has relevancy to a major question of Church-state relations on the contemporary scene. Here, let us be quite clear, is not an issue which belongs to an era that has come to an end, but to an era in Church-state relations that continues its unhappy course. Before the shades of night fall, let us give ourselves to reflection while the clouds, though lowering, are still high.

It should be made unmistakably clear that Communism does not have the answer for the ultimate problems of the human spirit and of human relations. It has no answer for man's hunger for spiritual freedom and the eternal God. Moreover, the Christian obligation to love others, whoever they be, and to admit them to one's circle of friends, is the crucial point where Christianity is superior to Marxism on the plane of human relations. A Marxist has no obligation to love another person as an individual, or to be his friend for his own sake, and not just for the sake of the Party and its goals. The classical biography of Karl Marx by Otto Rühle, himself a Marxist, makes clear that Marx had no use for people as individuals. He did not individualize. According to Rühle, the great Karl "detested social intercourse upon equal terms. He only cared to clink glasses with persons who praised and admired him. He took refuge in cynicism from any profounder manifestation of feeling." [17] And again, "the man who was a master of unsociability, and was incapable of true friendship, issued as a

[17] Otto Rühle, *Karl Marx, His Life and Work* (London: George Allen and Unwin, Ltd., 1929), p. 381.

watchword that all men were to be brothers." [18] It is upon this rock, the eternal imperative to show concern for other human beings for their own sake and to love them, that Marxist philosophy and its political counterpart will eventually be shattered.

For this very reason it is important that Christians and Christian Churches in a democratic society should demand the right to establish personal contact with fellow Christians in a Communist country with which their government has no diplomatic relations. To be concrete, the Government of the United States has refused and continues to refuse to allow American Churches to establish direct, personal contact with the Churches in China. Let the writer make this point clear by reaffirming a statement contained in the keynote address which he was privileged to deliver in Indianapolis, Indiana at a Joint Assembly of the Division of Christian Life and Work and the Division of Home Missions of the National Council of the Churches of Christ in America.

The words in question, which are as relevant today as when uttered in 1956, run as follows:

> We have reached a moment in the history of human relations, and of ecumenical relations in particular, when the eternal imperative of love to one's neighbor, who is also one's brother, should lead Christians around the world to establish contacts with fellow Christians and sister Churches in Communist lands. This has already been done, so far as regards contact with fellow Christians in Russia, Hungary, and Czechoslovakia, as well as in Rumania and Poland, and some other Communist-controlled countries. Thus far, however, the Churches of the West have not established contact with the Churches of China. It is absolutely imperative that this be done. Because of the essential unity of Christians in Christ, the Churches of the United States should proceed immediately to re-establish contact with brethren in the Peoples' Republic of China. We must delay no longer in meeting our Chinese Christian brethren face to face. It is a foundational principle of human relationship, which, alas, is not taken seriously in these sad years, that there can be no substitute for a face-to-face encounter between people who are estranged. It is doubly imperative that this principle be fulfilled when what is at stake is relations between

[18] *Ibid.*, p. 385.

Christians. Because of the traditional friendship between China and the United States, and the fact that so much of the Christian work in China today is the fruit of Christian missionary activity promoted from this country, the Churches of the United States have a great obligation to re-establish contact with Christians in China than do Christian Churches in any part of the world.

Christian Churchmen simply cannot regard as ultimate and permanently authoritative any Governmental edict that would force them to accept a situation which violates their Christian conscience and the eternal imperative of Christian love. We American Christians dare not, in loyalty to the mandate of Jesus Christ and the nature and unity of the Christian Church, accept any such ban so far as a visit from Christians to Christians is concerned. I trust that in this very gathering a process may be set in motion whereby we shall not wait for our Chinese Christian brethren to invite a delegation of American Churchmen to meet them face to face, but shall ourselves express to them our desire for such an encounter.[19]

It is a painful fact that, while the assembly in question gave overwhelming approbation to the proposed encounter between American and Chinese Christians, the General Board of the National Council, for reasons of ecclesiastical and political expediency, abstained from giving consideration to a proposal made by two of its major divisions. A year later the same group of distinguished Churchmen made clear that they did not endorse the action taken by another division of the Council which, at a national assembly in Cleveland, Ohio, advocated the diplomatic recognition of Communist China. The Council, moreover, has been backward in giving leadership to the Churches and the American people, in questions of inescapable importance for the Christian conscience, such, for example, as the current blockade of Cuba.

The problem of Communism cannot be dealt with in this negative fashion, by the mere creation of a void in the relations between peoples, or by making Communist nations suffer isolation and want. Official silence on the part of Church bodies, and their accommodation to state policies, when grave issues are involved

[19] "The Eternal Imperative in a World of Change," *Theology Today*, April, 1957.

that affect even the freedom of the Church to witness and to be "in very deed the Church," give grave concern.

Might Churches become puppets of the state in societies that glory in being "free?" Might they feel bound to do nothing and to say nothing that is not in clear accord with their institutional self-interest, because the Church establishment is so dependent for its existence upon members of the economic hierarchies by which government is controlled? Is the time approaching, in some democratic societies, when the cause of Christian truth, and loyalty to the one Lord, might call for a new Confessing Church and a "Barmen Declaration" addressed to the existing relationship between Church and state? That we cannot tell. But we can, and must, breathe this prayer: In the relations it maintains, in the functions it performs, in the vision of the Kingdom by which it lives, *let the Church be the Church.*

Forward Therefore!

epilogue

One thing has become clear. The Church Universal, in both its local and its ecumenical reality, must joyously accept its role to be a pilgrim Community, a fellowship of the Road, in every age and continent, in every society and state. Today, as in the turbulent time when Israel lived a crude existence, nearing the threshold of her national life, the words of that warrior daughter of Abraham, called Deborah, must take on contemporary significance: "That the leaders took the lead in Israel, that the people offered themselves willingly, bless the Lord!" (Judges 5:2).

In unity for mission, treading the ecumenical road towards the City of God, let the Christian pilgrims of today show themselves contemporary successors of those whose march was sung by an ancient bard of Israel in these rhapsodic words: "Blessed are the men whose strength is in Thee, in whose heart are the highways of Zion. As they go through the Valley of Baca,[1] they make it a place of springs. . . . They go from strength to strength" (Psalm 84:5–6).

Forward, therefore! More than poetry, more than romantic dreaming, is enshrined in Handel's Hallelujah chorus, "He shall reign—forever—and ever—and ever." That being certain, what

---

[1] A barren waste.

should be the Church's strategy today and tomorrow? In the exercise of its functions, in the maintenance of its relations, let Christ's Church, whatever be the place or time, or circumstance, in which its witness is given, strive, through the strength of Him who shall ultimately triumph, to be "in very deed the Church."

To expound the meaning of this imperative, and to explore its implications, for the Church and for the world, has been the design of this book. Notwithstanding its imperfections, which are manifold, may it contribute something to an understanding of the Church Universal and to the fulfillment of its ecumenical mission.

Bibliography

The bibliography is arranged in alphabetical order, by title. Books relating to the Faith and Order Movement, the International Missionary Council, the Life and Work Movement, and the World Council of Churches are alphabetically arranged under those headings within the section "Selected Guide to Further Reading."

SELECTED GUIDE TO FURTHER READING

Basileia: Walter Freytag Zum 60. Geburtstag. Jan Hermelink and Hans Jochen Margull, eds. Stuttgart: Evang. Missionsverlag, 1959. 515 pp. Wide range of articles by the leading figures of the worlds of ecumenics and missions. Very informative.

The Basis of Religious Liberty. A. F. Carrillo de Albornoz. New York: Association Press, 1963. 182 pp. Excellent study of ecumenical thought on the problems of religious liberty throughout today's world.

Beginning at Edinburgh: A Jubilee Assessment of The World Missionary Conference, 1910. Hugh Martin. London: Edinburgh House Press, 1960. 20 pp.

Beyond Religion: The Truth and Error in "Religionless Christianity." Daniel Jenkins. Philadelphia: The Westminster Press, 1962. 128 pp. Deals with the pros and cons of the relationship between true Christianity and the hyper-institutionalized and self-centered character of the Church today.

The Bible in World Evangelism. A. M. Chirgwin. New York: Friendship Press, 1954. 166 pp. Fine survey of the role of the Scriptures in the spread of the faith throughout Christian history.

*Biblical Authority for Today: A World Council of Churches Symposium
on "The Biblical Authority for the Churches' Social and Political
Message Today."* Alan Richardson and W. Schweitzer, eds.
London: SCM Press, 1951. 347 pp. Seven denominational interpretations of "the authority of the Bible," a survey of the status
of biblical theology and ethics at the time, six chapters on
hermeneutics, and six essays on application of the biblical view
to specific problems in social ethics. First rate.

The Biblical Doctrine of Justice and Law. Heinz-Horst Schrey and
others. London: SCM Press, 1955. 208 pp. Careful study of the
relationship of biblical righteousness and modern civil legisla-
tion.

Bibliography of the Theology of Missions in the Twentieth Century.
Rev. and enlarged. Gerald H. Anderson, comp. New York: Missionary Research Library, 1960. 79 pp.

The Biblical Doctrine of Man in Society. G. Ernest Wright and an
Ecumenical Committee. London: SCM Press, 1954. 176 pp.
Perceptive exegesis and interpretation of the biblical view, making it a companion volume to *Biblical Authority for Today*,
edited by Richardson and Schweitzer.

*Bridges to Understand: The "Academy Movement" in Europe and
North America.* Margaret Frakes. Philadelphia: Muhlenberg
Press, 1960. 134 pp. Excellent survey, more comprehensive than
subtitle indicates.

Brothers of the Faith. Stephen C. Neill. New York: Abingdon Press,
1960. 192 pp. Splendid interpretation of the range of 20th century ecumenical history in terms of the major personalities involved in the various aspects of the movement. (British edition,
SCM Press, *Men of Unity.*)

The Catholic Approach to Protestantism. George H. Tavard. New York:
Harper and Brothers, 1955. 160 pp.

*Catholic Ecumenism: The Reunion of Christendom in Contemporary
Papal Pronouncements.* Edward Francis Hanahoe. Washington,
D.C.: The Catholic University of America Press, 1953. 182 pp.
Fine doctoral dissertational survey of the pronouncements.

The Catholic Protestant Dialogue. Jean Bosc, Jean Guitton and Jean
Danielson. Trans. by Robert J. Olsen. Baltimore: Helicon Press,
1960. 138 pp. Bosc is a Protestant, the other two, Catholics.
Their discussions cover the meaning of Incarnation, the Church,
and authority, and of the role of the Scriptures.

The Challenge to Reunion. Robert McAfee Brown and David H. Scott.

New York: McGraw-Hill Book Company, 1963. 292 pp. Reactions and evaluations by numerous individuals, in various fields and from various points of view, to the "Blake-Pike Proposal" about church union in the U. S. A., made in 1960. A comprehensive and important study in American church history and church trends, with much value for understanding the contemporary scene in general, as well as unity and ecumenism in particular.

Christendom: The Christian Churches, Their Doctrines, Constitutional Forms, and Ways of Worship. Einar Molland. New York: Philosophical Library, 1959. 418 pp. Remarkable general survey of the major "families" of churches and leading sects.

The Christian Society. Stephen Neill. New York: Harper and Brothers, 1952. 334 pp. A survey of Christian history as a community rather than as an institution. Excellent for a different perspective than one normally gets.

Christian Theology: An Ecumenical Approach. Walter Marshall Horton. New York: Harper & Brothers, 1955. 304 pp. A synthesis of Protestant theologies.

Christian Unity in North America: A Symposium. J. Robert Nelson, ed. St. Louis: The Bethany Press, 1958. 208 pp. Variety of theologians and church leaders interpreting the status, problems, and prospects of unity in the U. S. A. and Canada.

Christian Unity in the Making: The First Twenty-Five Years of the Federal Council of the Churches of Christ in America, 1906–1930. Charles S. Macfarland. New York: Federal Council of Churches, 1948. 376 pp.

Christian Unity: Its Relevance to the Community. J(oseph) Quinter Miller. Strasburg, Va.: Shenandoah Publishing House, 1957. 122 pp. Lectures to the Association of Council Secretaries, discussing, meaningfully and practically, ways in which unity can be effected at local levels, through the channel of Councils of Churches.

Christianity and Revolution: The Lesson of Cuba. Leslie Dewart. New York: Herder and Herder, 1963. 320 pp. An unusual and provocative book, with useful sociopolitical insights as well as moral and religious interpretations, especially in an epilogue, "The Political Vocation of Christianity Today," and an appendix, "The Theology of Counterrevolution."

Christianity in a Revolutionary Age: A History of Christianity in the Nineteenth and Twentieth Centuries. 5 vols. Kenneth Scott

Latourette. New York: Harper, 1958–1962. 498, 532, 527, 568, 568 pp. An essential set of works for background and reference, by the foremost Christian historian.

Church and World Encounter: The Evangelical Academies in Germany and Their Meaning for the Ecumenical Church. Lee J. Gable. Philadelphia: United Church Press, 1964. 111 pp.

The Church of South India: The Movement Towards Union, 1900–1947. Bengt G. M. Sundkler. London: Lutterworth Press, 1954. 457 pp. Very comprehensive and able analysis of the most unique and significant church union in Protestant history, and the only voluntary union to comprehend all three basic forms of church polity: episcopal, presbyterian, congregational.

Church Unity and Church Mission. Martin E. Marty. Grand Rapids, Mich.: Wm. B. Eerdmans, 1964. 139 pp. A ringing challenge to the mid-twentieth century ecumenical movement to "stop looking at itself" and become immersed again in what gave it birth and life: the missionary obligation to witness to "one Lord."

The Churches and Rapid Social Change. Paul Abrecht. Garden City, N. Y.: Doubleday & Co., 1961. 216 pp. Second in a twin-volume study by the World Council of Churches, dealing specifically with the problems and obligations confronting the churches as a result of rapid social change. Two major contributions are (1) the way it sets forth the fact that the Church is by the nature of its faith involved in social, economic, political and international affairs, and (2) the way in which the "younger churches" are implicated in this responsibility along with the older churches. Final chapter discusses the obligation of the Church in discovering and implementing a "moral basis of a new society," within the context both of new social organisms emerging in the non-Christian societies and of the traditionally "Christian" societies.

The Church's Mission in the World. Vol. 102 in *The Twentieth Century Encyclopedia of Catholicism.* Louis and André Rétif. Trans. by Reginald F. Trevett. New York: Hawthorn Books, 1962. 156 pp. Grapples in a profound yet practical way with the problems of the Church in this era of world-wide industrialization and general social disorganization.

The Coming Great Church: Essays on Church Unity. Theodore O. Wedel. New York: The Macmillan Co., 1945. 160 pp. Thought-provoking articles on the Ecumenical Movement, the Protestant Liturgical Movement, "the Return to Orthodoxy," neglected but basic Christian doctrines, and "the Catholic-Protestant Chasm."

Conflict and Agreement in the Church. 2 vols. T. F. Torrance. Vol. One: *Order and Disorder.* 331 pp. Vol. Two: *The Ministry and the Sacraments of the Gospel.* 213 pp. London: Lutterworth Press, 1959, 1960. Collection of theological essays of a discriminating and important character.

The Conflict Between Church and State in Latin America. Frederick B. Pike, ed. New York: Alfred A. Knopf, 1964. 239 pp. Twenty pertinent essays by a wide variety of persons, comprehending the topic from the early 16th century to the present. Amazingly candid and self-critical. Editor is on the faculty of the University of Notre Dame.

The Council, Reform and Reunion. Hans Küng. Trans. by Cecily Hastings. New York: Sheed and Ward, 1961. 208 pp. Probably the most important general study on its subject, by a leading liberal Catholic scholar.

Creative Tension. Stephen Neill. London: Edinburgh House, 1959. 115 pp. Deals very constructively with some major tensions of faith (Christian and non-Christian), nation and Church, mission and Church, and partnership in obedience to the Great Commission.

Critical Bibliography of Missiology. (Vol. E 2 of *Bibliographia ad Usum*) Anastasius Disch and J. Wils, comps. of English edition. Nijmegen, Holland: Bestelcentrale der V.S.K.B., 1960. 118 pp. Good annotated list of 306 select works in Latin, German, French and English. On missionary theory, law, methodology, history, missiography ("progress, opposition, special difficulties, success or failure of certain methods"), and propaganda.

Death of a Myth: New Locus for Spanish American Faith. Kyle Haselden. New York: Friendship Press, 1964. 175 pp. The myth, or popular misconception, is that Spanish Americans are by nature not responsive to Protestantism. This little volume dispels any ground for such assumption, and also points up a number of contributions Protestantism could well receive from the Spanish American temperament and culture.

Digest of the Proceedings of the Consultation on Church Union for 1962 and 1963. Vols. I and II combined. 1963. 159 pp. George L. Hunt, comp. Available from P. O. Box 69, Fanwood, N. J. It is intended that this *Digest* will continue as an annual publication.

Documents Bearing on the Problem of Christian Unity and Fellowship, 1916–1920. London: S.P.C.K., 1920. 93 pp.

Documents on Christian Unity. G. K. A. Bell, ed. First Series, 1920–4.

London: Oxford University Press, 1924. 382 pp. Second Series, 1924–30. London: Oxford University Press, 1930. 225 pp. Third Series, 1930–48. London: Oxford University Press, 1948. 300 pp. Fourth Series, 1948–57. London: Oxford University Press, 1958. 243 pp.

Ecumenical Beginnings in the Protestant World Mission: A History of Comity. R. Pierce Beaver. New York: Thomas Nelson & Sons, 1962. 356 pp. Deals effectively with the meaning of the term "comity," the relationship between comity and unity, the distinctive forms assumed by comity in various geographical areas, and problems involved in the effort to practice comity.

The Ecumenical Era in Church and Society: A Symposium in Honor of John A. Mackay. Edward J. Jurji, ed. New York: The Macmillan Co., 1959. 238 pp. Very good symposium on theology, culture, missions, and ecumenism, with an appreciation of Dr. Mackay, a biographical note about him, and a selected list of his writings.

Ecumenical Foundations: A History of the International Missionary Council and Its Nineteenth-Century Background. William Richey Hogg. New York: Harper & Brothers, 1952. 466 pp. Still the only real history of the origins of the modern ecumenical movement. A storehouse of much valuable information and interpretation.

The Ecumenical Movement: What It Is and What It Does. Norman Goodall. London: Oxford University Press, 1961. 240 pp. Excellent brief interpretation.

Ecumenism and Catholicity. William Nicholls. London: SCM Press, 1952. 159 pp. Fine interpretation of the nature of the Church, with scholarly suggestions about steps toward unity through "theological integration."

Ecumenism and the Bible. Rev. ed. David Hedegard. London: The Banner of Trust Trust, 1964. Scholarly but very critical interpretation of the ecumenical movement and its teachings. Two new chapters have been added to the first (1953) edition: "Evangelical Missions in the Age of Ecumenism" and "The Second Vatican Council." Gives a sharply contrasting picture from that usually seen in works about the ecumenical movement, and therefore provides a basis for balance. Author is an ultra-conservative leader in Sweden, sometime lecturer in New Testament at the University of Lund.

FAITH AND ORDER MOVEMENT

A Documentary History of the Faith and Order Movement, 1927–1963. Lukas Vischer, ed. St. Louis: The Bethany Press, 1963. 246 pp. Excellent source book.

Faith and Order Findings. Paul S. Minear, ed. Minneapolis: Augsburg Publishing House, 1963. 228 pp. Reports made to the Fourth World Conference on Faith and Order, Montreal, 1963, by the commissions on Christ and the Church, Tradition and Traditions, Worship, and Institutionalism.

Faith and Order: Proceedings of the World Conference, Lausanne, 1927. H. N. Bate, ed. New York: George H. Doran Company, 1927. 534 pp. Report of the First World Conference of the Faith and Order Movement.

Fifty Years of Faith and Order: An Interpretation of the Faith and Order Movement. John E. Skoglund and J. Robert Nelson. New York: The Interseminary Movement, 1963. 113 pp. Brief, popular account designed chiefly as an introduction for seminary students.

The Fourth World Conference on Faith and Order. Patrick C. Rodger and Lukas Vischer, eds. New York: Association Press, 1964. 127 pp. A diary of the Montreal Conference, 1963 (by David M. Paton) and the five section reports made by the conference.

Institutionalism and Church Unity. Nils Ehrenstrom and Walter G. Muelder, eds. New York: Association Press, 1963. 378 pp. Significant papers prepared by the Study Commission on Institutionalism of the Commission on Faith and Order, World Council of Churches.

Minutes of the Faith and Order Commission and Working Committee: The Mandate from the Fourth World Conference on Faith and Order, Montreal, Canada, 1963. New York: World Council of Churches, 1963. 59 pp. Contains the Conference's numerous recommendations of questions for further study.

The Nature of the Unity We Seek: Official Report of the North American Conference on Faith and Order, 1957. Paul S. Minear, ed. St. Louis: The Bethany Press, 1958. 304 pp.

One Lord, One Baptism. Minneapolis: Augsburg Publishing House, 1961. 46 pp. Two reports made to the Fourth World Conference on Faith and Order, Montreal, 1963: on "The Meaning of

Baptism" and "The Divine Trinity and the Unity of the Church."
The Second World Conference on Faith and Order, Edinburgh, 1937.
    Leonard Hodgson, ed. New York: The Macmillan Co., 1938. 386
    pp.
The Third Conference on Faith and Order, Lund, 1952. Oliver S. Tom-
    kins, ed. London: SCM Press, 1953. 380 pp.

The First Decade: An Account of the Church of South India. Rajaiah
    D. Paul. London: Lutterworth Press, 1958. 294 pp.
*Foundations of the Conciliar Theory: The Contribution of Medieval
    Canonists from Gratian to the Great Schism.* Brian Tierney.
    New York: Cambridge University Press, 1955.
Foundations of the Responsible Society. Walter G. Muelder. New
    York: Abingdon Press, 1959. 304 pp. Thorough and excellent
    working out of the implications of the ethical thesis current in
    ecumenical circles: the responsible society. Deals with all
    aspects of the question in relationship to Western society. A
    very important work.
From Uniformity to Unity, 1662–1962. Geoffrey F. Nuttall and Owen
    Chadwick, eds. London: S.P.C.K., 1962. 423 pp. Discussions on
    problems involved in Establishment, Non-conformity, and
    rapprochement.
*The Greek East and the Latin West: A Study in the Christian Tradi-
    tion.* Philip Sherrard. New York: Oxford University Press, 1959.
    202 pp. Splendid theological-philosophical inquiry into the ideo-
    logical worlds into which Christianity was born, concluding
    that we are once again in a similar situation, and should there-
    fore understand the Church's task as within such a framework
    of reference.
*The Growth of the World Church: The Story of the Modern Missionary
    Movement.* Ernest A. Payne. London: Edinburgh House Press,
    1955. 174 pp. Simple but comprehensive and very good por-
    trait.
*The Historic Reality of Christian Culture: A Way to the Renewal of
    Human Life.* Christopher Dawson. New York: Harper & Broth-
    ers, 1960. 124 pp. Analysis of the relationship between Chris-
    tianity and culture, with a tracing of the course of growing
    secularization over the past 200 years which "has led to the
    present malaise," and an appeal for a new "organic union be-
    tween Christianity and civilization" as the ground for the re-
    newal of Christianity.

A History of the Ecumenical Movement, 1517–1948. Ruth Rouse and Stephen Charles Neill, eds. Philadelphia: The Westminster Press, 1954. 822 pp. The definitive and best history of the efforts toward unity from the Protestant Reformation to the formation of the World Council of Churches. An indispensable book, for reading and for reference.

A History of the Expansion of Christianity. 7 vols. Kenneth Scott Latourette. New York: Harper & Brothers, 1937–1945. 412, 492, 503, 516, 502, 526, 542 pp. Most definitive history of the spread of Christianity ever done. Essential.

History's Lessons for Tomorrow's Mission [No. 1–2, 1960 of *The Student World*] Philippe Maury, ed. Geneva: World's Student Christian Federation, 1960. 300 pp. One of the best survey-interpretations, both historical and contemporary, available. An essential book, many chapters of which should be re-read frequently.

Hope in Action: The Church's Task in the World. Hans J. Margull. Trans. by Eugene Peters. Philadelphia: Muhlenberg Press, 1962. 298 pp. Thorough, scholarly study of "the difficult problem of [understanding] evangelism theologically" and in the ecumenical milieu.

The Household of God. rev. ed. Lesslie Newbigin. London: SCM Press, 1964. Widely used and influential lectures on the nature of the church, first published in 1953. New edition has a new preface to up-date it.

Images of the Church in the New Testament. Paul S. Minear. Philadelphia: The Westminster Press, 1960. 294 pp. Best study of the views about the Church as reflected in the terminology and usage of the Bible. An essential book.

Evangelism: The Mission of the Church to Those Outside Her Life. Prepared by the World Council of Churches. London: SCM Press, 1954. 62 pp. One of the six preparatory studies for the Second Assembly of the World Council of Churches. Surveys the situation in evangelism at that time in the major areas of the world, then deals with problems and opportunities.

INTERNATIONAL MISSIONARY COUNCIL

The Ghana Assembly of the International Missionary Council, 1957–58: Selected Papers, with an Essay on the Role of the I.M.C. Ronald K. Orchard, ed. London: Edinburgh House Press, 1958. 240 pp.

The Jerusalem Meeting of the International Missionary Council, 1928. 8 vols. London: International Missionary Council, 1928. 424, 225, 305, 208, 167, 272, 126, 180 pp.

The Madras Series: Papers Based on the Meeting of the International Missionary Council at Tambaram, Madras, India, 1938. 7 vols. New York: International Missionary Council, 1939. 199, 281, 418, 412, 596, 314, 193 pp.

Missions Under the Cross: Addresses Delivered at the Enlarged Meeting of the Committee of the International Missionary Council at Willingen, in Germany, 1952; With Statements Issued by the Meeting. Norman Goodall, ed. London: Edinburgh House Press, 1953. 264 pp.

Renewal and Advance: Christian Witness in a Revolutionary World [Meeting in Whitby, Ontario, Canada, 1947]. C. W. Ranson, ed. London: Edinburgh House Press, 1948. 228 pp.

The Kingship of Christ: An Interpretation of Recent European Theology. W. A. Visser 't Hooft. New York: Harper & Brothers, 1948. 158 pp. Helpful background, with the always-fruitful creative insights of Visser 't Hooft himself.

The Kingship of Christ: The Story of the World Council of Churches. G. K. A. Bell. Baltimore: Penguin Books, 1954. 181 pp. An account by one intimately associated from the beginning with the movement culminating in the World Council of Churches.

The Latin American Churches and the Ecumenical Movement. John A. Mackay. Committee on Cooperation in Latin America.

Lausanne: The Will to Understand—An American Interpretation. Edmund Davison Soper. Garden City, N. Y.: Doubleday, Doran & Co., 1928. 156 pp. Lucid and useful personal response, by one well qualified.

The Layman Abroad in the Mission of the Church. Paul Loffler. London: Edinburgh House Press, 1962. 96 pp.

The Layman in Christian History. Stephen C. Neill and Hans-Ruedi Weber. London: SCM Press, 1963. 408 pp.

A Layman Looks at the Church. Kenneth Grubb. London: Hodder and Stoughton, 1964. 190 pp. One of the world's leading Christian laymen expresses his convictions about the Church and the role of the layman, showing how in history the layman has often been the pioneer in great movements of Christian reform and renewal.

LIFE AND WORK MOVEMENT

The Stockholm Conference, 1925: The Official Report of the Universal Christian Conference on Life and Work, 1925. G. K. A. Bell, ed. London: Oxford University Press, 1926. 971 pp.

Church, Community and State Official Conference Books:

Vol. I, *The Church and Its Function in Society.* W. A. Visser 't Hooft and J. H. Oldham.

Vol. II, *The Christian Understanding of Man.* T. E. Jessop, and others. 268 pp.

Vol. III, *The Kingdom of God and History.* H. G. Wood, and others. 217 pp.

Vol. IV, *Christian Faith and the Common Life.* Nils Ehrenstrom, and others. 195 pp.

Vol. V, *Church and Community.* Kenneth S. Latourette, and others. 259 pp.

Vol. VI, *Church, Community and State in Relation to Education.* Fred Clarke, and others. 234 pp.

Vol. VII, *The Universal Church and the World of Nations.* Marquess of Lothian, and others. 315 pp. Volumes I–VII: New York: Willett, Clark & Company, 1938.

Vol. VIII, *The Churches Survey Their Task: The Report of the Conference at Oxford,* July 1937. J. H. Oldham, comp. London: George Allen & Unwin, 1937. 314 pp.

Liturgical Renewal: Studies in Catholic and Protestant Developments on the Continent. J(ean) D(aniel) Benoit. Trans. by Edwin Hudson. London: SCM Press, 1958. 112 pp. Brief but good survey, covering only French-speaking Reformed Churches and the Roman Catholic Church.

Living Springs: New Religious Movements in Western Europe. Olive Wyon. London: SCM Press, 1963. 128 pp. Brief but valuable description of the newest and most significant trend in Christianity: "the idea of a religious community which inherits the peace and grace of the old monastic tradition, but which in rule and spirit meets twentieth century stirrings."

Local Church and World Mission. Douglas Webster. London: SCM Press, 1962. 92 pp. Originally designed for Anglican theological students, this book nonetheless has ecumenical value and contains much good thought on a very current consideration being encouraged by the World Council of Churches.

The Missionary Church: A Study in the Contribution of Modern Missions to Oecumenical Christianity. William Wilson Cash. London: Church Missionary Society, 1939. 326 pp. Fair general survey of the character of modern Protestant missions, and the way the universal church came into being quite unplanned by man.

Missionary, Go Home! A Reappraisal of the Christian World Mission. James A. Scherer. Englewood Cliffs, N. J.: Prentice-Hall, 1964. 192 pp. Re-examination of the whole range of questions relating to the Church in her missionary obligation today. Remarkable combination of Biblical, theological and practical perspective.

The Missionary Nature of the Church: A Survey of the Biblical Theology of Mission. Johannes Blauw. New York: McGraw-Hill Book Co., 1962. 182 pp. Excellent survey of the ablest exegetical and theological writing on the Bible and mission over the past 30 years. Thirty-six pages of Notes provide not only splendid bibliographical data but much valuable personal insight which the author felt should be precluded from the text because of the semi-official character of the book (done under the auspices of the Department of Missionary Studies of the World Council of Churches).

The Misunderstanding of the Church. Emil Brunner. Trans. by Harold Knight. Philadelphia: The Westminster Press, 1953. 132 pp. The most important single volume for understanding the Church and the doctrine of the Church in this day. Along with it should be read Jenkins' *The Strangeness of the Church.*

The Nature of the Church: Papers Presented to the Theological Commission of the World Conference on Faith and Order. R. Newton Flew, ed. London: SCM Press, 1952. 347 pp. Statements about the essential concept of the Church as held by the major denominations in Britain and the U. S. A.

A New Pentecost: Vatican Council II, Session 1. Vincent A. Yzermans. Westminster, Md.: The Newman Press, 1963. 376 pp. Very competent reporting on the Council.

The Noise of Solemn Assemblies: Christian Commitment and Religious Establishment in America. Peter L. Berger. Garden City, N. Y.: Doubleday & Co., 1961. 189 pp. Severe critique of religion in the U. S. A. today. Essential position is that contemporary "Christianity" in the United States is only an American culture religion, which nonetheless is as "established" as any State Church ever has been. Author, a trained sociologist of religion, holds that a new era must be precipitated which will be marked by transforming personal conversions, creatively new theological formulations, and radical involvement in Christian social responsibility.

No Other Name: The Choice Between Syncretism and Christian Universalism. W. A. Visser 't Hooft. London: SCM Press, 1963. 128 pp. Profound analysis of syncretism and of the Biblical attitude toward this innate human tendency. A very relevant and significant work.

The Oecumenical Movement and the Unity of the Church. Thomas [A.] Sartory. Trans. by Hilda C. Graef. Westminster, Md.: The Newman Press, 1963. 290 pp. Enlarged and adapted version of a German work (1955). In the first third of the book, the Roman Catholic scholar views the Protestant ecumenical movement historically, and in the last two-thirds he discusses theological points bearing on unity and union.

Ökumene in Mission und Kirche: Entwicklungslinien der Heutigen Ökumenischen Bewegung. Nils Karlstrom. München: Claudius Verlag, 1962. 280 pp.

Ökumenische Kirchenkundi: Lebensformen der Christenheit Heute. Peter Meinhold. Stuttgart: Kreuz-Verlag, 1962. 652 pp.

On the Road to Christian Unity: An Appraisal of the Ecumenical Movement. Samuel McCrea Cavert. New York: Harper & Brothers, 1961. 192 pp. Excellent study of the 20th century ecumenical movement, with analysis of the different participating groups and of the non-participating groups, and a look to the future.

One Church: Catholic and Reformed—Toward a Theology for Ecumenical Decision. Lewis S. Mudge. Philadelphia: Westminster Press, 1963. 96 pp. Fine reflections on theology and ecumenics.

The One Church in the Light of the New Testament. Clarence Tucker Craig. New York: Abingdon-Cokesbury Press, 1951. 155 pp. A New Testament scholar studies the contribution of that part of the Bible to Christian unity and union.

One Great Ground of Hope: Christian Missions and Christian Unity. Henry P. Van Dusen. Philadelphia: The Westminster Press, 1961. 205 pp. Fine summary of the way 19th century missions led to the growth of Christian unity, evaluation of the role of the "younger churches" in furthering unity, and an estimate of the "prospects for tomorrow."

One World, One Mission. William Richey Hogg. New York: Friendship Press, 1960. 164 pp. Study course book but still an excellent presentation of the relationship between mission, unity in the Church, and unity in the world.

Origin and History of the Federal Council of the Churches of Christ in America. Elias B. Sanford. Hartford, Conn.: The S. S. Scranton Co., 1916. 528 pp.

Outside the Camp. Charles C. West. Garden City, N. Y.: Doubleday & Company, 1959. 168 pp. First rate discussion of the obligation of the Church to those outside her membership in today's world.

Overcoming Christian Divisions. J. Robert Nelson. New York: Association Press, 1962. 126 pp. Revised edition of *One Lord, One Church* (Lutterworth, 1958), appealing for effort by the rank and file of Christians to labor to be "one" as Christ intended.

The Papal Council and the Gospel: Protestant Theologians Evaluate the Coming Vatican Council. Kristen E. Skydsgaard, ed. Minneapolis: Augsburg Publishing House, 1961. 213 pp. Studies in the Lutheran position toward ecumenism and toward church councils. Authors are mostly Europeans.

Partnership: The Study of an Idea. Max Warrne. London: SCM Press, 1956. 127 pp. Thoughtful and thought-provoking study of Christian interdependence.

The Pilgrim Church: An Account of the First Five Years in the Life of the Church of South India. Marcus Ward. London: The Epworth Press, 1953. 216 pp.

The Pressure of Our Common Calling. W. A. Visser 't Hooft. Garden City, N. Y.: Doubleday & Co., 1959. 90 pp. Excellent little volume about the "theology of the ecumenical movement."

The Problem of Catholicism. Vittorio Subilia. Trans. by Reginald Kissack. London: SCM Press, 1964. 190 pp. Succinct but comprehensive and profound interpretation of Reformed Christianity vis-à-vis Roman Catholicism, and what both need if real ecumenism is to emerge. This is an extremely important book, written by a Professor on the Waldensian Theological Faculty, Rome.

Progress and Perspective: The Catholic Quest for Unity. Gregory Baum. New York: Sheed and Ward, 1962. 245 pp. Thoughtful and solid inquiry by a Roman Catholic about the nature of the Kingdom and the Church, schism, Protestantism, the Christian and the Jews, ecumenism, and unity.

The Prospects of Christianity Throughout the World. M. Searle Bates and Wilhelm Pauck, eds. New York: Charles Scribner's Sons, 1964. 286 pp. Sixteen essays by notable personages around the world, all of whom were associated in some way with Union Theological Seminary in New York during the presidency of Henry Pitney Van Dusen.

The Radical Mutation in Theology: The Forthcoming Role of the Non-Christian Religious Systems as Contributory to Christian Theology. Herbert C. Jackson. New York: Missionary Research Library, 1961.

The Realm of Redemption: Studies in the Doctrine of the Nature of the Church in Contemporary Protestant Theology. J. Robert Nelson. London: The Epworth Press, 1951. 249 pp. Best survey and interpretation available on studies on the Church up to the time of its publication (1951), and still extremely significant.

The Recovery of Unity: A Theological Approach. Eric Lionel Mascall. New York: Longmans, Green & Company, 1958. 242 pp. Good tracing of basic theological points from the Middle Ages and interpretation of problems in theological disunity today.

Reformation and Catholicity. Gustaf Aulen. Trans. by Eric H. Wahlstrom. Philadelphia: Muhlenberg Press, 1961. 203 pp. Noted Swedish theologian undertakes to express the historical catholicity of the Church as understood by the Reformers, and apply this pristine attitude to problems in ecumenical relations and discussions today.

The Reintegration of the Church: A Study in Intercommunion. Nicolas Zernov. London: SCM Press, 1952. 128 pp. An Eastern Orthodox scholar (Oxford University) studies one of the most crucial points in the union of Christians in the churches.

Religion and Faith in Latin America. W. Stanley Rycroft. A basic book on the religious situation in Latin America.

The Renewal of the Church. W. A. Visser 't Hooft. London: SCM Press, 1956. 128 pp. Superb book, on the thesis that the Church is always in need of renewal, on the basis of which thesis the author analyzes the problem of the relation of the new to the old. Actually, a Biblical and theological study.

The Responsible Church and the Foreign Mission. Peter Beyerhaus and Henry Lefever. London: World Dominion Press, 1964. 199 pp. One of the very best recent studies in the missionary obligation and the role of the Church.

The Reunion of the Church. Rev. ed. Lesslie Newbigin. London: SCM Press, 1964. An extensively revised and really new edition. Deals chiefly with the Church of South India, inaugurated in 1947.

The Rise of Protestant Monasticism. François Biot. Trans. by W. J. Kerrigan. Baltimore: Helicon, 1963. 161 pp. Excellent contribution, by a Catholic priest, to the growing literature on monasticism in Protestantism, seeing it as a sign and means of renewal. Biot studies effectively the position of Luther, Calvin and other reformers, as well as of church confessions, traces the survival

expressions of monasticism in Protestantism, then describes the
resurgence of monasticism beginning with the Taizé Community.
The second half of this little volume deals with the theological
justifications for monasticism, the problem of the relationship
between the monastic community and "the world," and "Vocation, Basis of Community Life." The book closes with an analysis of Karl Barth's views on this Protestant phenomenon.

Schism in the Early Church. rev. ed. S. L. Greenslade. London: SCM
Press, 1964. New notes and a new preface being added to the
ablest work available on Christian schism.

*The Second Vatican Council: The Story Behind the Ecumenical Coun-
cil of Pope John XXIII.* Henri Daniel-Rops. Trans. by Alastair
Guinan. New York: Hawthorn Books, 1962. 160 pp. The noted
editor of The Twentieth Century Encyclopedia of Catholicism
(real name: Henri Jules Charles Petiot) provides here a good
perspective, surveying church councils from New Testament
times to the present, analyzing thoroughly what an ecumenical
council is (from a Roman Catholic point of view), and prog-
nosticates the effects of Vatican II.

Signs of Renewal: The Life of the Lay Institute in Europe. Department of the Laity, World Council of Churches. Geneva: World
Council of Churches, n.d. 63 pp.

*The Social Sources of Church Unity: An Interpretation of Unitive
Movements in American Protestantism.* Robert Lee. New York:
Abingdon Press, 1960. 238 pp. Excellent follow-up to H. Richard
Niebuhr's *The Social Sources of Denominationalism,* this book,
too, is necessary for an understanding of sociological processes
affecting Christianity.

The Social Sources of Denominationalism. H. Richard Niebuhr. New
York: Meridian Books, 1957. 304 pp. Standard and best analysis
of the Protestant phenomenon of denominationalism. Essential
for ecumenical understanding.

The Social Thought of the World Council of Churches. Edward Duff.
New York: Longmans, Green and Co., 1956. 339 pp. Scholarly
and superb analysis, with an outside perspective, for the author
is a Roman Catholic. This is an essential book.

The Soul of Greece. Raymond Etteldorf. Westminster, Md.: The Newman Press, 1963. 235 pp. An attempt by a Roman Catholic to
make a sympathetic comparative study of the Greek Orthodox
and Roman Catholic Churches.

The Strangeness of the Church. Daniel Jenkins. Garden City, N. Y.:
Doubleday & Co., 1955. 188 pp. A rare book indeed, and one

which should be read repeatedly, along with Brunner's *The Misunderstanding of the Church.*

The Study of Missions in Theological Education. 2 vols. Olav Guttorm Myklebust. Oslo, Norway: Forlaget Land og Kirke, 1955, 1957. 459, 412 pp. The only study of its kind. Most useful not only for informational purposes but as a guide to what is needed still by way of emphasis upon mission in theological education.

The Sufficiency of God: Essays on the Ecumenical Hope in Honor of W. A. Visser 't Hooft. Robert C. Mackie and Charles C. West, eds. London: SCM Press, 1963. 240 pp. An appreciation of the only General Secretary the World Council of Churches has had thus far (1964), and 14 first-rate essays on as many aspects of ecumenical concern by foremost thinkers and leaders in the ecumenical movement.

That They Go Forward: An Impression of the Oxford Conference on Church, Community and State. Eric Fenn. London: SCM Press, 1938. 104 pp. A discerning interpretation of one of the most important meetings in modern Christian history.

Theology Between Yesterday and Tomorrow. Josef L. Hromádka. Philadelphia: The Westminster Press, 1957. 106 pp. One of the ablest but most controversial figures in modern Christianity undertakes both to effect understanding between the two great segments of Christians (those in the Communist world and those outside it) and to break new ground for theological inquiry which grapples with contemporary problems and needs rather than merely reinterprets classical theology.

The Theology of the Christian Mission. Gerald H. Anderson, ed. New York: McGraw-Hill Book Co., 1961. 341 pp. A symposium covering the whole spectrum of views about the missionary obligation and about the approach to mission. More valuable for showing this gamut than for any inherent contribution in the material itself.

A Theology of the Laity. Hendrik Kraemer. London: Lutterworth Press, 1958. 191 pp. Survey of the status of the laity in the Church through Christian history, and an effective effort to set forth a theology that will reflect what the Scriptures envision, and Christian faith demands, as the role of the laity.

Toward World-Wide Christianity. O. Frederick Nolde, ed. New York: Harper & Brothers, 1964. 263 pp. A study volume prepared for the Interseminary Movement, this work has much material still of value for historical and interpretative purposes.

Trinitarian Faith and Today's Mission. Lesslie Newbigin. Richmond,

Va.: John Knox Press, 1964. 78 pp. Excellent essay grappling with the perplexities of those already committed to the Christian mission but confused by the problems and vagaries of the present situation.

Two Centuries of Ecumenism. George H. Tavard. Trans. by Royce W. Hughes. Notre Dame, Ind.: Fides Publishers, 1960. 239 pp. A leading Roman Catholic scholar on ecumenism delineates for the American public the genesis and development of modern Catholic ecumenism.

Two Centuries of Student Christian Movements, Their Origin and Intercollegiate Life. Clarence P. Shedd. New York: Association Press, 1934. 466 pp. Broader in scope than the Rouse book on the WSCF, this also gives a thorough picture of the range of student movements up to 30 years ago.

Under Orders: The Churches and Public Affairs. Roswell P. Barnes. Garden City, N. Y.: Doubleday & Company, 1961. 138 pp. An essential book for Christians in contemporary America, grappling practically with the principles enunciated in Muelder's *Foundations of the Responsible Society.*

The Unfinished Task. Stephen Neill. London: Edinburgh House Press, 1957. 228 pp. Excellent delineation of the Christian situation as of the date of writing (1957).

Unity: A History and Some Reflections. Maurice Villain. Trans. by J. R. Foster. London: Harvill Press, 1963. 381 pp. The history deals only with the 20th century Protestant ecumenical movement. A thought-provoking work by a French Catholic priest, designed for Catholics to aid rapprochement.

Unity and Reunion: A Bibliography. 2nd and enlarged ed. Henry R. T. Brandreth, comp. London: Adam & Charles Black, 1948, 158 pp.

Unity in Mid-Career: An Ecumenical Critique. Keith R. Bridston and Walter D. Wagoner. New York: The Macmillan Co., 1963. 211 pp. Insightful, and often severe, evaluation of the status of and trends within the Protestant ecumenical movement at the close of its first half-century.

Upon the Earth: The Mission of God and the Missionary Enterprise of the Churches. D. T. Niles. New York: McGraw-Hill Co., 1962. 269 pp. Companion volume to Blauw's *The Missionary Nature of the Church,* making practical the matter of applying to the contemporary situation the implications of the insights gained from biblical and theological study.

The Voice of the Church: The Ecumenical Council. Eugene R. Fair-

weather and Edward R. Hardy. Greenwich, Conn.: The Sea-
bury Press, 1962. 127 pp. Two Anglican scholars, a theologian
and a historian, provide a semi-popular delineation of the meaning and role of ecumenical councils in history, concluding that
only the whole Church can be the authority, and therefore the
ground for Christian unity.

Weltkirchen Lexikon: Handbuch der Ökumene. Franklin H. Littell
and Hans Hermann Walz, eds. Stuttgart: Kreuz-Verlag, 1960.
1755 pp. Essential reference tool.

Weltmission in Ökumenischer Zeit. Gerhard Brennecke, ed. Stuttgart:
Evang. Missionsverlag, 1961. 335 pp. First-rate survey of the
current status of Christianity and her mission, by 29 leading
missions scholars.

We the People: A Book About Laity. Kathleen Bliss. London: SCM
Press, 1963. 139 pp. Superb discussion about the whole relationship between the ecumenical awakening and the concomitant
awakening of the whole People of God, by the most brilliant
woman in church leadership.

We Witness Together: A History of Cooperative Home Missions.
Robert T. Handy. New York: Friendship Press, 1956. 273 pp.
The only work of its kind. Very useful.

Where in the World? Changing Forms of the Church's Witness. Colin
W. Williams. New York: National Council of the Churches of
Christ in the USA, 1963. 116 pp. Inquiry into the implications
of the theme, "The Missionary Structure of the Congregation,"
authorized by the Third Assembly of the World Council of
Churches.

*Witnesses Together: Official Report of the Inaugural Assembly of the
East Asia Christian Conference, 1959.* U. Kyaw Than, ed. Rangoon, Burma: East Asia Christian Conference, [1960?]. 179 pp.

WORLD COUNCIL OF CHURCHES

*The Christian Hope and the Task of the Church: Six Ecumenical
Surveys and the Report of the [Second] Assembly [of the
World Council of Churches].* Advisory Commission on the Main
Theme, ed. New York: Harper and Brothers, 1954. 402 pp.

*Ecumenical Missionary Conference, New York, 1900: Papers and Pro-
ceedings.* 2 vols. New York: American Tract Society, 1900. 558,
484 pp.

Evanston: An Interpretation. James Hastings Nichols. New York:
Harper & Brothers, 1954. 155 pp. Good digest of the Second

Assembly of the World Council of Churches, by one eminently qualified to make an interpretation.

The Evanston Report: The Second Assembly of the World Council of Churches. W. A. Visser 't Hooft, ed. New York: Harper and Brothers, 1955. 360 pp.

Evanston Speaks: Reports from the Second Assembly of the World Council of Churches. New York: World Council of Churches, 1954 71 pp.

Evanston to New Delhi, 1954–1961: Report of the Central Committee to the Third Assembly of the World Council of Churches. Geneva: World Council of Churches, 1961. 288 pp.

Man's Disorder and God's Design: The Amsterdam Assembly Series. [4 volumes in 1.] New York: Harper & Brothers, 1948. 856 pp.

New Delhi Speaks—about Witness, Service, and Unity: The Message, Appeal, and Section Reports of the Third Assembly of the World Council of Churches, 1961. W. A. Visser 't Hooft, ed. New York: Association Press, 1962. 124 pp.

What Did the World Council Say to You? Harold A. Bosley. New York: Abingdon Press, 1955. 127 pp. An outstanding pastor undertakes to bring the meaning of the Second Assembly of the World Council of Churches to the grass roots.

World Missionary Conference, Edinburgh, 1910. 9 vols. New York: Fleming H. Revell Company, 1910. 452, 380, 467, 337, 341, 567, 191, 243, 367 pp.

World Mission Windows. Oliver Barres. Staten Island, N. Y.: Alba House, 1963. 209 pp. Excellent semi-popular study of the world situation today vis-à-vis Christianity, calling unashamedly upon Christians and the Church to shoulder the tremendous missionary challenge of our day, sending forth many more missionaries (clergy as well as laity) whose avowed object will be conversion. Author is a former Protestant minister now on the staff of the Roman Catholic Society for the Propagation of the Faith.

The World's Student Christian Federation: A History of the First Thirty Years. Clara Ruth Rouse. London: SCM Press, 1948. 332 pp. Solid historical survey of very important background for ecumenics.

Zinzendorf, the Ecumenical Pioneer: A Study in the Moravian Contribution to Christian Mission and Unity. A. J. Lewis. Philadelphia: The Westminster Press, 1962. 208 pp. Beautifully written portrayal of the life and influence of one who, long before the

20th century, saw Christian faith, mission, and unity as an inseparable entity. Inspires new heights of vision and concern.

PERIODICALS

(Select List of Major Pertinent Periodicals)

Bulletin of the Division of Studies of the World Council of Churches, (semi-annual).
150 Rue de Ferney
Geneva 20, Switzerland
Concept, (occasionally).
Department of Studies in Evangelism
World Council of Churches
150 Rue de Ferney
Geneva 20, Switzerland
The Ecumenical Courier, (bi-monthly).
World Council of Churches
475 Riverside Drive
New York, New York 10027
Ecumenical Press Service, (weekly).
World Council of Churches
475 Riverside Drive
New York, New York 10027
The Ecumenical Review, (quarterly).
150 Rue de Ferney
Geneva 20, Switzerland
The Ecumenist: A Journal for Promoting Christian Unity, (Roman Catholic, (bi-monthly).
Glen Rock, New Jersey
Faith and Order Trends, (quarterly).
National Council of the Churches of Christ in the U. S. A.
475 Riverside Drive
New York, N. Y. 10027
Information Service, (bi-weekly).
Bureau of Research and Survey
National Council of the Churches of Christ in the U. S. A.
475 Riverside Drive
New York, N. Y. 10027
The International Review of Missions, (quarterly).
150 Rue de Ferney
Geneva 20, Switzerland

Occasional Bulletin, (monthly).
   Missionary Research Library
   3041 Broadway
   New York, N. Y. 10027
Journal of Ecumenical Studies, (3 times a year).
   Duquesne University Press
   Pittsburgh, Pennsylvania
The Student World, (quarterly).
   World Student Christian Federation
   150 Rue de Ferney
   Geneva 20, Switzerland

Index